TAX AND TIME

Tax and Time

On the Use and Misuse of Legal Imagination

Anthony C. Infanti

NEW YORK UNIVERSITY PRESS

New York

NEW YORK UNIVERSITY PRESS
New York
www.nyupress.org

References to Internet websites (URLs) were accurate at the time of writing. Neither the author nor New York University Press is responsible for URLs that may have expired or changed since the manuscript was prepared.

Library of Congress Cataloging-in-Publication Data
Names: Infanti, Anthony C., 1968–   author.
Title: Tax and time : on the use and misuse of legal imagination / Anthony C. Infanti.
Description: New York : NYU Press, 2022. | Includes bibliographical references and index.
Identifiers: LCCN 2021014420 | ISBN 9781479800346 (hardback) | ISBN 9781479800391 (ebook) | ISBN 9781479800414 (ebook other)
Subjects: LCSH: Time (Law)—United States. | Taxation—Law and legislation—United States. | Tax administration and procedure—United States. | Time (Law) | Taxation—Law and legislation.
Classification: LCC KF6289 .I493 2022 | DDC 343.7304—dc23
LC record available at https://lccn.loc.gov/2021014420

New York University Press books are printed on acid-free paper, and their binding materials are chosen for strength and durability. We strive to use environmentally responsible suppliers and materials to the greatest extent possible in publishing our books.

Manufactured in the United States of America

10 9 8 7 6 5 4 3 2 1

Also available as an ebook

For Hien and Rose Mai

CONTENTS

List of Figures   ix

Preface   xi

Introduction   1

1. Time Travel   29

2. Time Travel Avoided (or, Justice Denied)   63

3. Time as Money   95

4. Bartering with Time   125

5. Fearing the Power of Tax Time   156

Conclusion   181

Notes   193

Index   241

About the Author   253

LIST OF FIGURES

Figure 1.1   Redemption of Stock   46

Figure 1.2   Related Party "Sale"   48

Figure 1.3   Post–Related Party "Sale"   48

Box 1.1   Internal Revenue Code § 304: Redemption Through
          Use of Related Corporations   49

PREFACE

The idea for this book can be traced back to the Law & Society Association's 2016 annual meeting in New Orleans. Though the annual meeting now has a full complement of tax panels, I like to visit panels that have nothing to do with tax but just sound intriguing. What intrigued me at the New Orleans meeting was a panel titled "Law and Time." The presentations turned out to be fascinating, and I walked away spurred to think about the myriad of ways in which questions of time and timing pervade tax law. My mind was spinning with ideas as I enthusiastically recounted my experience to my dinner companions that evening. But because I had just begun working on a different book project, I wasn't immediately able to pursue this new and exciting avenue of inquiry and decided instead to jot down a few notes in the file where I keep track of potential areas for future research.

Two years later, with that earlier book nearing publication and the thirst to explore the relationship between tax and time never quenched, I looked back at my notes and began to think more deeply about the relationship between tax and time. Following some preliminary research, I realized that, aside from the many obvious overlaps between tax and time, there are unrecognized or underappreciated ways in which time surfaces in tax law that not only deserve exploration and explication but also merit interrogation regarding their impact on the justness of the tax system. This book has now grown from these early intellectual seeds.

My work on this book neared its conclusion as the COVID-19 pandemic set in, with me working from home more than usual but now accompanied by my partner and young daughter, who had also begun working and schooling from home. But the pandemic did more than merely change my daily routine of research and writing. It also gave a project with philosophical overtones a renewed relevance to everyday life. As the pandemic disrupted lives around the world, it brought into sharp relief the lines of discrimination and disadvantage that exist here in the United States and in other countries. As governments eventually undertook halting efforts to return their societies to the prepandemic "normal," calls were issued to view the crisis not as something to be overcome so that we might return to a deeply flawed "normal" but rather as an opportunity to correct the social injustices that led the most vulnerable segments of the population to bear the brunt of the health, social, and economic impacts of this deadly disease. These calls asked us to imagine and work toward a more just world—one that would be better, stronger, and more resilient in the face of crisis. These calls to recognize and remedy inequalities were then underscored by the tragic death of George Floyd at the hands of Minneapolis police, triggering protests in the United States and around the world regarding the police's (and, in turn, the state's) treatment of minorities that called for action to put an end to these injustices.

Urging us all to collectively imagine—and create—a more just world has always been the focus of this project (and much of my other work). Taxes are not only central to the creation and shaping of the structure of society but also act as a reflection of who we are and what we aspire to be. Thus, at a time when so many are focused on using a moment of profound crisis as an opportunity for collective self-reflection and self-assessment—to reimagine our relationships with each other as human beings and the type of society that we wish to share together—taking stock of our tax system couldn't be more important. As the pages of this book explore, imaginings and reimaginings have long been part of the stock-in-trade of tax law. Unfortunately, the tax imagination has not always been used to work toward forging a more just society; to the contrary, it has been used as a tool to reinforce or work injustice. Hopefully, this book will deepen and further the conversations that are taking place around the world about working not simply to return to the flaws of our past but to imagine and create more just societies in which we can all flourish together.

As with any project of this size and scope, the help of others is necessary to bring it to fruition. There are thus many to whom I owe thanks. For comments on draft chapters of this book, thanks go to Linda Beale, Phil Hackney, and Katie Pratt. For comments on the full manuscript, thanks go to Bridget Crawford, whose friendship and scholarly input, output, and joint enterprise have been so invaluable to me and my development as a tax scholar. Likewise, thanks go to the two anonymous reviewers who read and commented on both the initial proposal for this book and later the full manuscript. For support in locating resources and checking the citations throughout this book, thanks go to the University of Pittsburgh's Barco Law Library and its staff of faculty research fellows; to library staff Linda Tashbook, Pat Roncevich, and Helen Jarosz; and to my able research assistants Alison Forsyth, Jessica Lusamba, Michael Mawhinney, and Kimberly Seskin. Thanks for help in figuring out how to track historical Twitter trends for chapter 5 go to Dan Camarda in Pitt's University Communications and Marketing Department (and to Pitt Law's Cori Parise for connecting me with Dan). For financial support of this project, thanks go to the University of Pittsburgh School of Law for summer research stipends as well as to the University of Pittsburgh's European Studies Center for a generous research grant that allowed me to travel to France and Spain to complete the comparative research for this project.

Thanks go to my editor at New York University Press, Clara Platter, for her interest in this project and for her hard work in shepherding it through the editorial process. And above all, thanks go to my family for their patience and understanding during the time that I was working on this project.

—Anthony C. Infanti
Pittsburgh, May 2021

Introduction

Time. Its texture, nature, and qualities have long perplexed and preoccupied scientists and philosophers alike. Indeed, as Paul Horwich put it in the preface to his book *Asymmetries in Time: Problems in the Philosophy of Science*: "Time is generally thought to be one of the more mysterious ingredients in the universe. Perhaps some of the reason for this is that *understanding* is often a matter of finding analogies. But time is unique; there's nothing else remotely like it."[1]

In the scientific realm, Albert Einstein famously upended preexisting notions of time and space when he published his theory of special relativity in the early twentieth century. Horwich's warnings notwithstanding, Einstein later wrote a book explaining his complex theories for a nonexpert audience.[2] While hardly beach reading,[3] *Relativity: The Special and General Theory* endeavored to unravel some of the mysteries of time for the general reader, including the idea of the "relativity of simultaneity." Einstein illustrated this seemingly paradoxical notion using a simple example, explaining that a passenger traveling in a train would not perceive simultaneous lightning strikes at opposite ends of the railway line as having occurred simultaneously because the passenger would be traveling toward one of the lightning strikes and away from the other while the light from the strikes was traveling toward the train.[4]

Before and after publication of Einstein's theory of relativity, continental philosophy—which is notoriously less accessible reading than *Relativity: The Special and General Theory*—likewise engaged with questions of time and temporality. In fact, in the introduction to *Time and Philosophy: A History of Continental Thought*, John McCumber described continental philosophy in all its "boisterous diversity" as "the philosophical resonance of time itself."[5] McCumber continued:

> For time is the slipperiest of topics, and one of its aspects—the future—is by definition unknowable, an inscrutable source of unimagined surprise.

New ways of understanding it are thus inevitable. Moreover, if a single method, or even family of methods, for understanding the future could be settled on, continental philosophy would have discovered a truth or truths held for all time, and would itself become traditional. The proliferation of different ways of conceiving not only the future, but also the past and present, is thus part and parcel of continental philosophy's temporalized approach.[6]

For most of us, however, the passage of time doesn't seem slippery or mysterious. It just seems normal and natural, calling for no great introspection such as that engaged in by Einstein or continental philosophers. We take time for granted as we live our lives. We set off to, and later return home from, work, school, or errands each day. As we proceed through our routines, the sun reliably rises and sets each day, and as the days accumulate, one season, year, or even stage of life passes to the next, occupying no more than the background of our life stories. This is not to say that we are wholly oblivious to the passage of time, because our perception and experience of time do occasionally vary and thus become noticeable to us. For example, time can seem to move at different speeds in different situations—whether excruciatingly slowly, remarkably quickly, or perhaps even not at all, as so many of us were reminded when confined to our homes during the COVID-19 pandemic in 2020 and 2021.[7] Or, we might occasionally find ourselves lost in reverie regarding real or imagined times past, present, or future.[8] Nonetheless, we tend to take time as a given in our daily lives and operate within and through time without giving it much thought.

When we do give thought to time, whether in life or in law, we generally perceive it as linear; that is, we think of time as moving from the past through the present and into the future—such as the progression from morning to evening; from one day or week to the next; and, over the course of our lifespans, from birth to death—with no possibility of reversing this flow. Just consider how we talk about time: we characterize it as *flowing, passing, going by*, or even *flying by*.[9] As anthropologist Carol Greenhouse has put it:

> "We" moderns are supposed to know that time is "really" linear and infinitely so. We are supposed to know that time is about motion,

change, mortality, and progress. We are supposed to know that linear time rationalized the periodicity of cyclical time and lifted the veils of timelessness from the now-visible face of human experience, and that the clock is the essential technology of modern life. But "we" have also devised a strategy for resisting linear time: we imagine that there exist people not preoccupied with change; we are supposed to know that some of *them* are happier, more sociable, more provincial, more attuned to nature and less skeptical of their rituals. If we are romantics, we imagine ourselves experiencing this liberation in love, faith, or travel to exotic places. If we are *post*-moderns, though, we also know that we are not supposed to think this. The difficulty of developing intellectual strategies for dismantling the privileges of linear time cross-culturally and, even more so, in the examination of more familiar cultural terrain, is compounded by such contemporary Western engagements with the idea of time.[10]

But as we will explore in the pages of this book, there is no need to fall in love, to embrace religion, to vacation on a tropical island, or even to embrace a postmodernist perspective in order to liberate ourselves from the linear representation of time that ostensibly rules our daily lives and our laws. To witness and experience the plasticity of time, we need look no further than the tax system. You might be asking yourself: "Tax? What is so important about tax law that merits a book considering the relationship between time and tax law? Why should we care about how time is used in tax law?" The answer to these questions is simple: tax law is simultaneously omnipresent in our lives, the essential lifeblood of the society that we share together, and a tangible expression of what and whom our society values. Itself a powerful presence in our lives, time intertwines with tax law in a myriad of ways—some easily seen, others unnoticed, but all eminently pliable and capable of remodeling. These interactions between time and tax law can affect how the burden of funding public goods is distributed and serve to shape the messages that the tax system sends about what and whom society values. How we choose to manage—and, often, to creatively manipulate—these interactions between time and tax law thus implicates fundamental questions of social justice that should concern—and be brought to the attention of—all members of society.

The Importance of Examining Tax Time

Unlike many other areas of law, tax law touches each of our lives on a daily basis.[11] To take the United States (where I live) as an example: Americans interact with the tax system as they go about their routines each day, whether they realize it or not. When they run errands (in virtual or real life), they often pay sales taxes on the goods or services they purchase.[12] When they work, they create income and/or payroll tax liabilities—a fact that is driven home each pay period by withholding that their employers subtract from their wages and pay over to the government (or, for the self-employed, through quarterly payments of estimated taxes to the government).[13] When they fill up the gas tank in their car, they pay excise taxes.[14] When they find a place to live, they pay property taxes (directly or indirectly) on the roof over their heads.[15] Even births and deaths can trigger tax consequences; for instance, they can claim a newborn child as a dependent for income tax purposes and can trigger estate or inheritance tax obligations when they pass away.[16]

Without all of the taxes that are paid every day, we wouldn't have police to protect us, public transportation or highways to drive on, schools to send our children to, courts to settle our disputes, or any of the other physical and social structures that government provides to facilitate our lives together and to ensure that society runs as smoothly as possible. Moreover, taxes are not only ubiquitous and necessary to fund the provision of public goods but also serve an important expressive function.[17] Each member of society does not contribute equally to funding public goods, because so-called head taxes are seen as neither a popular nor a fair way of distributing the tax burden. Instead, in crafting a tax system that allows for differing contributions to the common good based on ability to pay, a society expresses its collective notion of what a fair distribution of the tax burden looks like. Whether those who have reaped greater benefit from the socioeconomic structures that government has created are called upon to contribute more—or less—than those who have been left out or left behind speaks volumes about a society. Moreover, the choices made regarding precisely what, whom, and how to tax say things about what and whom a society values. Placing a tax imprimatur on someone or something is no empty statement; after all, tax encouragement or approval comes in the form of tangible financial benefits (e.g., tax exemptions, deductions, or credits). Conversely, tax discouragement or disapproval results in a heavier exaction that is experienced through the sting of a tax penalty.

Unsurprisingly, then, how a country uses time in its tax laws sends important messages about its political, social, and cultural context. We will discover through our exploration of "tax time" that, far from linear or even romantic, time in tax law is really what we make of it—and what has been made of it, particularly in the United States, resembles more the fantastical creations of literary fiction than it does run-of-the-mill legal fictions.[18] As with literature, studying manipulations of time in and through US tax law helps to reveal the character of Americans as a people, by shining a light both on their good intentions in imagining a more just world and on the more sinister side of the tax imagination that uses time to entrench and exacerbate existing inequalities in US society.

But in the limited space of these pages, we will not be able to examine the relationship between time and all of the different taxes that exist in the United States. Rather, the primary focus here will be on examining select aspects of the relationship between time and the income tax, as it "raises particularly interesting issues because income is a concept defined by reference to time."[19] Furthermore, the income tax is perhaps the most salient of taxes in the United States as well as the source of more than half of all US federal tax revenue—not to mention a significant source of revenue in other countries too.[20]

The remainder of this introduction begins our study of tax time by first discussing some of the obvious ways in which time surfaces in US federal income tax law—from the need to determine the appropriate period for reporting tax to establishing methods of accounting for allocating income and expenses among reporting periods to more esoteric questions about the "time value of money." Having acknowledged the practical timing questions that face taxpayers, their tax advisers, and the Internal Revenue Service, this introduction then makes clear that the focus of this book is *not* on revisiting this well-trodden ground. Instead, this book opens tax law to a burgeoning area of research that explores the deeper and more complicated connections between law and time. A brief survey of US contributions to this line of research is provided to give the reader a sense of the types of interesting and thought-provoking questions already being examined outside the tax arena—from how law constructs time to questioning the linear representation of time to revealing the multiplicity of ways in which time can be seen as operating through and within law.

The final section of this introduction then lays out the basic idea underpinning this book and sketches out how that idea will be explored in the coming chapters. Put simply, the basic thesis of this book is that *time can be seen as surfacing in tax law in important ways that are untethered from conventional notions of time and that are more akin to creative acts of legal imagination*. Upending taken-for-granted linear notions of time, we will explore how, through tax law, it is possible to travel back in time by rewriting the past and then to act upon that rewritten past in the tax present and future as if it had actually occurred. We will consider how time is converted into a currency in tax law—a currency that taxpayers can use to purchase valuable benefits and one that is regularly dispensed by government as a reward. And showing that we do not (and should not) always take time for granted, we will examine how taxpayers sometimes react to exercises of the tax imagination, fearing the ways in which the imaginative power of tax time might be used against them. As a US tax academic, my main focus is on exploring the intersection of tax and time in US law; however, given my interest in comparative tax law,[21] throughout these chapters we will also consider examples from other countries when those examples might enrich the discussion by reinforcing a point or by providing an interesting contrast to the US approach to dealing with tax time.

As a self-identified critical tax scholar—that is to say, as someone who is concerned with the operation of our tax laws on marginalized groups and in working to advance tax and social justice—I also consider throughout this book the broader normative questions raised by these examples of the tax imagination at work. After all, as Emily Grabham and Siân Beynon-Jones have observed, "analyzing the 'making' of legal temporalities, if anything, only intensifies our accountability and responsibility to act in and on the world in ways that work toward social justice."[22] With this admonition in mind, once freed from the bonds of convention and empowered to imagine a world that is simultaneously within and beyond time, I ask to what end this imaginative power has been brought to bear. Has the power to reimagine time been used to serve ends of justice or injustice? Having created a socially constructed notion of time that directly affects the doling out of tax benefits and the imposition of tax burdens, what do the choices made in deploying the tax imagination say about society—about what and whom society values and, conversely, about what and whom society ignores or devalues? With a heightened awareness of the unbounded nature of tax time, I argue that a systematic examination needs to be undertaken to assess and reimagine how society engages with and deploys time in and through tax law.

With these questions in mind and a basic sense of where the analysis is headed, we are now ready to embark on our journey into the imaginative realm of tax time.

Timing Issues in Tax Law

Time pervades tax law just as it pervades our lives. In the basic federal income tax course that I teach every fall, an entire chapter of the textbook is devoted to questions of timing.[23] And when I was working on my Master of Laws (LLM) degree in taxation many years ago, an entire course was devoted to timing issues in the income tax.[24] When taught to students in these courses—and even when discussed in policy circles or in the academic tax literature—the questions of timing that merit consideration are practical in focus and take the legally and culturally prevalent linear representation of time as a given. In other words, time is simply seen as part of the natural background against which tax law operates.[25] And mimicking nature, the choices that have been made in adapting US tax law to linear time often create their own rhythms and patterns akin to the cyclical time that we experience in the repetitive passage from day to night or from one season to the next as we proceed through our lives.

Reporting Period

At their most basic level, these timing questions involve the *when* of income taxation. Once it has been decided who will be subject to tax, what income will be taxed, and how that income will be taxed, it must be determined *when* income taxation will occur. Should taxpayers report their income on a transactional basis or at periodic intervals? And if income is to be reported periodically, what interval should be chosen? Should income be reported every day, every year, once a decade, once in a lifetime—or at some other interval? With April 15 etched in the American consciousness as "tax day"—an annual ritual that has come to mark the cyclical passage of time from one tax "season" to the next—it likely comes as no surprise that the United States has settled on an annual reporting period.[26]

Of course, tax law being what it is, there are exceptions to this annual accounting framework that aim to mitigate some of the hardships of having a system too rigidly tied to linear time.[27] These exceptions are designed to make the income tax fairer from the taxpayer's perspective, the government's perspective, or sometimes both. An example of each type of exception follows.

To aid taxpayers, Congress enacted the deduction for net operating losses early in the history of the income tax.[28] Generally, net operating losses can now be carried forward indefinitely (before 2018, net operating losses were generally carried back two taxable years and forward twenty taxable years).[29] As the United States Supreme Court has explained, this deduction aims to benefit taxpayers by "ameliorat[ing] the unduly drastic consequences of taxing income strictly on an annual basis. [The deduction was] designed to permit a taxpayer to set off its lean years against its lush years, and to strike something like an average taxable income computed over a period longer than one year."[30] In this way, the deduction operates in linear time but extends the periodicity of the income tax. Before 2018, the net operating loss deduction extended the income tax's periodicity over a finite segment of linear time that included both the past and future. Now, the deduction extends that periodicity only into the future but over a potentially lengthier segment of linear time (i.e., the life of an individual or the virtual life of an entity).[31]

A second exception to the annual accounting framework is the so-called *Arrowsmith* doctrine, which stems from a case "holding that taxpayers who reported capital gain on the complete liquidation of a closely held corporation could not deduct from ordinary income their subsequent payment of corporate obligations that had been neglected at the time of liquidation."[32] This exception protects the government by preventing taxpayers from reporting gain on a transaction as capital gain taxed at preferential rates in one year and then, in a later taxable year, reporting a related payment as an ordinary deduction that is freed from the limitations imposed on capital losses and, therefore, can be used to offset income taxed at higher rates.

Yet a third example of an exception to the annual accounting framework is the "tax benefit rule," which can protect either the taxpayer or the government (or occasionally both at the same time). The tax benefit rule protects the government by taxing recoveries of amounts previously deducted (e.g., refunded state or local income taxes) when the earlier deduction produced a tax benefit.[33] By increasing income in the year of the recovery, the tax benefit rule makes the government roughly whole for the revenue lost due to the (now seemingly inappropriate) deduction in the earlier year. Conversely, the rule protects the taxpayer by shielding the recovery from taxation if the earlier deduction produced no tax benefit. Again quoting the Supreme Court: "The basic purpose of the tax benefit rule is to achieve rough transactional parity in tax . . . and to protect the Government and the taxpayer from the adverse effects of reporting a transaction on the basis of assumptions that an event in a subsequent year proves to have been erroneous."[34]

Despite requiring the taxpayer or the government to take a peek at an earlier tax return, both the *Arrowsmith* doctrine and the tax benefit rule continue to operate strictly within the annual accounting framework and thus within linear time. In other words, neither the *Arrowsmith* doctrine nor the tax benefit rule permits the taxpayer to go back in time and reopen or amend an earlier return. Instead, both simply require a look back at past events to determine the appropriate reporting of an amount on the current year's tax return.[35]

Accounting Methods

Once the appropriate periods for reporting income and paying tax to the government have been established, questions arise about how to determine during which year an item of income or deduction should be reported. The basic methods of accounting are (1) the cash receipts and disbursements method and (2) the accrual method.[36] The cash method is commonly used by individual taxpayers, and it requires income to be reported in the year when received and allows deductions to be taken when payments are made.[37] The accrual method is used more commonly by businesses; in fact, some business are prohibited from using the cash method and are thus effectively required to use the accrual method.[38] Under the accrual method, income is reported in "the taxable year when all the events have occurred that fix the right to receive the income and the amount of the income can be determined with reasonable accuracy," and deductions are generally allowed "in the taxable year in which all the events have occurred that establish the fact of the liability [and] the amount of the liability can be determined with reasonable accuracy."[39] Accordingly, reporting of income and deductions under the accrual method need not track when income is received or expenses are paid, as happens under the cash method.

To maintain the integrity of these two methods of accounting, concepts from one method are sometimes incorporated into the other. Thus, to prevent those on the cash method from simply turning their back on income in order to receive it in a later year (when, for instance, the taxpayer might expect to be in a lower tax bracket or to have more deductions), the Internal Revenue Service (IRS) has created a rule under which "[i]ncome although not actually reduced to a taxpayer's possession is constructively received by him in the taxable year during which it is credited to his account, set apart for him, or otherwise made available so that he may draw upon it at any time, or so that he could have drawn upon it during the taxable year if notice of intention to withdraw had been given."[40] And to prevent accrual method taxpayers from manipulating the "all events" test for accruing deductions, Congress adopted an "economic performance" requirement in 1984 that in a variety of situations (e.g., payment of tort claims, jackpots and prizes, and taxes) effectively puts accrual method taxpayers on the cash method by deferring deductions until expenses are actually paid.[41]

Of course, these general methods and their complexities do not address all the questions taxpayers might have regarding when to report income or deductions. Indeed, the regulations specify that the "term 'method of accounting' includes not only the overall method of accounting of the taxpayer but also the accounting treatment of any item."[42] The regulations go on to provide that, apart from the cash and accrual methods of accounting, the "methods of accounting for special items include the accounting treatment prescribed for research and experimental expenditures, soil and water conservation expenditures, depreciation, net operating losses, etc."[43] In addition, the IRS is empowered to require larger businesses to use inventories where necessary "clearly to determine the income of any taxpayer," raising timing issues regarding whether the items of inventory sold each year are determined on a first-in, first-out basis or a last-in, first-out basis (these are known in the trade as "FIFO" and "LIFO").[44] Furthermore, the IRS has been granted a more general and wide-ranging power to dictate a taxpayer's method of accounting if the method that the taxpayer has adopted "does not clearly reflect income."[45]

Rules regarding the timing of income inclusion and of reporting deductions can also crop up implicitly, as they do in the requirement that gains and losses from property transactions must be reported upon the occurrence of a "realization" event (i.e., a sale or other disposition of property).[46] This rule largely places timing in the hands of the taxpayer and serves as a key source of tax planning and, as explored in chapter 4, tax avoidance.[47] In fact, "loss harvesting" is such a common tax planning strategy that it is often included among the end-of-year tax tips offered to newspaper readers around the country each December.[48] But the common denominator of all of these accounting rules is the attempt to determine the appropriate period within linear time for reporting an item on the tax return.

Time Value of Money

As Lawrence Lokken observed in the first few lines of his treatise-length law review article on the subject, "heightened sensitivity to the importance of interest and the time value of money" coupled with rising tax shelter activity in the 1970s and 1980s led to a complex web of tax rules dealing with disguised payments of interest.[49] Among them are the "original issue discount" rules that recharacterize discount on the issuance of debt as interest and require that interest to be accrued ratably over the debt instrument's term.[50] Other rules similarly recharacterize amounts as interest when debt is issued in the context of a sale or exchange of property.[51] Yet another set of rules imputes interest (both for income and, where relevant, gift tax purposes) on: (1) below-market loans between employers and employees or corporations and shareholders, (2) gift loans (i.e., "where the forgoing of interest is in the nature of a gift"), and (3) tax-avoidance loans.[52] Of course, there are also rules that aim to prevent taxpayers from manipulating the use of interest deductions to artificially depress their income.[53]

In addition to addressing the appropriate taxation of disguised interest, "time value of money" operates as a broader rubric that likewise encompasses taxpayers' appreciation that they can benefit from accelerating deductions (i.e., tax savings) and deferring income (i.e., tax burdens). As Mary Louise Fellows has put it: "'Time value of money' is a shorthand reference to the simple principle that a person prefers a dollar today over one tomorrow, because, by investing today's dollar, that person tomorrow will have not only the dollar but also an investment return on it."[54] In an earlier (and different) time and context, these time-value-of-money considerations were downplayed as relatively unimportant.[55] Indeed, the noted economist Henry Simons famously referred to "the argument that income must be allocated to the right period, in order to eliminate the 'interest saving' from deferral, 'this mosquito argument,' at which he had 'several times swatted . . . [and] must now swat once more, [albeit] not to kill the pest.'"[56] Underpinning Simons's view was his avowed skepticism regarding the possibility that income might "be allocated precisely among short time-intervals"[57] and his concomitant favoring of multiyear income averaging over a strict (and manipulable) annual accounting system.[58]

Taxpayers and their tax advisers, however, have become acutely aware of (and have actively exploited) the opportunities to minimize taxation that are available when the tax system is viewed through a time-value-of-money lens—and Congress and the IRS have fought back against these attempts to reap unwarranted and unintended tax benefits.[59] For instance, exploitation of time-value-of-money considerations lay at the heart of the individual tax shelters that bedeviled Congress and the IRS in the 1970s and 1980s.[60] For a far longer period—which still continues, despite changes to the law—time-value-of-money considerations have been at the core of multifaceted gamesmanship with the US international tax regime, which has involved the use of corporate entities to shift profits offshore and then keep them offshore to defer US taxation.[61]

As was the case with the accounting methods discussed earlier, the common denominator of all of these time-value-of-money schemes is their heavy reliance on the linear representation of time. Whether taxpayers are attempting to convert interest into another form of (presumably more lightly taxed) income or to accelerate deductions or defer income, the background against which these schemes operate is the linear distinction between, and juxtaposition of, the past, present, and future.

Amending Returns

Yet, even within a tax system ostensibly wedded to linear time, we can glimpse the legal imagination chafing at the restrictions imposed by time's arrow. For instance, after filing an original income tax return, a taxpayer may amend that return "to modify, supplement, or supplant the taxpayer's original return [or] to claim a refund."[62] The Internal Revenue Code (Code) neither specifically authorizes nor requires taxpayers to amend an erroneous return; rather, as the Supreme Court has observed, "an amended return is a creature of administrative origin and grace."[63] Regulations encourage—but do not require—the filing of an amended return when a taxpayer discovers a mistake in the original return.[64] Because amended returns are a creature of the administrative imagination, the IRS is not bound to accept them and has the discretion to reject them.[65]

Through amended returns, the IRS seems to provide taxpayers with a vehicle for traveling back in time to correct past mistakes and clean up the historical record. However, the mechanism for amending the return actually constrains taxpayers' ability to travel through time, illustrating the influence of linear time over even this limited exercise of the tax imagination. In the United States, individuals are generally required to file Form 1040 by April 15 each year.[66] Once a Form 1040 is filed, a taxpayer wishing to amend that return does not submit a new Form 1040. Instead, the taxpayer completes a different form—Form 1040-X—that includes both the original *and* the corrected information along with an indication of the net change in what was originally reported.[67] In this way, the taxpayer is not really permitted to travel back in time but is afforded the more limited power to write in the margins of history. In fact, the IRS makes this very point in the context of providing a "tip" to taxpayers about how most easily to complete Form 1040-X: "Many find the easiest way to figure the entries for Form 1040-X is to first make the changes in the margin of the return they are amending."[68] Accordingly, an amended return is less a rewriting of the past and more an admission of past error in the here and now.

The Supreme Court underscored the limited nature of an amended return's power to rewrite the past when it squarely rejected taxpayers' suggestions that the filing of a fraudulent original return should be cured through the filing of an honest amended return.[69] The only situation in which an amended return may supersede a mistaken original is when the amended return is filed before the due date for the original return (e.g., before the April 15 deadline for individual returns).[70] In that situation, it seems that the past is not yet past; that is, it has not yet been indelibly written and is capable of erasure and correction—but only until the point when the filing deadline is reached along time's arrow.

Despite itself being a product of imagination, the amended return—much like the other aspects of tax time described earlier—is both influenced and confined by the rigid strictures of linear time. But this peek at the tax imagination at work foreshadows much more powerful—and often more hidden—displays of creativity that will be explored in coming chapters as we delve more deeply into the relationship between time and tax law.

The Deeper Relationship Between Law and Time

All of these various timing aspects of taxation are undeniably important because they continuously raise issues for taxpayers and policy makers to address, both in the United States[71] and in other countries.[72] Nevertheless, the purpose of this book is not to add yet another set of footprints to this well-trodden ground. Rather, picking up on the glimpse of the tax imagination witnessed in the discussion of amended returns, this book strikes off on a different path by contributing to a growing body of research that has moved beyond examining the practical, surface-level relationship between law and time[73] and progressed toward a focus on the deeper, more complicated connections between them.

Contributions to this line of research from the United States have, among other things, contested how time is taken as a given, questioned the linear representation of time that predominates in US law and culture, revealed the multiplicity of ways in which time can be conceptualized and in which it can operate in and through law, and even considered the ways in which law structures time in the United States. In the coming chapters, this book will likewise cast doubt on the conventional acceptance of linear time that was so clearly on display in the preceding discussion of timing issues in tax law. To lay the groundwork for these efforts to shake the unquestioning acceptance of time as "natural" or a "given" when constructing, interpreting, and applying tax laws, the following sections sketch how this same work has been done by US researchers outside the realm of tax law. Before proceeding, it is worth noting that US scholars are not the only ones who have explored the deeper relationships between law and time;[74] however, for the sake of brevity and focus, the US line of research in this area will be spotlighted here.

Time and Lawmaking

A portion of this line of research exploring the deeper relationships between law and time outside of the tax context focuses on the relationship between time and lawmaking and demonstrates just how varied—and nonlinear—the temporalities of lawmaking can be. For instance, approaching the subject from a political science perspective, Bruce Peabody has used examples of constitutional and statutory interpretation to demonstrate how "it is intellectually productive to think of the present as having an impact on the past—in ways that go beyond mere (re)interpretation."[75] Put more directly, Peabody claimed to show how "the hands of the present grasp and transform the past."[76]

In an interesting example of this phenomenon, Peabody examined the debate over former president Bill Clinton's eligibility to serve as vice president.[77] According to the Twenty-Second Amendment to the US Constitution, "No person shall be elected to the office of the President more than twice . . . ."[78] On its face, this amendment seems to prevent Clinton only from being elected president and not from being elected vice president.[79] Yet, Peabody pointed to arguments made by those questioning Clinton's eligibility for the vice presidency who asserted that the Twenty-Second Amendment must be read in conjunction with the Twelfth Amendment, which provides that "no person constitutionally ineligible to the office of President shall be eligible to that of Vice-President of the United States."[80] These critics argued that Clinton's ineligibility for election as president (because he had already served two terms) rendered him ineligible for election as vice president.[81] Peabody contended that this argument serves to illustrate the extent to which some legal arguments implicitly assume that contemporary legal structures can transform the original content and significance of past law. Whatever the Twelfth Amendment's eligibility restrictions meant when it was formally approved in 1804, they presumably did not include the terms of the Twenty-Second Amendment—ratified almost 150 years later. Nevertheless, arguments that Clinton is ineligible to serve as vice president seem based on an assumption that the ratification of the Twenty-Second Amendment altered the basic, initial terms of the Twelfth Amendment's eligibility provisions; the claim is not that the Twenty-Second Amendment simply legally amended or supplemented the existing language of the Twelfth Amendment, but that it helped to define the very parameters and authority of the earlier provision.[82]

Overall, Peabody maintained that "the American legal system's common law foundations, as well as its formality and commitment to serving as both a constitutive and aspirational endeavor, make it especially conducive to meaningful reversals of the traditional path of 'time's arrow.'"[83]

Considering lawmaking through the courts, anthropologist Carol Greenhouse has attempted to shake linear time from its privileged position through an exploration of time's varying implications in the succession of United States Supreme Court justices.[84] For Greenhouse, "[j]udicial succession is particularly relevant . . . in that it is precisely in succession that multiple temporalities—of the law, personal lifetimes, and public lives—and their indeterminacies must be worked out."[85] As Greenhouse observed, Supreme Court vacancies are usually related to the justices' personal lifetimes—that is, they are caused by a justice's death or decline—and these lifetimes have distinct beginning and ending points as well as a linear direction.[86] But the finite, linear time frame of individual justices' lifetimes contrasts with the temporality of law, which the justices are supposed to embody, because law exists in "a form of timelessness, or, more accurately, *all-times*, a form of time which stipulates time as social, but not with geometric metaphors."[87] Further complicating matters is the question of how and when an individual *becomes* a Supreme Court justice:

The special temporal symbolism of the law requires a special "kind" of person, one who will find the law, not make it; know the law, but not preach it; be a representative of the national community, but have no causes of his or her own. These three temporal charters are by no means easily reconciled. Their reconciliation is possible only with the deft management of essential temporal symbols, that is, by downplaying or suppressing altogether aspects of a judicial "career" that entail *becoming*. It is in *becoming* a judge that any tensions between individuality and a judicial persona would be most evident.[88]

In a later book, *A Moment's Notice: Time Politics Across Cultures*,[89] Greenhouse continued her examination of *becoming* a Supreme Court justice as part of a larger project regarding the role of time (and particularly linear time) in ethnographic studies. Greenhouse described this larger project as challenging how, in anthropology, "linear time stands relatively unquestioned as self-evident, a social time but also 'the time.' Part of [her] experiment [was] to consider linear time as equally a social time, to demonstrate how reexoticizing linear time affects one's approach to other time forms elsewhere."[90] Greenhouse revisited Supreme Court succession as part of this project because it implicated "at least three essentially different forms of time"[91]: (1) the general perception of time as infinite, linear, and irreversible (what Greenhouse called "the time of biographies and national histories, among other things"); (2) the time of the law, which is without a fixed endpoint and is reversible (both in the sense that past precedent can control present decisions and in the sense that past precedent can be reversed); and (3) the finite life of the individual judge.[92] To explore the interaction of these different forms of time, Greenhouse examined the role of autobiography in the confirmation hearings of Robert Bork and Clarence Thomas.[93]

In examining Bork's confirmation hearings, Greenhouse focused on Bork's "retraction problem" with some of his earlier writings and the resulting clash between, on the one hand, the senators who were placing Bork, his past experiences, and his future judicial decision-making on the Supreme Court in an implicitly linear time framework and, on the other hand, Bork, who initially resisted that framing. "While committee members seemed to expect to 'meet' Bork somewhere on a continuous time line between his past and his future, he came to them from a discontinuous past as an individual who had successfully fulfilled multiple professional roles and looked forward to the possibility of others."[94] Ultimately, Bork lost "control over his autobiographical narrative in the face of committee pressure to reconstitute his life story as a sequence of personal choices, rather than a series of professional commitments."[95] Greenhouse continued: "In successfully translating his self-presentation into conventional male autobiographical form, the committee reinterpreted his life story as one of successive engagements; his supporters and critics differed only as to their characterization of these engagements and his effectiveness in representing the interests they involved. The adversarial aspects of the hearings became, in this respect, a collaborative project to make Bork's life representative. In this way, the senators improvised a vocabulary that spoke directly through Bork to the contests between a conservative executive branch and a relatively more liberal legislative branch."[96]

In examining Clarence Thomas's first set of confirmation hearings, Greenhouse considered how "his biography was repeatedly invoked to assert that his identity as an African American was proof of his ability to represent, through memory, African Americans' struggles for civil rights and social justice in his future tenure on the Supreme Court."[97] The senators who supported his nomination, as well as Thomas himself, used the linear framework of his biography "as a way of defining African American identity as an identity of discrimination, celebrating Thomas's personal success, and expanding the conceptual frame around the substantive issues on which he might be challenged, to narrow and contain them."[98]

Reflecting on both sets of confirmation hearings, Greenhouse asserted:

> Because the temporal element was so explicit in them, the Bork and Thomas hearings are useful illustrations of the extent to which notions of judicial succession in the United States are highly charged with issues of individuality, nationhood, sacredness, and the nature of textuality, among other things. But there is more. The unprecedented relevance of nominees' autobiographies must . . . be understood in relation to the public and highly politicized construction of the United States as a diverse and increasingly culturally fragmented society. The individual autobiographies were constructed in the hearings in such a way as to highlight particular issues and images associated, in Bork's case, with the intensely ideologized battles over reproductive choice in the middle to late 1980s

leading up to the 1988 presidential election and, in Thomas's case, with
the Bush administration's effort to confound liberal opposition by nomi-
nating an African American—and a conservative.[99]

Greenhouse closed both the case study in *A Moment's Notice* and her
earlier essay with the following observation: "'The law' is cultural
not only, or not first, in its patterned processes and outcomes, but in
its constitution in multiple temporalities and their indeterminacies.
Specifically, law, as an idea, carries cultural force because it engages
these temporalities and their critical incongruities so directly."[100] In the
case study, she then elaborated on this observation by focusing on the
differing temporalities of the nation and the individual in the larger context of the idea of justice that lies beyond time: "These incongruities are
reinforced in the United States, where democratic rhetorics stress the
capacity of public institutions to represent collective personal interests.
The contemporary view of the United States as culturally divided adds
to the premium and power of the symbols that fuse individual life stories
to the linear time of the state."[101]

Others concerned with the intersection between time and lawmaking
have ruminated on the tensions between the increasingly harried (and
hurried) pace of modern life and the traditionally staid and slow-moving
pace of legal development through common law decision-making by
judges.[102] Approaching the topic from the perspective of an active judge,
Andrew Wistrich has explored the influence of both the past and future
on the law—for example, how lawyers study past precedent to shape
future conduct or to predict how a court might rule in a given situation.[103] But Wistrich mostly sketched what he saw as a general shift of
lawmaking in the United States toward a predominantly future-oriented
approach and mindset:

> The overall trend is clear: in lawmaking of every sort, and in the relative pro-
> portions in which the methods of lawmaking are employed, the role of the
> past is waning, and the role of the future is waxing. The common law has
> been dethroned, and statutes, treaties, and regulations have been enthroned
> in its place. As a consequence, law today is surprisingly future-oriented, and
> it is rapidly becoming more so. Law's memory of past law still matters, of
> course, but the influence of the past in the lawmaking process is declining.[104]

Wistrich detected this shift not only in the means used for lawmaking (i.e., the rising use of statutes, treaties, and regulations as opposed to common law decision-making) but also in the method of common law decision-making itself (e.g., the erosion of the force of precedent, the ability of the Supreme Court to set its own agenda by choosing the cases that it will review, and the rise of "institutional reform litigation" that turns judges into administrators).[105] Though aiming to be even-handed in his treatment of the relationship between time and lawmaking, it is hard not to detect in Wistrich's prose an undercurrent of wistful longing for a time when things moved a bit more slowly and his own profession—judging—was on top of the lawmaking heap.[106]

Instrumental Time

Other contributions to this line of research outside the tax context have considered how time can be used as a tool to achieve a goal or even to inflict punishment. David Engel provides an example of the former approach, highlighting how time can be manipulated to achieve desired ends. Engel challenged the dominant linear framework of time and demonstrated how time can be used as a tool in advocating for (or resisting against) social change through his documentation of how different groups within a single county "constructed their versions of the community's past, present, and future"—and the role of law and legal institutions in it—using different temporal perspectives.[107] The more conservative, traditional groups in the county embraced an iterative notion of time in which repeated cycles (in this case, of seasonal farming) reinforced community values, whereas more progressive groups advocating for change (in this case, those who supported the location of an industrial plant in the county) embraced a linear notion of time against which change could be measured.[108] These different temporal lenses "played complementary roles in shaping the local culture and in marking out the temporal field in which . . . events could be viewed and interpreted."[109] Concretely demonstrating the socially constructed nature of time, Engel described how the conflict between these groups over whether an industrial plant should be located in the county brought to the fore "conflicting ideas about time and change," with the more conservative group valuing stability and arguing "that change implied the erosion and loss of their traditional culture and values," whereas the more progressive group wished to avoid stagnation and argued that failing to bring the plant to the community "implied a failure of vision and will and hence a cultural deterioration."[110]

Illustrating a different way in which time can be used instrumentally, Jonathan Goldberg-Hiller and David Johnson have considered criminal punishment through a temporal lens.[111] In their essay "Time and Punishment," Goldberg-Hiller and Johnson "describe[d] some of the ways that attention to time deepens our appreciation of the pain associated with punishment and . . . offer[ed] new perspectives from which to understand and critique time's role in the administration of justice."[112] For example, they tapped into religion when considering the role that belief in an afterlife might play in different countries' continued support for, or abandonment of, capital punishment.[113] They noted the irony in leveling the harshest punishments for premeditated murders when, "in one of the many contradictions of capital punishment, states kill in a manner that is far more premeditated than even the most precisely planned murder"—and do so in ways that use time to inflict additional punishment (e.g., by having a death sentence hang over the head of the convicted for decades in the United States or by having the precise date and time of execution kept from the convicted in Japan until just before the execution takes place).[114] And tapping into literature describing a day in a prisoner's life in a Soviet labor camp and Supermax inmates' experience of a day, Goldberg-Hiller and Johnson showed how "presumptions about just calculations of time often fail to account for the inner time of incarceration, in many cases producing an overabundance of pain."[115]

Law's Role in Constructing Time

Demonstrating that time is not simply a received, natural phenomenon but is shaped and molded by human hands, other contributions to this line of research outside the tax context have examined the "law of time"—that is, how law regulates the organization and use of time. In *A Time for Every Purpose*, Todd Rakoff explored how law has been used for such varied purposes as to standardize how to tell time (e.g., by "zone" and through daylight saving time); to carve out community and family time (e.g., through adoption of so-called blue laws that legally mandate rest on Sundays); and to limit hours of work (e.g., through enactment of the Fair Labor Standards Act and the embrace of the forty-hour work week).[116] As Rakoff explained:

> Social time . . . is not made up of undifferentiated minutes. Chunks of time are organized so that the efforts of many people can be coordinated with each other; so that groups can establish the rhythms that help maintain both their activities and the groups themselves; and so that different meanings can be assigned to periods of time for various culturally significant purposes. The specifics of any particular pattern are, of course, open to debate, but that there ought to be some such organization is beyond doubt. In particular, in a society such as ours in which we expect individuals to play many different social roles in a variety of social settings, it is desirable that there be many different organizations of time to support these various activities.[117]

Disjunctures between the various domains of organized time (e.g., between work time and family time or between a parent's work time and a child's school time) can lead to conflicts and problems that implicate "not only specific rules of law, but a whole additional set of mechanisms by which the law shapes our social uses of time."[118] According to Rakoff, it is important to recognize that "[a] central function of the law, especially in a society as wedded to the law as ours, is to help organize the society. As generations before us have tried to do, we, too, should use our power of creating law to help us shape a structure of time that will, in turn, help us to live fulfilled lives."[119]

Earlier, in *American Indians, Time, and the Law*, Charles Wilkinson examined law's ability to construct time from an entirely different perspective when he showed how law has been used to construct barriers against the passage of time, effectively holding time at bay to create space for the governments of Indian tribes to develop and change over time. Wilkinson described Indian law as a "time-warped field" in which "many of the basic rights of Indian tribes depend upon constructions of treaties, statutes, and executive orders promulgated during the nineteenth century or even eighteenth century."[120] According to Wilkinson: "[E]xcept for the Reconstruction era civil rights statutes, Indian law has been the vehicle for the modern analysis of laws enacted during the nation's first century of existence more frequently than any other body of law."[121] These "old laws" aimed "to create a measured separatism"—Indian tribes were to be "largely free from interference by non-Indians or future state governments" but were to be subject to supervision by, and were to receive support from, the federal government.[122] Yet, as Wilkinson explained, it was not merely a matter of freezing time through "efforts to enforce solemn promises of another age."[123] "The tribes . . . have sought and obtained a substantial measure of insulation from many of the negative effects of the passage of time. Concurrently, however, they have attempted to make time work in their favor by seeking to establish a vigorous, modern tribal sovereignty with actual powers far beyond those exercised at the time of the treaties and treaty substitutes."[124] Wilkinson saw the Supreme Court's "recognition of rules providing for insulation against time, a tribal right to change, and special Indian law canons of construction" as both "appropriate" and "necessary" to fostering the "principled growth of those organic governmental documents [i.e., the treaties and treaty substitutes entered into between the federal government and the tribes] in much the same way as the Constitution evolves."[125] Law had thus constructed a seemingly paradoxical bulwark against the passage of time that actually allowed time to pass and change to occur.

Tax Law and Time

This book extends this line of research on the complex relationships between law and time into the tax arena. Without purporting to be exhaustive in examining the relationship between tax and time, my aim in the coming chapters is to show how, after we move beyond obvious connections and shed the strictures of conventional notions of the relationship between tax and time, it becomes clear that, as James Boyd White has put it:

[T]he activities which make up the professional life of the lawyer and judge [and, in the tax context, of the legislator and others participating in the making and interpretation of tax law] constitute an enterprise of the imagination, an enterprise whose central performance is the claim of meaning against the odds: the translation of the imagination into reality by the power of language. Its art is accordingly a literary one, most obviously perhaps in the demand that one master the forces and limits of what we have called the legal language system—speaking, as it does, in a set of official voices, reducing people to institutional identities, insisting on repetition of inherited patterns of thought and speech (most frustratingly in its use of the rule) and reposing an impossible confidence in its fictional pretenses. The art of the lawyer is perhaps first of all the literary art that controls this language. To say as much, and to ask how that language can be controlled—what the lawyer can do with it—is to say that the lawyer is at heart a writer, one who lives by the power of his imagination.[126]

This power of the legal—and, more particularly, tax—imagination will be on display throughout the pages of this book. We will begin our journey through tax time in chapters 1 and 2, which together consider the venerable US tax law doctrine of "substance over form" and its statutory incarnations from the perspective of time. In chapter 1, freed from the confines of linear time, we will witness how this doctrine is used to travel back in time to rewrite the course of past events and then to act upon that reimagined course of events as if it had actually occurred when determining past, present, and future tax consequences related to, or based on, those events. Illustrating that no single tax actor possesses a monopoly on the power to use the tax imagination to travel through time, we will examine judicial applications of the doctrine at the urging of the IRS as well as Congress's own attempts to legislate time travel through the enactment of statutory antiabuse rules. Although our primary focus will be on US federal tax law, chapter 1 also provides comparative context to show that the United States is not alone in its embrace of substance-over-form principles and the necessary rejection of a strict adherence to linear representations of time that those principles entail.

Because this power to turn back time is deployed ostensibly to achieve greater justice and fairness in the application of the tax laws, it is important to question whether that is the end to which the power of the tax imagination is actually put to use. It is to this task that chapter 2 turns. The power to travel back in time and rewrite history—fettered only by one's own imagining of what "really" happened or what a "fair" application of the tax laws dictates—opens the door to arbitrary, unfair, or plainly discriminatory applications of substance-over-form principles.

This possibility becomes concerning particularly when one moves beyond conventional applications of tax policy principles, such as those explored in chapter 1, that focus on economic considerations and measure tax equity solely by reference to taxpayers' income.[127] When one takes a broader view and recognizes the reality that taxpayers are more than merely the sum of their financial transactions, it becomes clear that tax law, much like other areas of law, can have differential—and notably adverse—impacts based on race, ethnicity, socioeconomic class, gender and gender identity/expression, sexual orientation, disability, and immigration status.[128] To illustrate this phenomenon at the intersection of tax and time, chapter 2 focuses on the element of choice in the doctrine of substance over form; that is to say, when tax actors choose to use the tax imagination to turn back time—and when not. As examples of situations in which a choice was made *not* to apply substance-over-form principles to correct manifest tax (and intertwined nontax) injustices perpetrated against disadvantaged groups, chapter 2 considers the IRS's refusal to recognize domestic partnerships and civil unions after the Supreme Court's marriage-equality decisions as well as its slow recognition of the incompatibility of racial discrimination with classification of an organization as a tax-exempt charity. Despite having rejected application of substance-over-form principles in both of these cases, the IRS nonetheless managed to engage the tax imagination in other creative ways that manipulated time for the benefit of those possessed of power and privilege based on their race and sexual orientation (not to mention other characteristics).

Moving from the fantastic to the mundane, chapters 3 and 4 give new meaning to the old adage "time is money." These chapters consider the ways in which the power of the tax imagination is deployed to convert time into a form of currency—not using time to commodify labor in the usual sense of "time is money" but instead reifying time itself and turning it into a tradeable commodity. Each of these two chapters draws together and combines the two lines of tax policy analysis that were explored separately in chapters 1 and 2. In other words, they marry the more conventional economic focus of "traditional" tax policy analysis with a more "critical" approach that considers the impact of commodifying time on members of disadvantaged groups (e.g., based on their race, ethnicity, gender, or sexual orientation).

Chapter 3 focuses on another key concept in tax law: capital cost recovery—the notion that investments in income-producing assets ought to be recovered over time, whether through depreciation, amortization, depletion, or some other mechanism. The general purpose of capital cost recovery is to obtain a better measure of a taxpayer's income that ought to be subject to tax. But capital cost recovery can be manipulated easily in ways that turn time into money that the government can hand out to favored taxpayers. Demonstrating that this is not uniquely a US pastime, chapter 3 explores examples both from the United States—where there has been a shift away from recovering cost over time and toward the immediate expensing of investments—and from Spain—where early twenty-first century changes to the rules for amortizing goodwill on foreign stock acquisitions aimed to give Spanish companies a leg up in acquiring foreign enterprises. Naturally, when the government hands out money only to certain persons, especially when the payment is less than transparent, questions arise regarding who is receiving the money and whether the payments are being made to advance tax justice or to reward privilege.

In chapter 4, attention shifts to the ways in which taxpayers can use time to barter with the government in exchange for desired tax results. There are a number of instances in the Internal Revenue Code where time is treated as a commodity—that is, where a taxpayer will be afforded tax results that Congress might otherwise deny or be suspicious of due to the potential for abuse, so long as sufficient time has passed. In other words, if the taxpayer is willing to—and can afford to—give up a specified amount of time, then the taxpayer can have its desired tax benefits. Again, where transactions are taking place in less than transparent contexts, questions naturally arise regarding who is afforded the special opportunity to shape their tax results in ways that they deem beneficial and whether this opportunity is being afforded for reasons that advance tax justice or reward privilege.

Chapter 5 approaches the power of the tax imagination from a different angle: from the perspective of those who fear its application to them. By way of example, chapter 5 considers the role of withholding as a mechanism for income tax collection. Withholding is essentially a matter of timing; it does not impact final tax liability but simply determines whether taxes are to be paid now (e.g., through withholding when wages are received) or later (e.g., when a tax return is filed after the end of the year). Reactions to two recent experiences with withholding are used as illustrations. First, the chapter describes the reaction in the United States to revisions made to withholding tables to implement the 2017 Tax Cuts and Jobs Act (the signature legislative achievement of the Trump administration that included tax cuts favoring corporations and wealthy individual taxpayers). There were early charges that these changes were politically motivated to gain an advantage in the 2018 midterm congressional elections. Later, during the spring 2019 tax filing season, the changes triggered a public backlash when widespread attention was drawn to the drop in the overall number and size of tax refunds. The chapter next underscores once again that issues of tax time are not unique to the United States by exploring the constellation of worries voiced by French politicians, taxpayers, and even the government itself arising out of the replacement of the country's long-standing delayed-payment regime for collecting income tax with a new withholding regime. The existence of these fears shows not only that the tax imagination can shape time to serve specific ends but also how readily we can recognize the existence of this power when it appears on the surface of the tax system. It should require only small steps—with this book hopefully being the first such step—for us to open our collective eyes so that we might see and question other, less visible manipulations of tax time as well.

In the conclusion, the book closes by drawing together these examples of the tax imagination at work along with the broader discussions of whether we have been using our power to reimagine time in tax law to work toward greater tax and social justice (or not). Taking Carol Greenhouse's admonition that "time is cultural" in a different direction than she might have intended,[129] the conclusion likewise examines the cultural aspects of tax time.[130] It analyzes and considers what the choices that have been made in deploying the tax imagination say about society—about what and whom society values and, conversely, about what and whom society leaves out or does not value as highly. In light of these choices and the messages that they send, it is contended that a systematic examination and reimagination of how we engage with and deploy time in and through tax law is long overdue—and especially relevant at a moment of widespread soul-searching regarding the existence and dismantlement of structural inequalities, occasioned by a combination of the global CO-

VID-19 pandemic and public anger at acts of violence by law enforcement against minorities in the United States and elsewhere.

* * *

Through this book I hope to bring a fresh perspective to readers inside and outside tax academia who are interested in the relationship between law and time, as well as to those interested more generally in the operation and fairness of the tax laws—a group that should include all members of society. For readers interested in the relationship between law and time, this book places needed focus more squarely on statutes through its sustained examination of the intersection of time with complex tax legislation. This examination opens new frontiers in thinking about the relationship between law and time by demonstrating how, even within a single legal domain, time can simultaneously move in multiple directions and be converted into an inert (yet valuable) commodity. Throughout, this examination highlights the creative aspects of the use of time in tax law, exploring how Congress, the federal courts, the IRS, and even taxpayers and their tax advisers bend and shape time to achieve desired tax goals.

Of interest to a broader audience, this book continues my past work debunking the myth that tax is an arcane subject knowable only by an initiated few. My aim is to explain tax in a way that is accessible to nonexperts because everyone deserves to be educated about how the tax system operates. As the lifeblood of government and the foundation of society, a country's tax system embodies and conveys its values, expressing the nation's sense of self as a society. This book highlights these cultural aspects of taxation by shining a spotlight on the power and influence of time on tax law—and, conversely, of tax law on time—while bringing to the fore a simple notion: the way in which a country chooses to use time in its tax laws sends messages about its society and is thus deserving of attention from and questioning by *all* members of that society.

As we will explore in the coming pages, there is no need to fear the power to manipulate time in and through tax law. Instead, with greater awareness of the depth and breadth of that power, we should together take steps to harness that creativity to imagine—and then work toward—a more just society for all, rather than paying lip service to the idea of furthering justice while entrenching and exacerbating socioeconomic inequalities in and through tax law.

1

Time Travel

In tax law, the past is never truly past. The US federal government—
and sometimes even taxpayers—can travel back in time to rewrite the
course of past events to achieve a more just tax result in the present.
This chapter explores two different means of tax time travel, one created
by the courts and the other by Congress. This chapter first explores the
doctrine of substance over form, which is a judicially created mechanism for reenvisioning the past that is nearly as old as the federal income
tax itself. Then, it explores § 304 of the Internal Revenue Code, which,
though created by Congress, is based on the same principles as the judicial doctrine and operates as an antiabuse rule aimed at situations where
stock is redeemed through a related corporation.

Though arising from different sources, both of these mechanisms for
tax time travel ostensibly aim to further the fairness of the tax system
and to maintain its integrity against attack or abuse.[1] Speaking with reference to *Gregory v. Helvering*, a case that will be discussed at length
in the first part of this chapter, the United States Tax Court described
the basic conundrum inherent in applying substantive-over-form and
related principles as follows:

> *Gregory*, like much of the caselaw using the economic substance, sham
> transaction, and other judicial doctrines in interpreting and applying tax
> statutes, represents an effort to reconcile two competing policy goals. On
> one hand, having clear, concrete rules embodied in a written Code and
> regulations that exclusively define a taxpayer's obligations (1) facilitates
> smooth operation of our voluntary compliance system, (2) helps to ren-
> der that system transparent and administrable, and (3) furthers the free
> market economy by permitting taxpayers to know in advance the tax
> consequences of their transactions. On the other side of the scales, the
> Code's and the regulations' fiendish complexity necessarily creates space
> for attempts to achieve tax results that Congress and the Treasury plainly

never contemplated, while nevertheless complying strictly with the letter of the rules, at the expense of the fisc (and other taxpayers).[2]

The conflict here is thus between the core tax policy goals of administrability and equity, that is, between striving for a workable tax system and striving for a fair tax system—one that treats taxpayers engaging in similar transactions similarly and that prevents some taxpayers from artfully shirking their tax obligations and effectively foisting them on others.

As foreshadowed in the introduction, the tax policy principles explored in this chapter are of a very "traditional" sort. They focus on ascertaining the economic realities of the situation at hand in order to avoid adverse economic impacts on taxpayers and to avoid a potentially vicious circle of adverse economic and reputational impacts on the tax system as a whole (and, in turn, on the government for which it is the lifeblood). Chapter 2, which should be read in tandem with this chapter, picks up this story by offering a complementary (though definitely not complimentary) "critical" perspective that calls into question the extent to which substance-over-form principles are used to advance tax and social justice as opposed to simply entrenching extant structures of power and privilege. Concomitantly, chapter 2 explores the alternative (and more nefarious) manipulations of tax time that have filled the vacuum left when a deliberate choice has been made *not* to use the tax imagination to rework the past in an effort to arrive at a more just tax present and future.

The Judicial Doctrine of Substance over Form

As one court has described it: "The principle of looking through form to substance is no schoolboy's rule; it is the cornerstone of sound taxation . . . ."[3] The doctrine of substance over form, which was created by the courts, generally aims to prevent taxpayers from manipulating the facts and the law to obtain unwarranted benefits from an income tax in which so much hinges on classification. For instance, tax consequences can differ markedly depending on whether a transaction is classified as a sale, a lease, or a license; on whether an instrument is labeled debt or equity; or on whether an item of income is characterized as wages, a gift, or capital gain. These classifications can determine, among other things, whether an item must be included in income, the applicable tax rate, and the availability of deductions for payment of that item or related amounts.

Of course, there are many situations in which the taxpayer's chosen form will be honored and determine a transaction's tax consequences. This is particularly true where Congress has chosen to bestow a benefit on, or has ascribed a certain result for, taxpayers who avail themselves of a specified form.[4] But form (and substance) can also bedevil taxpayers and the Internal Revenue Service—particularly where the same end can be achieved through a variety of forms that entail different tax consequences. In fact, in addressing such a potentially unfair and inefficient application of different tax consequences to equivalent transactions in the area of partnership mergers, divisions, and incorporations, Heather Field has urged that taxpayers be permitted to elect among a menu of different possible forms, regardless of the form the transaction actually took.[5] This purely fictional approach would level the playing field by granting all affected taxpayers the power to travel back in time to rewrite the past by choosing among a variety of stock stories that could fundamentally rework the path taken to their lived present.

In many other situations, however, the doctrine of substance over form allows the IRS and the courts to look past the form chosen by the taxpayer to determine what "really" happened and to apply the appropriate tax consequences to what is asserted to be the true nature of the transaction. In adjudicating a case concerning a gold mining tax shelter, the United States Court of Appeals for the Seventh Circuit colorfully described the doctrine and its pervasiveness:

> The freedom to arrange one's affairs to minimize taxes does not include the right to engage in financial fantasies with the expectation that the Internal Revenue Service and the courts will play along. The [IRS] Commissioner and the courts are empowered, and in fact duty-bound, to look beyond the contrived forms of transactions to their economic substance and to apply the tax laws accordingly. That is what we have done in this case and that is what taxpayers should expect in the future.[6]

Before delving into such a case in detail to illustrate the doctrine's relationship to time, it is worth noting that protection of the fisc is not the exclusive purpose of the doctrine of substance over form, as the doctrine can also be used to protect the integrity of the tax system from the taxpayer's perspective. For instance, in the mid-1950s, the IRS issued a ruling that looked past form to substance to aid taxpayers wishing to fall within a provision in the Internal Revenue Code that permits the tax-free exchange of like-kind properties.[7]

Normally, to qualify as an *exchange*, a "transaction must be a reciprocal transfer of property, as distinguished from a transfer of property for a money consideration only."[8] Despite the existence of this regulation—which would seem to disqualify any transaction that takes the form of a sale—the IRS chose to disregard sales for cash where the intent of the taxpayer was to effect an exchange of properties. In the ruling, the estate of an individual under guardianship included farmland that "became valuable for residential development."[9] The individual's guardian did not wish to have the estate invest in a speculative venture such as real estate development, so the guardian arranged to acquire other farmland from its owner. Under local law, the guardian did not have the power to enter into an exchange of one parcel of farmland for the other, but the guardian was permitted to sell the estate's farmland for cash and then immediately purchase the new farmland with the same cash. To avoid clouding the title of the estate's farmland, the guardian chose to engage in this back-to-back sale arrangement, with both sales being concluded on the same day. Invoking the doctrine of substance over form, the IRS ruled that, "since the sale was only a necessary step in reaching the ultimate desired exchange, the transaction was an exchange within the provisions of section 1031 of the Code."[10]

And the IRS is not alone in possessing the power to invoke the doctrine of substance over form to rework past events in ways that benefit taxpayers. Taxpayers themselves possess that power too; however, the hurdles that taxpayers face when invoking the doctrine of substance over form vary from court to court and can be difficult to overcome.[11] For this reason, the Tax Court has described the hurdles facing taxpayers in the following geographic terms: "Petitioner argues that a taxpayer may go beyond what appears on the face of an agreement, just as the Commissioner may do so. We do not disagree. However, the so-called 'two-way street' seems to run downhill for the Commissioner and uphill for the taxpayer. The Commissioner must be permitted to go beyond mere form to substance in order to protect the revenue; but taxpayers have the opportunity at the outset to choose the most advantageous arrangement."[12]

The doctrine of substance over form and a few others created by the courts (e.g., sham transaction, business purpose, and step transaction) have been collectively described as "so pervasive that they resemble a preamble to the Code, describing the framework within which all statutory provisions are to function. But these judicial presuppositions, like the canons of statutory construction, are more successful in establishing attitudes and moods than in supplying crisp answers to specific questions."[13] As Joseph Isenbergh has explained: "A justification frequently offered for extrastatutory or remedial forays by the courts in tax cases is that the tax laws cannot possibly reach all the artful forms of transaction used by taxpayers to reduce taxes and, therefore, that the courts have an important function in filling gaps left open by an imperfectly expressed congressional intent. Few myths so persistent are as easily dispelled. It is hard to think of a single case that has ever permanently staunched any fissure in the congressional dyke."[14] Notwithstanding Isenbergh's profound skepticism about its utility (a skepticism shared by others, particularly those favoring textualist interpretation of statutes[15]), the doctrine of substance over form has retained such importance—and hovers so ominously in the background of all that tax lawyers do[16]—that I cover it in the first few weeks of the basic federal income tax course to prepare students for the many times that it will be called upon in class discussions, in that and other tax courses.

Substance-over-Form Principles in Comparative Context

The United States is not alone in its concern with questions of substance versus form in the administration of its tax laws. Many other countries embrace the principle that substance should generally control when determining tax consequences. Nevertheless, the scope and method of the inquiry, the labels applied, the parties who can invoke substance over form, and the results achieved can differ greatly from one country to another and do not break down along neat geographic or civil law/common law lines.[17] A brief discussion of substance over form in Canada (generally a common law country, as is the United States) and

France (a civil law country) will illustrate the importance of substance-over-form principles in other countries. It will also show how countries take divergent—and at times unexpected—approaches when embracing substance-over-form principles. For instance, the typical common law and civil law approaches to judging appear to be reversed here, with French courts taking a more active role (much like their US counterparts) and Canadian courts taking a less active role in developing the law in this area.

CANADA

Canada, unlike the United States, has had a long history of strict, textualist construction of its taxing statutes that has proved to be "highly conducive to tax avoidance."[18] "Since courts were generally unwilling to interpret statutory provisions in light of their purpose, legislative drafters developed a detailed and prolix drafting style in order to prevent judicial misunderstanding—a process . . . that became 'self-perpetuating' . . . as detailed legislative provisions encouraged courts 'to conclude that the treatment of the subject is exhaustive, and that the legislation is meant to say exactly what it says and does not mean to say anything that it omits.'"[19] In the 1970s and 1980s, however, Canadian courts began to depart from this interpretive tradition by taking a more purposive approach to interpreting and applying Canadian tax law and by "display[ing] a much greater willingness to question the characterization of transactions and relationships according to their legal form."[20]

In 1988, the Canadian legislature enacted a general antiavoidance rule (GAAR) to nudge the country's courts further toward embracing substance-over-form principles.[21] Accordingly, in cases of abusive tax avoidance, the GAAR provides that "the tax consequences to a person shall be determined as is reasonable in the circumstances in order to deny a tax benefit that, but for [the GAAR], would result, directly or indirectly, from that transaction."[22] Nonetheless, following the enactment of the GAAR, the Supreme Court of Canada backtracked in its decisions to which the GAAR did not yet apply and then circumscribed the application of the GAAR in its early decisions applying the rule.[23] It is only in recent decisions—some thirty years after enactment of the GAAR—that the Supreme Court of Canada appears to have begun to embrace the spirit of the GAAR.[24]

FRANCE

In France, there are two primary avenues for the tax authorities to apply substance-over-form principles.[25] First, under court decisions, the tax authorities may set aside tax consequences (e.g., deny the deductibility of losses or expenses) resulting from an *acte anormal de gestion* (literally, an "abnormal act of management").[26] Under this rubric, the tax authorities may not second-guess any and all management decisions, even ones that might be characterized as mismanagement; rather, the authorities may disregard only those actions that are taken not in the business's interest but in the interest of third parties.[27] For more than twenty-five years, the tax authorities were also permitted under this rubric to disregard actions of a business—and to nullify the claimed tax consequences of those actions—when the actions entailed "manifestly excessive risk."[28] Because of its malleability, this latter ground for finding an *acte anormal de gestion* proved both popular with the tax authorities and quite controversial; however, in 2016, it was largely disavowed by the Conseil d'État, France's highest administrative court.[29]

The other avenue available to the French tax authorities to apply substance-over-form principles is code-based, namely, the procedural provision regarding abuse of tax law (*abus de droit fiscal*).[30] Following a decision by the Conseil d'État holding that the tax authorities could disregard a transaction as a fraud on the law even when the abuse-of-tax-law provision did not apply,[31] the French legislature amended the statute in 2008 to take account of that judicial decision as well as to render the law and procedures in this area more broadly applicable, more certain, and fairer to taxpayers.[32] Following that amendment, the tax authorities may recharacterize an abusive transaction if either (1) it is fictitious in nature or (2) the sole purpose for engaging in the transaction was to avoid or reduce tax through a literal application of the tax laws that is contrary to legislative intent.[33] Notably, the courts take a relaxed interpretation of "sole purpose," disregarding negligible or minimal nontax purposes offered by the taxpayer.[34] In 2019, the French legislature itself prospectively expanded the second ground for recharacterizing an abusive transaction by adding a new provision that requires tax avoidance to be only a principal—rather than the sole—purpose for engaging in the transaction.[35] At the same time, the legislature implemented a European Union directive by adding a general antiabuse provision to the corporate tax that disregards tax-motivated arrangements that lack a valid business purpose and are inconsistent with the purpose of the tax law.[36] One commentator has argued that this general antiabuse provision along with other specific antiabuse rules have come to reoccupy the ground ceded by the Conseil d'État when it abandoned "manifestly excessive risk" as a basis for finding an *acte anormal de gestion*.[37]

* * *

These are but two examples among many of countries embracing substance-over-form principles. In fact, the International Fiscal Association, which engages in an annual comparative study of a chosen tax topic, has on a number of occasions either directly or indirectly studied substance over form, with the most recent sustained and direct focus on the topic having occurred in 2002.[38] That 2002 report included twenty-seven different country reports, including reports on Canada, France, and the United States.[39] These country reports were accompanied by a general report that compared and contrasted the national experiences "to highlight important similarities and differences in approaches to the issue of form and substance, with an effort to investigate whether and to what extent general patterns can be found, and to analyse whether and how differences in approach lead to differences in practical solutions."[40] As the general reporter observed at the outset of his report: "Form and substance in tax law is a subject of a basic theoretical nature and at the same time a very practical one. On the one hand, it raises fundamental questions of methodology. On the other hand, questions concerning form and substance arise frequently in court and administrative cases."[41]

With this observation in mind and now having established the importance of the doctrine of substance over form not only in the United States but also in other countries, we are prepared to undertake a close reading of *Gregory v. Helvering*, which is the seminal judicial decision in this area of tax law in the United States. A careful reading of *Gregory* through a temporal lens will permit us to explore in greater depth how the doctrine of substance over form gives flight to the tax imagination by permitting all involved in a tax dispute—the taxpayer, the IRS, and the courts—to travel through time. Our reading of *Gregory* will further reveal how these tax imaginings complicate the conventionally accepted relationship between tax and time described in the introduction.

Gregory v. Helvering

During the earliest days of the federal income tax, the United States Supreme Court embraced the notion that substance should generally control over form.[42] But the judicial touchstone on questions of substance over form remains the case of *Gregory v. Helvering*, which was not decided until the income tax was more than two decades old.[43] The series of judicial decisions that ultimately led the *Gregory* case to the Supreme Court dates to the early 1930s, a time when judges were taking a more "realist" approach to statutory interpretation and evincing less tolerance of tax avoidance; the Great Depression had "led to a renewed emphasis in public discourse and public cultural perceptions of the immorality of tax avoidance"; and the largest tax evasion scandal of the period was unfolding in the form of the trial of corporate titan and former treasury secretary Andrew Mellon.[44] Because of its enduring importance, *Gregory v. Helvering* provides a convenient lens for understanding how the doctrine of substance over form facilitates tax time travel and thoroughly complicates the unthinking embrace of linear time as a natural, taken-for-granted part of US tax law.

THE FACTS

Given our temporal focus, it is interesting to begin by noting what was *not* in dispute in *Gregory v. Helvering*, namely, the facts. The Board of Tax Appeals (the predecessor of the current US Tax Court[45]) stated at the outset of its opinion at the trial level that "[t]here is no dispute about the facts, both parties having agreed that they are essentially as set forth in the report of a revenue agent."[46] Thus, the IRS and the taxpayer—and, of necessity, the courts adjudicating the dispute between these parties— did not differ regarding the events that had transpired or their sequence in the linear conceptualization of time that serves as the unstated background against which the facts in a tax dispute are normally ordered and described.

We are told that events proceeded as follows: Evelyn Gregory owned all of the stock of the United Mortgage Corporation.[47] Among United Mortgage's assets were shares of the Monitor Securities Corporation.[48] In 1928, the opportunity arose to sell the Monitor Securities shares at a profit; however, if United Mortgage did so, it would have resulted in two layers of tax (i.e., a tax on the gain recognized by United Mortgage when it sold the stock, and a tax on the dividend of the proceeds to Gregory when she received it).[49]

To minimize the tax on the transaction, Gregory was advised to structure the transaction as a spin-off.[50] The spin-off entailed several steps. First, on Tuesday, September 18, 1928, the Averill Corporation was created. Next, on Thursday, September 20, 1928, United Mortgage transferred all of its Monitor Securities shares to Averill, which then issued shares of its own stock directly to Gregory. Finally, on Monday, September 24, 1928, Gregory (1) completed the liquidation of Averill, which had been set in motion immediately after the company's stock was issued to her the prior Thursday; (2) received the Monitor Securities stock in a liquidating distribution from Averill; and (3) sold the Monitor Securities stock for $133,333.33.[51]

On her 1928 tax return, Gregory took the position that the spin-off qualified as a tax-free corporate reorganization and that the only gain to be reported was on Averill's liquidating distribution of the Monitor Securities stock to her.[52] This resulted in the elimination of the corporate-level income tax that United Mortgage would have owed had it sold the stock directly, and it reduced the shareholder-level income tax that Gregory would have owed because the liquidating distribution was treated for tax purposes not as a dividend but as an exchange of Averill stock for Monitor Securities stock.[53] By structuring the transaction as a tax-free spin-off followed by a liquidation, Gregory was able to (1) use part of the tax basis in her United Mortgage stock as an offset against the amount realized on the liquidation of Averill, thereby reducing the reported income from $133,333.33 to $76,007.88; and (2) significantly reduce the tax rate applied to that income because gain on a liquidation was taxed at capital gain rates that were half the maximum ordinary income rates that applied to dividends.[54] According to Assaf Likhovski, the restructured transaction would have reduced the tax on the sale of the Monitor Securities stock by more than two-thirds.[55] The final fact that was beyond dispute was that Gregory structured the transaction in this way—creating, involving, and then dissolving Averill in less than a week—for the sole purpose of tax minimization.[56]

This carefully engineered series of events was designed to satisfy the ritualistic demands of written law. Most important to observe will be the varying judicial and administrative responses to these events and how each legal actor involved in this drama chose to wield (or not) an acknowledged power to reimagine and rewrite the past in an effort to achieve a fairer and more just tax present and future. In describing these reactions, we will not be pigeonholed by linear time, which would dictate describing the responses to Gregory's tax planning in their temporal order along time's arrow. To do so would only reinforce the implicit hierarchy among the actors—a hierarchy that is irrelevant to this inquiry—and detract from the real focus, which is the variety of possible responses conjured by the tax imagination, not which actor had which response when or even which response prevailed at the end of the day.

THE IRS'S MULTIPLE REWRITINGS OF TIME

Framed in this way—as a matter of choice—it is interesting to explore how and why some legal actors chose to deploy the power to reimagine and rewrite the past and others did not. The most powerful application of the doctrine of substance over form was urged by the IRS in its argument that Averill's participation in the transaction should be disregarded as "a mere device or instrumentality formed and availed of solely to avoid a tax which was clearly intended to be imposed."[57] Before the Board of Tax Appeals, the IRS contended that disregarding Averill's participation meant that Gregory "must be taxed as upon a dividend consisting of the amount received upon the sale of the Monitor shares as if such amount had been distributed by the United corporation directly to her."[58] This represents a complete reimagining of the sequence of events that Gregory undertook. The spin-off would be effaced from the past, and so would Gregory's own sale of the Monitor Securities stock. The IRS used the doctrine of substance over form to imagine an entirely different course of events that would replace the "real" events with an alternate course of history—and of the future. Gregory's tax bill would be recomputed as if United Mortgage had held on to the Monitor Securities stock, sold it to the purchaser itself, and then distributed the proceeds as a dividend that would be taxable in full to Gregory at the higher ordinary income rates.[59] But this new past would not simply affect Gregory's immediate tax bill, because it could also trigger an attempt to increase United Mortgage's own tax bill. As a separate taxpayer and the person now considered to have sold the

Monitor Securities stock, United Mortgage would be the one to pay tax on the large resulting gain (because United Mortgage itself had a relatively low basis in the Monitor Securities stock).[60] This alternative course of events would also have future impacts on Gregory, because the portion of the basis in the United Mortgage stock that she had allocated to her Averill stock (and that she had used as an offset against the amount realized on Averill's liquidation) would now revert to the United Mortgage stock, reducing any gain or increasing any loss realized on a later sale of that stock. Accordingly, this act of legal imagination would have tangible effects on all of those involved, not just Gregory, and those effects would not be confined to the tax past but would reverberate in the tax present and future.

This was not, however, the only alternative timeline imagined by the IRS. Later in the process, the IRS—continuing to argue that the participation of Averill should be disregarded on substance-over-form grounds—contended that United Mortgage should be treated as having distributed the Monitor Securities stock directly to Gregory as a dividend prior to the stock sale.[61] This alternative would ignore the spin-off yet still treat Gregory as the person who sold the Monitor Securities stock. And it would entail somewhat different tax consequences in the tax present and future than the IRS's first reimagining of the past. Gregory's tax bill would still go up by the same amount because she would be considered as having received the Monitor Securities stock as a dividend. But United Mortgage would no longer be concerned with potential fallout from this new tax past because it would not have been taxed on the distribution of the Monitor Securities stock to Gregory.[62]

ANOTHER ALTERNATIVE: STRIPPING THE PAST OF MEANING

These two alternatives hardly exhaust the tax imagination. The United States Court of Appeals for the Second Circuit, reviewing the ruling by the Board of Tax Appeals that favored Gregory, engaged in its own reimagining of the past, coming up with a third alternative tax past with effects in the tax present and future. The Second Circuit refused to rewrite the events that had occurred or their sequence: "[W]e cannot treat as inoperative the transfer of the Monitor shares by the United Mortgage Corporation, the issue by the Averill Corporation of its own shares to the taxpayer, and her acquisition of the Monitor shares by winding up that company. The Averill Corporation had a juristic personality, whatever the purpose of its organization; the transfer passed title to the Monitor shares and the taxpayer became a shareholder in the transferee."[63] But the Second Circuit did not leave the past completely undisturbed. Despite respecting the events that had occurred as being "real" (to use the court's own adjective for describing their nature),[64] the court stripped a ritualistic sequence of events that had been carefully organized and executed to effectuate a tax-free corporate reorganization of their performativity.

The Second Circuit stated that merely because the "facts answer the dictionary definition of each term used in the statutory definition" of a *reorganization* did not mean that Congress intended to treat the events as a tax-free reorganization.[65] The Second Circuit asserted instead that "the meaning of a sentence may be more than that of the separate words, as a melody is more than the notes, and no degree of particularity can ever obviate recourse to the setting in which all appear, and which all collectively create."[66] In this instance, the larger context persuaded the court that Congress intended to confine tax-free reorganizations to situations where businesses rearrange their holdings, which remain in corporate solution, "for reasons germane to the conduct of the venture in hand."[67] With this larger context in mind, it was clear to the Second Circuit that "[t]o dodge the shareholders' taxes is not one of the transactions contemplated as corporate 'reorganizations.'"[68] Thus, even though "[a]ll these steps were real, and their only defect was that they were not what the statute means by a 'reorganization,'" the Second Circuit concluded that Gregory should be taxed on the value of the Averill shares that she received as part of the putative spin-off rather than receiving them tax-free.[69] The Second Circuit felt compelled to offer its alternative reimagining of the past even though it would result in the same change to Gregory's tax bill as the IRS's suggestion that Gregory be treated as having received the Monitor Securities stock as a dividend distribution from United Mortgage.[70]

Stripping this carefully choreographed sequence of events of its performativity is no less radical a change to the past than was the complete reimagining of past events that the IRS urged the Board of Tax Appeals to adopt. Imagine if you were to go through the rituals necessary to marry but then discovered years later that there was a legal defect in the marriage that called its validity into question. (This was the fear lived by some in the LGBTQ+ community who watched President Donald Trump and a Republican-majority Senate tilt the Supreme Court noticeably rightward, fulfilling Trump's campaign promise to consider appointing justices who would overturn the Supreme Court's marriage-equality decisions.[71]) Such a legal realization—which would not have changed the past course of events any more than the Second Circuit's decision in *Gregory* did—would represent a shock that would change the nature and course of your past and how you view it, not to mention the course of your present and future.

REFUSING TO TRAVEL THROUGH TIME

It was for essentially this reason that the Board of Tax Appeals chose to eschew the use of the doctrine of substance over form in *Gregory*. According to the Board: "Whatever can be said of the wisdom of recognizing the corporate device, the taxing statutes have so plainly accepted it and provided the detailed methods of taxing its transactions, that to disregard it in a case like this would vary the time, method and amount of tax which the statute imposes."[72] Relying on past precedent, the Board was not persuaded that the presence of a tax avoidance motive, the short life of the corporation, or the fact that Gregory was the corporation's sole shareholder made any difference in the application of the statute.[73]

To the contrary, the Board stated: "A statute so meticulously drafted must be interpreted as a literal expression of the taxing policy, and leaves only the small interstices for judicial consideration. The general legislative plan apparently was to recognize the corporate entity and, in view of such recognition, to specify when the gains or losses would be recognized and upon what basis they should be measured. We may not destroy the effectiveness of this statutory plan by denying recognition to the corporation and thus preventing consideration of its transactions."[74] Accordingly, the Board of Tax Appeals had its own, differing view of how best to preserve the integrity of the tax laws—that is, by honoring a detailed and carefully drafted statute as it was written. Rather than ignoring the form of the transaction in favor of searching for its substance, the Board chose not only to leave the past course of events untouched but also to honor the performative quality of the ritualistic steps that Gregory took to achieve her desired tax results.

Another actor in this drama chose the same course of action as the Board of Tax Appeals: Evelyn Gregory. As described earlier, the IRS and the courts are not the only ones who can avail themselves of the doctrine of substance over form. Taxpayers may likewise avail themselves of the doctrine to disavow the form of their transaction and to travel back in time to offer reimagined pasts with differing (and presumably more advantageous) tax consequences than the actual course of events. However, Gregory, like the Board of Tax Appeals, chose not to disturb the past—but for her own, more personal reasons. In light of the significant tax planning surrounding these transactions, Gregory and her advisers likely decided that the already written past provided greater tax advantages to her than any alternative they might conjure up during audit and litigation.

HOLDING TIME IN SUSPENSE

There is one actor in this drama—the United States Supreme Court—whose reaction has yet to be considered. From a temporal perspective, its approach may be the most interesting of all. After setting forth the facts and procedural history of the case, the Supreme Court expressed its agreement with the Second Circuit's reasoning and conclusion that what had occurred did not meet the definition of a *reorganization* within the intent of Congress.[75] But having rejected the choices by the Board of Tax Appeals and the taxpayer *not* to revisit the past, the Supreme Court did not make clear in its opinion whether it agreed with the reimagined course of events offered by the Second Circuit or with one of the IRS's proffered alternatives.

While the Supreme Court agreed with the Second Circuit that the steps undertaken by Gregory should be stripped of their performativity, it seemed to go farther when exploring the substance of the situation:

> Putting aside, then, the question of motive in respect of taxation altogether, and fixing the character of the proceeding by what actually occurred, what do we find? Simply an operation having no business or corporate purpose—a mere device which put on the form of a corporate reorganization as a disguise for concealing its real character, and the sole object and accomplishment of which was the consummation of a preconceived plan, not to reorganize a business or any part of a business, but to transfer a parcel of corporate shares to the petitioner.[76]

This passage seems to focus on the Monitor Securities shares received by Gregory and not the receipt of the Averill shares, which was the Second Circuit's focus. Further credence is lent to this interpretation by the next sentences of the opinion: "No doubt, a new and valid corporation was created. But that corporation was nothing more than a contrivance to the end last described. It was brought into existence for no other purpose; it performed, as it was intended from the beginning it should perform, no other function. When that limited function had been exercised, it immediately was put to death."[77] In the end, the Supreme Court concluded tantalizingly that "the facts speak for themselves and are susceptible of but one interpretation"[78]—but the real question that the Court leaves open is, Which one? After all, we have discussed here at least three possible alternative pasts.

Hanging on as we are, hoping for guidance and a resolution, the Supreme Court then cryptically added that "[t]he whole undertaking . . . was in fact an elaborate and devious form of conveyance masquerading as a corporate reorganization, and nothing else," and simply affirmed the Second Circuit's judgment reversing the Board of Tax Appeals' decision in Gregory's favor.[79] But even this simple affirmance does nothing to resolve the doubt about which reimagined course of events the Supreme Court deemed to have occurred, because the Second Circuit ended its own opinion by explaining that, even though it agreed with the end result urged by the IRS, it differed starkly in terms of how it reimagined the past events that arrived at that result.[80]

Therefore, what is most striking about the Supreme Court's opinion is how it seems to leave time suspended. We know the tax present that the Court wished Evelyn Gregory to inhabit—owing much more in taxes than she had hoped for—but we don't know how exactly she was deemed to have arrived at that present or where her tax future would lead (not to mention the tax futures of those, such as United Mortgage, whose stories intersected with and depended on Gregory's story). Gregory's tax past was now a mystery. She might have arrived at the spot in which the Court placed her by taking one of several different paths. And although those different paths might portend the possibility of similarly divergent futures, the Supreme Court leaves us wondering no less about what the future might hold than what the past has already written. Along with Evelyn Gregory, we stand suspended simultaneously inside and outside time—inhabiting a tax present without a definite past or an ascertainable future. What *Gregory* teaches us, then, is not only that the past is never truly past in tax but also that the tax present is evanescent, being forged out of and connected with an ever-changing, limitless array of potential tax pasts and futures.

Statutory Antiabuse Rules: Section 304

The federal courts are not alone in introducing a mechanism for time travel into the Internal Revenue Code. Congress, too, sometimes wishes to unfetter itself from the strictures of linear time. To this end, Congress has codified specific statutory applications of the doctrine of substance over form. These provisions aim to forestall abusive behavior by requiring taxpayers to travel back and forth along time's supposedly irreversible arrow and, in the process, to inscribe (sometimes repeatedly) Congress's own reimagination of the past—a past that we conventionally believe can be remembered but not revisited in such a way—all in order to produce a more just tax present.

The following sections consider a single example of such an antiabuse provision—Code § 304, which recharacterizes certain sales of stock as redemptions in order to determine the appropriate tax consequences of the transfer. Many other examples of codified time travel exist, all with the aim of rewriting the past to protect the fisc.[81]

Redemptions: Sale or Dividend Distribution?

Before examining the inner workings of § 304, a bit of background is necessary to understand the abuse that Congress was targeting when it enacted this provision in 1950.[82] A redemption—which, as depicted in figure 1.1, is defined as a corporation's purchase of its own stock from one of its shareholders[83]—can resemble either a sale of stock or a distribution of a dividend, depending on the circumstances.[84]

On the one hand, where a minority shareholder in a widely held, publicly traded corporation sells half of a small block of stock back to the corporation, the shareholder is in roughly the same position as if the stock had been sold to a third party. In other words, the shareholder's interest in corporate earnings and potential corporate growth and the

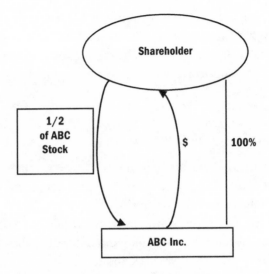

Figure 1.1. Redemption of Stock

shareholder's say in corporate affairs have all been diminished in much
the same way that they would have been had the stock been sold to
someone else.[85]

On the other hand, where a shareholder owns all of a corporation's
stock and sells half of that stock back to the corporation (the scenario
depicted in figure 1.1), the shareholder's 100 percent ownership of the
corporation continues undisturbed. In other words, it makes no difference whether the shareholder holds all hundred shares of a corporation's stock or, after the redemption, all fifty shares of the corporation's
stock—in either case, the shareholder is entitled to all of the corporation's earnings and growth potential and has complete say over its affairs
because the shareholder owns all of the corporation's outstanding stock.
The shareholder is in no different position than if the corporation hadn't
engaged in a repurchase transaction at all but instead simply distributed
the same amount of its earnings as a dividend to the shareholder.[86]

The distinction between these two characterizations of the same basic
transaction is important because the Code ascribes different tax consequences to sales of stock than it does to corporate distributions. A
sale of stock will normally generate capital gain or loss.[87] In the hands
of individuals, capital gains are taxed at preferential rates—currently a

maximum rate of 20 percent as compared to the top ordinary income rate of 37 percent—provided that the stock was held for more than a year before it was sold.[88] In contrast, a corporate distribution is treated as a dividend to the extent of the corporation's earnings and profits.[89] Since 2003, many dividends qualify for the same preferential tax rates that apply to capital gains.[90] Nonetheless, corporate distributions remain less advantageous than sales of stock, even after equalization of the tax rates, because of the differing ability to recover the shareholder's tax basis (i.e., investment) in the stock tax-free.[91] In the case of a sale of stock, a shareholder reports a gain only if the sale proceeds exceed the shareholders' basis in the stock.[92] Put differently, the sale proceeds are first treated as a tax-free return of the taxpayer's investment in the stock and are taxed only after the shareholder has received back all of that investment tax-free. In the case of a corporate distribution, however, the distributed funds are taxable as a dividend to the extent of the corporation's current and accumulated earnings and profits.[93] As a result, the proceeds of the distribution are first treated as taxable, and it is only if the corporation does not have sufficient earnings and profits to cause the entire distribution to be taxed that the shareholder can be treated as receiving a tax-free recovery of the basis in the stock.[94] Thus, the ordering is reversed: on a sale, tax-free basis comes out first; on a distribution, tax-free basis comes out second—if it comes out at all.

To provide shareholders and corporations with a measure of clarity when determining how a redemption should be treated—whether as a sale or as a distribution—Congress enacted a set of tests now found in Code § 302. But because a *redemption* is defined as a corporation's purchase of *its own stock* from one of its shareholders (as earlier depicted in figure 1.1), taxpayers realized that they could circumvent these tests when they might result in disadvantageous dividend treatment simply by having another corporation that they control purchase the stock from them instead. By way of example and to set out the hypothetical that will be examined later, figure 1.2 depicts a related-party purchase involving "brother-sister" corporations. (The maneuver can be accomplished just as easily in the context of a parent-subsidiary relationship. Indeed, that was the first maneuver that Congress blocked when it enacted the predecessor of § 304 in 1950.) Figure 1.3 then shows how the shareholder's ability to control the two brother-sister entities is unaffected by the

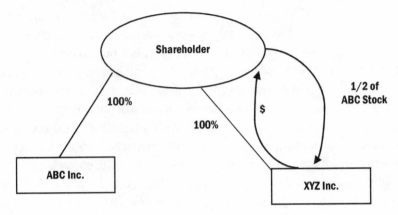

Figure 1.2. Related Party "Sale"

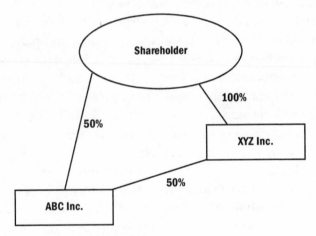

Figure 1.3. Post–Related Party "Sale"

purchase—direct control merely having been swapped for a combination of direct and indirect control. Nevertheless, the shareholder would be able to claim that the transaction should automatically be treated as a sale for tax purposes in keeping with the transaction's form.

When the IRS attacked this maneuver in the parent-subsidiary context and lost in court,[95] Congress recognized that the transaction was in substance (if not in form) a redemption and enacted the predecessor of § 304 to prevent this abusive end run around the tests that it had set up for distinguishing redemptions treated as sales from those treated as distributions.[96] Initially having addressed only the parent-subsidiary context, Congress amended § 304 four years later to likewise cover redemptions in the brother-sister context.[97] Interestingly, in both situations, Congress stepped in to protect the fisc where the courts had, in Congress's view, failed to apply the tax laws to the substance of a transaction. With the enactment of § 304, Congress effectively mandated the application of substance-over-form principles in the context of redemptions through related corporations. We will explore here how the codification of substance-over-form principles in § 304 bends the fabric of time in a different way from that witnessed in our close reading of *Gregory v. Helvering.*

Section 304

Like many antiabuse rules, § 304 is a highly complex statutory provision. To give a sense of the provision's complexity and to allow the reader to follow along with my analysis, the text of § 304 is set out in box 1.1. Please bear in mind that this discussion provides only a glimpse of § 304's complexity, as I have omitted more than 900 words of the provision's text because they are not directly relevant to analyzing the following hypothetical example.

---

§ 304: Redemption Through Use of Related Corporations.

(a) **Treatment of certain stock purchases**
  (1) **Acquisition by related corporation (other than subsidiary)**
     For purposes of sections 302 and 303, if—
       (A) one or more persons are in control of each of two corporations, and
       (B) in return for property, one of the corporations acquires stock in the other corporation from the person (or persons) so in control,
     then (unless paragraph (2) applies) such property shall be treated as a distribution in redemption of the stock of the corporation acquiring such stock. To the extent that such distribution is treated as a distribution to which section 301 applies, the transferor and the acquiring corporation shall be treated in the same manner as if

the transferor had transferred the stock so acquired to the acquiring corporation in exchange for stock of the acquiring corporation in a transaction to which section 351(a) applies, and then the acquiring corporation had redeemed the stock it was treated as issuing in such transaction.

(2) Acquisition by subsidiary
For purposes of sections 302 and 303, if—
   (A) in return for property, one corporation acquires from a shareholder of another corporation stock in such other corporation, and
   (B) the issuing corporation controls the acquiring corporation,
then such property shall be treated as a distribution in redemption of the stock of the issuing corporation.

(b) Special rules for application of subsection (a)
   (1) Rules for determinations under section 302(b)
      In the case of any acquisition of stock to which subsection (a) of this section applies, determinations as to whether the acquisition is, by reason of section 302(b), to be treated as a distribution in part or full payment in exchange for the stock shall be made by reference to the stock of the issuing corporation. In applying section 318(a) (relating to constructive ownership of stock) with respect to section 302(b) for purposes of this paragraph, sections 318(a)(2)(C) and 318(a)(3)(C) shall be applied without regard to the 50 percent limitation contained therein.
   (2) Amount constituting dividend
      In the case of any acquisition of stock to which subsection (a) applies, the determination of the amount which is a dividend (and the source thereof) shall be made as if the property were distributed—
      (A) by the acquiring corporation to the extent of its earnings and profits, and
      (B) then by the issuing corporation to the extent of its earnings and profits.

. . .

(c) Control
   (1) In general
      For purposes of this section, control means the ownership of stock possessing at least 50 percent of the total combined voting power of all classes of stock entitled to vote, or at least 50 percent of the total value of shares of all classes of stock. If a person (or

persons) is in control (within the meaning of the preceding sentence) of a corporation which in turn owns at least 50 percent of the total combined voting power of all stock entitled to vote of another corporation, or owns at least 50 percent of the total value of the shares of all classes of stock of another corporation, then such person (or persons) shall be treated as in control of such other corporation.

(2) Stock acquired in the transaction

For purposes of subsection (a)(1)—

(A) General rule

Where 1 or more persons in control of the issuing corporation transfer stock of such corporation in exchange for stock of the acquiring corporation, the stock of the acquiring corporation received shall be taken into account in determining whether such person or persons are in control of the acquiring corporation.

(B) Definition of control group

Where 2 or more persons in control of the issuing corporation transfer stock of such corporation to the acquiring corporation and, after the transfer, the transferors are in control of the acquiring corporation, the person or persons in control of each corporation shall include each of the persons who so transfer stock.

(3) Constructive ownership

(A) In general

Section 318(a) (relating to constructive ownership of stock) shall apply for purposes of determining control under this section.

(B) Modification of 50-percent limitations in section 318

For purposes of subparagraph (A)—

  (i) paragraph (2)(C) of section 318(a) shall be applied by substituting "5 percent" for "50 percent", and

  (ii) paragraph (3)(C) of section 318(a) shall be applied—

    (I) by substituting "5 percent" for "50 percent", and

    (II) in any case where such paragraph would not apply but for subclause (I), by considering a corporation as owning the stock (other than stock in such corporation) owned by or for any shareholder of such corporation in that proportion which the value of the stock which such shareholder owned in such corporation bears to the value of all stock in such corporation.

Box 1.1. Internal Revenue Code § 304: Redemption Through Use of Related Corporations

A HYPOTHETICAL EXAMPLE

To demonstrate the application of § 304 and its approach to tax time travel, let's consider a simple example based on the illustrations in figures 1.2 and 1.3. Shareholder wholly owns two different corporations: ABC Inc. and XYZ Inc. Assume that both ABC and XYZ are profitable corporations and that Shareholder wishes to get access to ABC's $100 of profits (to choose a round number to simplify calculations; for a more realistic scenario, simply add zeroes to this number). Shareholder could have ABC distribute the profits as a dividend; however, that would mean that the profits would be taxed first in the hands of ABC (currently at a rate of 21 percent) and then again in Shareholder's hands when the dividend is received (currently at the same 20 percent maximum rate that applies to capital gains).[98] As a result, ABC would pay $21 of tax on its profits ($100 x 21 percent), leaving only $79 to be distributed to Shareholder. Shareholder would then pay an additional $15.80 in tax on the $79 dividend ($79 x 20 percent), leaving Shareholder with only $63.20 of the $100 in profits at the end of the day.

If each share of ABC stock were worth exactly $79 (i.e., the corporation's after-tax profits) and Shareholder had a basis of $20 in each share of stock, Shareholder could significantly reduce the tax bite if the distribution were instead cast as a sale of the ABC stock. In the case of sale treatment, the reported gain would not be the full $79 received but only $59 (i.e., the $79 sale proceeds less Shareholder's $20 basis in the stock).[99] Assuming the stock had been held for more than one year, this would reduce the tax imposed on Shareholder from $15.80 to $11.80 ($59 x 20 percent), for a tax saving of $4 (or more than 25 percent).[100] Naturally, a larger basis would allow for even greater tax savings. For instance, a $40 basis would reduce Shareholder's tax by slightly more than half. But given that Shareholder wholly owns ABC, a redemption of stock by ABC could never achieve the desired sale treatment because Shareholder would fail all of the applicable statutory tests for treating a redemption as a sale.[101]

Still wishing to obtain a tax-free return of basis to reduce the tax, Shareholder could cause XYZ, which also has ample earnings, to purchase the ABC stock. This transaction would take the form of a sale and would not meet the definition of a *redemption* because XYZ would be purchasing the stock of another corporation and not its own stock.[102]

We will next consider whether this maneuver can achieve the sought-after sale treatment and tax-free recovery of basis and find that § 304 frustrates Shareholder's attempt to circumvent the tests for distinguishing redemptions taxed as distributions from redemptions taxed as sales. In the course of this analysis, we will examine what the operation of § 304 tells us about the complex relationship between tax and time and witness the ingenuity of the tax imagination at work as § 304 repeatedly—and seemingly impossibly—moves us back and forth along time's otherwise unbendingly linear, constantly forward-moving arrow.

DOWN THE RABBIT HOLE: § 304'S PREREQUISITES

For § 304 to apply in the brother-sister corporation context,[103] one or more persons must be in control of two corporations.[104] *Control* is defined as "ownership of stock possessing at least 50 percent of the total combined voting power of all classes of stock entitled to vote, or at least 50 percent of the total value of shares of all classes of stock."[105] As depicted in figure 1.2, Shareholder is in "control" of both ABC and XYZ because shareholder at all relevant times possesses at least one-half of the voting power and value of ABC and XYZ. Shareholder thus clearly meets the control requirement.

Before proceeding further with the analysis of this hypothetical example, it bears observing that constructive ownership rules apply for purposes of determining whether control exists under this test.[106] The constructive ownership rules involve a bit of time travel and imagination of their own, which is why taking a short diversion to discuss them is worthwhile. The constructive ownership rules treat one person as if that person actually owned stock that is owned by another.[107] For instance, if Shareholder's children held 51 percent of the stock of one or both of these corporations—which would bring Shareholder's ownership under the 50 percent threshold of control needed for § 304 to apply—it would make no difference. Under the constructive ownership rules, Shareholder would be treated as owning the children's stock and, therefore, as being in sole control.[108]

Interestingly, this reimagination of past events (which effaces the children's acquisition and ownership of stock of one or both of the corporations from Shareholder's tax timeline) is not the only path that time is deemed to take here. The constructive ownership rules also apply in reverse, treating each of the children as owning all of the stock owned by Shareholder.[109] Thus, multiple other past paths to the tax present coexist with Shareholder's reimagined tax past. To construct these alternate paths, Shareholder's ownership in ABC and XYZ would be repeatedly effaced and attributed to each of the children separately—and simultaneously. Accordingly, the concept of control employed for purposes of § 304 imagines a series of separate and distinct timelines that easily coexist rather than compete with each other for our attention.

To return now to the hypothetical example depicted in figure 1.2, there is an additional condition that must be satisfied in order for § 304 to apply to the transaction: one of the two controlled corporations must acquire stock in the other corporation from the controlling shareholder(s) in exchange for "property."[110] Here both ABC and XYZ are controlled by Shareholder, and XYZ has acquired stock in ABC from Shareholder in exchange for cash. Cash qualifies as *property* for this purpose.[111] Thus, the property requirement has likewise been satisfied.

With both the control and property requirements satisfied, § 304 will apply to the transaction depicted in figure 1.2. Before examining the tax consequences that § 304 ascribes to the transaction and the relation of § 304's operative rules to linear time, it is worth observing what is missing here—namely, any assessment of the taxpayer's subjective intent. Although § 304 is aimed at combatting abusive behavior, there is no requirement that the taxpayer have an intent to avoid tax by structuring the transaction as a sale of stock between related corporations. Some antiabuse rules do specifically target intentionally abusive behavior, while others contain exceptions for situations that lack a tax avoidance motive.[112] However, § 304, like many antiabuse rules,[113] aims to deter tax avoidance yet is written broadly enough to apply to taxpayers that have no intent to avoid tax at all. In fact, the lack of any need for a tax avoidance motive combined with the complexity of the provision led one of the attorneys whom I worked for while in practice to warn that § 304 acts as a trap for unwary taxpayers—and their tax advisers. The absence of an intent requirement will also be important for us to bear in mind as we next consider the role that § 304 plays in manipulating tax time.

FURTHER DOWN THE RABBIT HOLE: RECASTING THE SALE AS A REDEMPTION

When § 304 applies to a sale of stock in one controlled corporation to another, the property that is received in exchange for the stock by the controlling shareholder is "treated as a distribution in redemption of the stock of the corporation acquiring such stock."[114] To put this in terms of our example, the cash that Shareholder received from XYZ in exchange for one-half of Shareholder's ABC stock is treated as if XYZ had instead distributed that cash in redemption of *its own* (i.e., XYZ) stock. This is quite a fanciful reimagining of the events depicted in figure 1.2, but one with a very specific purpose. By recasting the actual events as a redemption by XYZ of its own stock, § 304 effectively forces Shareholder to determine the tax treatment of the cash proceeds under the rules in § 302 that apply for determining whether a redemption is more akin to a sale of stock or a corporate distribution.[115] Through this reimagining of past events, § 304 prevents Shareholder from circumventing the tests in § 302, which was the purpose for involving XYZ in the first place.

From a temporal perspective, what is interesting is *when* this reimagination of the actual events occurs. Because § 304 applies to any transaction that meets the control and property requirements without regard to the presence or absence of a tax avoidance motive, the recharacterization of the sale as a redemption happens automatically. In other words, even as the sale is taking place, § 304 causes the present that is becoming past to immediately be overwritten and rewritten. This is a far different approach to time from that embraced by the courts in the creation and application of the doctrine of substance over form, as described earlier. In the judicial creation, some action or intervention by the taxpayer, the IRS, and/or the courts is necessary before the doctrine of substance over form can be used to rewrite the past.

Time—sometimes a significant amount of time—will pass between the actual events and the decision to invoke the doctrine of substance over form to rewrite past events. Consider *Gregory v. Helvering* again as an example. In that case, the actual events occurred in September 1928. The return on which Gregory would have reported the transaction— either in keeping with the actual facts or invoking the doctrine of substance over form—was not due until almost six months later, on March 15, 1929.[116] In fact, Gregory did wait until March 1929 to file her return.[117] Under the law then in effect, the IRS was permitted two years beginning with the date the return was filed to examine the return and assess a deficiency.[118] The IRS, too, waited until near the deadline to send Gregory a notice of deficiency, having sent that notice disregarding the form of the transaction and instead assessing tax based on the transaction's substance in February 1931.[119] Gregory then had sixty days to file a petition with the Board of Tax Appeals contesting the IRS's proposed deficiency.[120] Again, Gregory waited nearly that long, filing her petition in April 1931.[121] More time passed as each successive court considered Gregory's case. The Board of Tax Appeals rendered its decision in December 1932.[122] The Second Circuit decided the appeal from the Board's decision in March 1934.[123] And the Supreme Court rendered the final decision in the case in January 1935.[124] Thus, more than six years passed between the actual events and their finally being disregarded in favor of the substance of the transaction, with a variety of different approaches to the reimagining and rewriting of time having been offered along the way. In the end, no final answer was reached regarding which of these rewritten pasts actually prevailed. (As you may recall, the Supreme Court seemed to leave time in suspense in the *Gregory* case.)

In § 304, Congress has neither required human intervention nor allowed for such a large time lag nor brooked uncertainty in how past events might be reimagined and rewritten. In lieu of a protracted process involving unpredictable human intervention—or even the messiness attendant to considering human motivation—§ 304 was designed to operate mechanically and automatically. Given its experience with the courts in this area, Congress chose not to leave the reexamination and rewriting of the past to chance. Instead, Congress dictated the reimagined past in advance, writing a future past to be later superimposed over the actual past without further intervention. Upon satisfaction of the control and property requirements, § 304 automatically and instantaneously processes and etches into tax memory a series of preprogrammed changes to the past.

Yet, belying its appearance as the only correct interpretation of events, § 304's preprogrammed rewriting of the past has undergone changes of its own. Congress has repeatedly fine-tuned its retelling of the past through § 304, making minor and major changes to its writing of the future past to better combat abuse.[125] This history and the automated processes we will next consider for determining the tax consequences of sales recast as redemptions are no less conflicted and confusing a product of the tax imagination than those that followed when the doctrine of substance over form unleashed the legal imaginations of so many different tax actors in *Gregory*.

HOW FAR DOWN DOES THE RABBIT HOLE GO?

The fictions at the heart of § 304 do not end with recharacterizing the sale of stock as a redemption. As suggested by the earlier discussion of why redemptions are sometimes likened to sales and sometimes to distributions, the distinction between these characterizations is made by reference to whether the redemption caused a "meaningful reduction" in the shareholder's interest in the redeeming corporation.[126] But making this determination by reference to Shareholder's interest in XYZ stock seems to make little sense when XYZ is involved only as an accommodation and none of its stock actually changed hands. Accordingly, despite the initial fiction that Shareholder's sale of ABC stock to XYZ is to be treated as a redemption by XYZ of its own stock, § 304 requires the determination of whether there has been a meaningful reduction in Shareholder's interest to be made by reference to Shareholder's ABC stock (and *not* by reference to Shareholder's XYZ stock).[127]

In other words, the rules of § 302 that characterize redemptions as sales or distributions are applied by comparing Shareholder's ownership of ABC stock before and after the fictional redemption. Because § 302 employs the same constructive ownership rules as § 304, its rules that characterize redemptions for tax purposes will treat Shareholder as having experienced no reduction in interest in the ABC stock.[128] These rules reflect the reality that Shareholder has merely traded direct control of 100 percent of ABC's stock for a combination of direct and indirect control of 100 percent of ABC's stock, as depicted in figure 1.3. Shareholder's interest in ABC thus remains undiminished; that is, there has been no actual reduction in Shareholder's interest in ABC, let alone a meaningful reduction. Shareholder's redemption is, therefore, classified as a corporate distribution rather than as a sale of stock.

Consequently, § 304 has rewritten and overwritten the past once again. What began, in form, as a sale by Shareholder of ABC stock to XYZ was first converted into a redemption by XYZ of its own stock from

Shareholder in order to trigger the application of the rules in § 302 for characterizing the redemption as a sale or distribution. Once those rules were triggered, the redemption by XYZ was erased and replaced with a redemption by ABC of its own stock for purposes of applying the § 302 rules to characterize the redemption as a sale or distribution.

But we still have not exhausted § 304's power to rewrite and overwrite past events. Congress preprogrammed § 304 to rewrite the past yet again immediately upon a determination that the fictional redemption will be treated as a corporate distribution. Now, what was ostensibly a distribution from ABC to Shareholder is treated instead as if ABC were not directly involved at all. To take into account XYZ's actual ownership of the ABC stock—both at the end of the "real" course of events and into the future—Shareholder is treated as having contributed the ABC stock to XYZ in exchange for fictional XYZ stock in a tax-free transaction. This newest turn of events is designed to trigger rules that (1) provide XYZ with an appropriate basis in the actual ABC stock that it purchased and (2) provide Shareholder with an appropriate basis in the fictional XYZ stock.[129]

XYZ is then treated as if it had redeemed the fictional XYZ stock in exchange for the sales proceeds that were provided to Shareholder in the beginning of this repeatedly rewritten course of events.[130] Based on our earlier analysis, that redemption is to be treated as a distribution and will be taxed as a dividend to the extent of corporate earnings and profits.[131] Only if there are insufficient earnings and profits to characterize the entire distribution as a dividend will Shareholder be able to recover any of the basis in the fictional (and fictionally redeemed) XYZ stock.[132] (By way of aside, the fictional XYZ stock will have the same basis that the ABC stock sold to XYZ had, because of the fictional tax-free contribution of the ABC stock to XYZ.[133]) Any unused tax basis from the fictional (and fictionally redeemed) XYZ stock is transferred to Shareholder's actual XYZ stock.[134]

If your head still hasn't begun spinning, rest assured that additional rewriting of the past awaits. When determining whether there are earnings and profits to support dividend treatment of the distribution, Shareholder must first look to the earnings and profits of XYZ.[135] This makes logical sense because it carries the most recent rewriting of the past to its natural conclusion. (In case you are losing track of all of the rewritings, this latest reimagined past is the one that involves the contribution of ABC stock to XYZ in exchange for fictional XYZ stock that is promptly—and fictionally—redeemed by XYZ.) If XYZ is thought to be making a distribution to Shareholder in the context of a redemption of its own stock, one would naturally expect that dividend treatment of that distribution would be determined by reference to XYZ's earnings and profits. But what if XYZ doesn't have sufficient earnings and profits to characterize the entire distribution as a dividend? Will Shareholder finally get to recover basis tax-free? Not necessarily, because Shareholder is required to look to the earnings and profits of ABC as well as those of XYZ in determining the extent to which the distribution will be characterized as a dividend.[136] Shareholder will thus be entitled to a tax-free recovery of basis only if the distribution exceeds the combined earnings and profits of both XYZ and ABC because these two corporations are, in effect, treated as having collectively made the distribution.

In this way, we have stumbled into an even more extreme rewriting of the past. Where past rewritings have repeatedly shifted the transaction from one corporation to the other, this final rewriting seems to efface the separate identities of the two corporations altogether. It is as if Congress, after struggling with several drafts of a story that has repeatedly been written and rewritten, has tired of working with the basic facts depicted in figure 1.2. In place of those facts, Congress appears to have decided to start all over again from the beginning of the story. Congress has, once and for all, dispensed with the pretense of working within the fiction of separate corporate identities and has displaced that fiction with another fictional story—namely, that the two corporations' businesses and profits should be merged into one, as if Shareholder had never created the two separate entities of ABC and XYZ to begin with but instead had created a single corporate shell to house both businesses together. It is this new story, and our last move back and forth along time's supposedly unbending arrow, that allows the earnings and profits of the two corporations to be pooled so that they can support what Congress appears to deem the appropriate end of the story—dividend treatment of as much of the distribution as possible (without actually inventing earnings and profits as well!).

Imagination Unleashed

This chapter's exploration of the judicial doctrine of substance over form through the seminal case *Gregory v. Helvering* and the congressional codification of the doctrine in § 304 has revealed how, notwithstanding conventional wisdom, federal tax law is in no way ruled by linear time. Federal tax law demonstrates an openness to far more imaginative and creative approaches to dealing with time, bending its fabric in ways that permit all tax actors—the Congress that writes the law; the taxpayers who, with the help of their tax advisers, must comply with the law; the IRS that must administer the law; and the courts that must interpret the law—the opportunity to travel through time to rewrite the tax past in ways that are deemed to lead to more just results in the tax present and future.

In *Gregory*, we witnessed how the judicial doctrine of substance over form permits taxpayers and their tax advisers, the IRS, and the courts to unleash their tax imaginations. Each of these tax actors was permitted to allow its mind to wander and to consider whether or not to offer new and different paths through the tax past to the tax present. And, as we witnessed with the IRS's proffer of multiple rewritings of the past in *Gregory*, there is no inherent limit on a single tax actor's ability to imagine and reimagine the past in different ways. For this reason, it is a bit misleading to refer to taxpayers, their tax advisers, the IRS, and the courts as tax "actors," even though that word is used here in the neutral sense of someone who is a "participant" or "takes part in any affair."[137] The word "actor" cannot help but carry the connotation of someone playing a role written by another. Yet, the actors involved in the tax drama that played out in *Gregory* were not merely following a script—playing their part as taxpayer, tax adviser, tax enforcer, or tax interpreter. Instead, more like authors, they were engaged in the creative endeavor of writing and rewriting the final script of a drama that had already played out.

As new paths were offered in place of the acknowledged "real" course of events, these tax actors/authors were able to argue over which among a variety of paths should be treated as the "true" path to the correct tax results—or whether there should be a discernible "true" path at all. Far from being bound to accept the previous points on time's arrow as real or given, for all of the actor/authors in *Gregory*, the past was a contested site that was open—not to figuring out what had "really" happened (because all involved, without qualms, had accepted the factual course of events) but to figuring out what ought to be considered as having happened in a reimagined past that would have concrete consequences in both the present and the future. It is as if the rewriting of the past in *Gregory*—the paradigmatic case applying substance-over-form principles—had been crowdsourced in order to obtain a fictional creation that best fit a collectively crafted idea of how to achieve a just tax result despite—not in light of—the actual events that had occurred or even tax law's putative embrace of linear time.

In contrast, § 304 involves the imagination of a single (albeit collective) tax actor/author: Congress. Nonetheless, we still witnessed conflict in the rewritings of the past embodied in § 304. These conflicts were not among competing stories offered by different actor/authors, as happened in *Gregory*, but among different versions of the same story as it was repeatedly rewritten in wholly new and different ways by a single actor/author. Congress preprogrammed § 304 to automatically unleash a process of congressional creation—or, in this case, repeated re-creation—of the tax past. Each succeeding version of the tax past is rewritten and then overwritten to move the taxpayer quickly and often jarringly back and forth along time's arrow, but always slowly inching closer to what Congress deems a just end result—a result that the crowdsourced writing entailed in the judicial incarnation of substance-over-form principles had earlier failed to achieve in the context of redemptions through related corporations. Thus, even with a single tax actor/author in control and the rewritten past preprogrammed in advance, the journey to reimagining the tax past through § 304 proved no less nakedly fictional and creative and no less twisted and conflicting than it did in *Gregory*.

This examination of judicial and statutory applications of substance-over-form principles, which have been heralded in the United States as the "cornerstone of sound taxation,"[138] demonstrates just how little taxpayers, their tax advisers, the IRS, the courts, and Congress feel bound by linear time. Given how deeply embedded substance-over-form principles are in US tax law, these tax actors freely take on the role of authors, bringing their creative energies to bear as they travel through time—or step outside time—to reimagine and rewrite the past in ways that they hope will bring about a more just tax present and future, whether for themselves, other taxpayers, or the tax system as a whole. But even if these tax actors embrace the role of author without giving it much thought, there is always an element of choice involved in applying and employing substance-over-form principles. Chapter 2 will view these choices through a critical lens, considering instances in which the IRS made the decision *not* to apply substance-over-form principles when the tax imagination was called on to address the tax aspects of battles for civil rights and social justice. More than just drawing attention to the IRS's failure to engage the tax imagination to correct injustices perpetrated against disadvantaged groups, chapter 2 demonstrates how the IRS has employed the tax imagination to manipulate time in ways that actually serve to channel and further entrench inequality and privilege that harms disadvantaged groups.

2

Time Travel Avoided (or, Justice Denied)

Chapter 1 applied a temporal lens to examine the application of substance-over-form principles in legislation and judicial decision-making in the United States. That chapter explored how a variety of tax actors can employ those principles to travel back in time to rewrite the course of past events in an effort to achieve what, in their eyes, is a more just or correct result in the tax present and future. From this perspective, substance-over-form principles are seen as a force for good, enhancing the perceived fairness of the tax system by protecting the public fisc and taxpayers alike.

But because just as much can be learned from the choice not to act as from the choice to act, this chapter takes a different approach to substance-over-form principles by examining instances in which the Internal Revenue Service chose *not* to apply those principles in the context of battles for civil rights and social justice. The two examples explored here are: (1) the IRS's decision to deny recognition to civil unions and domestic partnerships following the United States Supreme Court's marriage-equality decisions and (2) the IRS's shifting position regarding the tax-exempt status of segregated private schools following the Supreme Court's landmark *Brown v. Board of Education* decision. These examples demonstrate how the IRS's choice not to employ substance-over-form principles—in the face of sometimes very specific urging to do so—worked manifest injustice and did so in ways that illustrate how the creativity of the tax imagination can be used to further iniquitous ends as easily as it can be used as a force for good.

For some readers, this chapter may feel distinctly different from chapter 1, but that is only because conventional tax policy analysis is premised on the myth that tax law is uniquely "neutral"—an area in which the only concern relevant to developing policy is taxpayers' relative income. According to this view, any discussion of taxpayers' noneconomic characteristics (e.g., race, gender, or sexual orientation) is quite simply out of bounds; however, as I have explained at length elsewhere—and as this chapter will pointedly demonstrate—this view is profoundly misguided.[1] In both of the examples explored here, the IRS faced questions that seem to be of a purely tax nature, namely, which couples should qualify as a taxable unit and which organizations should be classified as tax-exempt charities. What brings race and sexual orientation into the discussion is the historic privilege enjoyed by some at the expense of subordinating others—and the ongoing battles for civil rights and social justice aimed at dismantling that privilege and ending that subordination—that shaped and influenced both the IRS's answers to these tax questions and the messages that those answers send about US society. Placed in this larger context, the IRS's decision to refuse to apply "cornerstone" tax principles to basic tax questions affecting members of minority groups conveys the message that a lesser (and, at first blush, seemingly less imaginative) standard of tax justice and fairness applies to members of these groups than applies to other taxpayers.

Yet, the story in this chapter is about more (and, in truth, is much worse) than just a refusal by the IRS to engage the tax imagination to rewrite the past either to (1) place same-sex couples' domestic partnerships and civil unions on equal footing with different-sex marriages or (2) acknowledge and repudiate the financial support that the federal government provided to segregated private schools. Compounding the harm done by its refusal to use the tax imagination to enforce the spirit (if not the letter) of Supreme Court decisions, the IRS actively manipulated tax time in both of these situations in ways that entrenched and enhanced the very forms of power and privilege—and the concomitant subordination of the "other"—that these judicial decisions aimed to dismantle. Thus, by delving into what initially might seem like an absence of imagination or creativity on the part of the IRS, this chapter actually reveals a different—and far darker and more insidious—side of the creativity of the tax imagination.

Defining *Marriage*

Historically, federal tax law deferred to state law when determining marital status.[2] For more than eighty years, this meant that same-sex relationships were not recognized for federal tax purposes because no state permitted same-sex couples to marry. Following a 1993 Hawaii

Supreme Court decision, however, Congress grew concerned that this deference to state law might soon force the federal government to legally recognize same-sex relationships.[3] In response, Congress enacted the Defense of Marriage Act (DOMA), which defined *marriage* for purposes of federal law as "only a legal union between one man and one woman as husband and wife."[4] When states eventually began to extend legal recognition to same-sex couples, DOMA denied them access to the relative tax certainty that marriage affords and instead relegated them to a wilderness in which the tax treatment of their relationships was uncertain, burdensome, and fraught with legal peril.[5]

As it turned out, Massachusetts—and not Hawaii—became the first state to permit same-sex couples to marry.[6] Before and after Massachusetts extended marriage to same-sex couples, a small group of other states created alternative legal relationships for same-sex couples, using labels like "domestic partnership" or "civil union" because extending marriage to same-sex couples was then politically risky and/or legally impossible.[7] Some of these states chose to permit different-sex couples to enter into these marriage alternatives too.[8]

Because DOMA presented no barrier to treating different-sex couples in civil unions and domestic partnerships as married, H&R Block sent an inquiry to the IRS in 2011 asking whether a different-sex couple who had entered into an Illinois civil union could file a joint federal income tax return. In keeping with substance-over-form principles discussed in chapter 1, the IRS responded that the different-sex couple could file jointly because, notwithstanding the difference in nomenclature, civil unions and marriages are legally equivalent under Illinois law:

> In general, the status of individuals of the opposite sex living in a relationship that the state would treat as husband and wife is, for Federal income tax purposes, that of husband and wife. Section 20 of the Illinois Religious Freedom Protection and Civil Union Act provides that "[A] party to a civil union is entitled to the same legal obligations, responsibilities, protections, and benefits as are afforded or recognizes [*sic*] by the law of Illinois to spouses . . . ." . . . Accordingly, if Illinois treats the parties to an Illinois civil union who are of opposite sex as husband and wife, they are considered "husband and wife" for purposes of Section 6013 of the Internal Revenue Code, and are not precluded from filing jointly . . . .[9]

Word of this position treating civil unions and marriages entered into by different-sex couples as in substance the same circulated quickly among the tax bar, and the Illinois Department of Revenue even publicly advised different-sex civil union couples that they could file joint tax returns at both the federal and state levels.[10]

Marriage-Equality Decisions

Two years later, in 2013, the Supreme Court decided *United States v. Windsor*, which declared unconstitutional the portion of DOMA that defined *marriage* for purposes of federal law and required the recognition of valid same-sex marriages for federal tax purposes.[11] Because the majority of states then refused to recognize same-sex relationships, the IRS promptly issued a revenue ruling drafted by lawyers in its Chief Counsel's Office to clarify which same-sex relationships would be recognized for federal tax purposes following *Windsor*.[12] After addressing same-sex marriages at length and taking an expansive view of which of these marriages would be recognized for federal tax purposes, the IRS closed the ruling by stating that any relationship "not denominated as a marriage" under state law would be denied legal recognition.[13] The IRS permitted taxpayers, at their option, to apply the revenue ruling retroactively to open tax years, which allowed different-sex couples who had entered into marriage alternatives to replace earlier "married filing jointly" returns with separate "single" returns if it proved to their tax advantage (e.g., to obtain a refund of a marriage penalty).[14]

Surprisingly, in deciding to exalt form over substance in this way, the IRS neither mentioned its earlier position in the widely disseminated letter to H&R Block nor provided any legal analysis that might support its reversal of position.[15] At the time, it seemed possible that the IRS might have adopted its new position to provide an incentive for states to permit same-sex couples to marry (as opposed to creating or maintaining an alternative status for them that would not be recognized for federal tax purposes). Indeed, a New Jersey court quickly cited the IRS's refusal to recognize New Jersey civil unions in support of its decision extending the right to marry to same-sex couples in that state.[16] But this impetus for denying recognition to civil unions and domestic partnerships disappeared with the Supreme Court's 2015 decision in *Obergefell v. Hodges*, which required all states to permit same-sex couples to marry.[17] Nonetheless, the IRS quickly extinguished any hope that its new position was merely an opportunistic effort to advance the cause of marriage equality.

Proposed Regulations

A few months after the decision in *Obergefell*, the IRS proposed regulations that reaffirmed its post-*Windsor* position.[18] In those regulations, principally drafted by its Chief Counsel's Office, the IRS proposed to recognize "[a] marriage of two individuals . . . for federal tax purposes if the marriage would be recognized by any state, possession, or territory of the United States."[19] The regulations went on to provide that "[t]he terms *spouse, husband,* and *wife* do not include individuals who have entered into a registered domestic partnership, civil union, or other similar relationship not denominated as a marriage under the law of a state, possession, or territory of the United States."[20] For the first time, the IRS articulated its reasons for denying legal recognition to marriage alternatives: (1) States that created marriage alternatives "have intentionally chosen not to denominate those relationships as marriages"; (2) recognizing domestic partnerships and civil unions might upset the expectations of couples who entered into those relationships to reap greater federal benefits (e.g., under Social Security) than they would if they were "married"; and (3) "no provision of the [Internal Revenue] Code indicates that Congress intended to recognize as marriages civil unions, registered domestic partnerships, or similar relationships."[21]

THE REACTION

The IRS received only a handful of comments regarding the proposed regulations. Of greatest interest here are the comments from those who opposed the IRS's decision to refuse to recognize marriage alternatives. These comments came from the Human Rights Campaign, a national LGBTQ+ rights organization; the American Bar Association's (ABA) Section of Taxation, which is "the largest, most prestigious group of tax lawyers in the country";[22] and Donald Read, a longtime tax practitioner and then a member of the IRS Advisory Council.

The Human Rights Campaign urged the IRS to recognize marriage alternatives both because other federal agencies (e.g., the Social Security Administration) already recognized those relationships and because "marriage remains out of reach for many same-sex couples due to fear of discrimination."[23] Donald Read assailed the IRS's rationale for refusing legal recognition to marriage alternatives as "contrived and unpersuasive,"[24] and the ABA Tax Section similarly described the IRS's decision to deny recognition as "seriously flawed."[25] As explored in the following sections, a recurring theme in both Read's and the Tax Section's comments is how the IRS's articulated reasons for refusing to recognize marriage alternatives conflicted with substance-over-form principles that should (and, before 2013, did) lead to recognizing relationship statuses other than marriage.

DEFERENCE TO STATE LAW

With respect to the first justification proffered by the IRS, Read contended that "[t]he proposed regulations do not show the deference to state domestic relations law that the [IRS] asserts. The proposed regulations do violence to the principles of *Windsor* and *Obergefell*. And they violate [the] longstanding 'cornerstone' tax principle that substance should prevail over form."[26] Read continued: "Inexplicably, the [IRS] ignores the spirit of *Windsor* by insisting on the label 'marriage,' even where all of the legal substance of marriage is present."[27] He further provided the IRS with examples of how its decision to deny recognition to marriage alternatives left the tax treatment of same-sex couples in these relationships just as it was under DOMA—that is, both uncertain and "vexatious."[28] Read pleaded with the IRS to reconsider its position: "Before the invalidation of DOMA there was nothing the [IRS] could do about this. But with DOMA now declared an unconstitutional violation of equal protection and due process, the [IRS] should not continue this discrimination, as it did without explanation in Rev. Rul. 2013-17."[29]

Like Read, the ABA Tax Section observed that the IRS was not actually deferring to the states as it purported to be doing:

> The state legislatures were in most cases limited in their ability to recognize same-sex relationships either as a political matter or by a state constitutional provision that banned them from enacting legislation extending "marriage" to same-sex couples. It is also important to bear in mind that when they first appeared on the scene, civil unions and domes-

tic partnerships were heralded as granting full equality to same-sex couples, but within a short time came to be seen as doing nothing more than relegating same-sex couples to a second-class, separate-but-equal status. With this history in mind, it becomes clear that to deny legal recognition to these relationships based on the label applied to them . . . would make the [IRS] a party to the very sort of discrimination that the U.S. Supreme Court declared unconstitutional in *Obergefell* and *Windsor* . . . .[30]

The Tax Section argued that, "[t]o truly defer to the states, the [IRS] should ignore the labels applied to these alternative relationships and be guided instead by their legal equivalence to marriage under state law in determining their federal tax treatment."[31]

FRUSTRATED EXPECTATIONS

With respect to the second justification proffered by the IRS, Read explained that the idea of frustrated expectations was nothing more than a red herring. Before *Windsor*, the only couples who possessed a choice between marriage and an alternative relationship status were different-sex couples.[32] Until *Windsor*, DOMA prevented *any* legal relationship entered into by a same-sex couple—whether called "marriage," "civil union," "domestic partnership," or something else—from being recognized under federal law. Moreover, Read insisted that different-sex couples' "expectation to avoid the tax or Social Security consequences of the substance of their legal relationship—that of spouses—because of the artifice of a different label is not deserving of deference."[33]

The ABA Tax Section further noted that, even after the Supreme Court's marriage-equality decisions, some same-sex couples remained trapped in alternative statuses and were unable to marry because of the death or incapacity of one of the partners (and the same was true of those whose relationships broke down before marriage became legally available but who did not split until afterward). These couples never had a choice among relationship statuses that the IRS would be honoring— their only choice was between a marriage alternative or no legal recognition at all.[34] Compounding the IRS's disregard for this legacy of unconstitutional discrimination, the Tax Section pointed out that the actual expectation of *all* couples in civil unions and domestic partnerships prior to 2013 was—based on the IRS's own guidance—that these

relationships *would* be recognized for federal tax purposes.[35] If anything, it was the IRS's reversal of position post-*Windsor* that frustrated
taxpayer expectations.[36]

Additionally, both Read and the ABA Tax Section opposed the
idea that interpretation of the tax laws should be dictated by couples'
expectations regarding the benefits that they might achieve through
abusive behavior that takes advantage of gaps in the law. The Tax Section observed that the doctrine of substance over form was designed
precisely to combat such behavior.[37] What's more, as Read remarked,
"it is not clear that their device works—Social Security bases spousal
status for benefits on whether one person would take from the other
under intestacy laws, which, in California, registered domestic partners clearly do."[38]

CONGRESSIONAL INACTION

With respect to the final justification proffered by the IRS, both Read
and the ABA Tax Section argued that it was untenable for the IRS to
base its guidance on congressional inaction in this area. Read pointed
out that Congress had not addressed marriage alternatives "because
it previously enacted an unconstitutional law that prevented same sex
domestic partners from being treated as married. Now that DOMA is
unconstitutional, the [IRS] needs to interpret the Code based on basic
tax principles—principally substance over form. If Congress does not
like that interpretation, it can change the law and overrule the regulations."[39] Likewise, the Tax Section's remarks relied heavily on the
gap-filling function of substance-over-form principles:

> [U]ntil the *Windsor* decision, Congress refused to treat even married
> same-sex couples as spouses for federal tax purposes. It is implausible to
> expect that Congress would have enacted a provision indicating that if
> the federal Defense of Marriage Act were ever struck down, only married
> spouses and not registered domestic partners or parties to a civil union
> could be treated as married. Moreover, the lack of a specific provision
> in the Code addressing the exact situation faced by a taxpayer has never
> been a barrier to the application of the principle of substance over form;
> indeed, the inability of Congress to timely address every situation faced
> by taxpayers is the *raison d'être* of that principle.[40]

Final Regulations

One might have expected that strong opposition from a national LGBTQ+ rights organization, the leading organization of tax lawyers in the United States, and a member of its own Advisory Council would have given the IRS pause in continuing to adhere to its post-*Windsor* position regarding marriage alternatives. Reconsideration was particularly appropriate given that the arguments in opposition were grounded repeatedly in the fundamental tax principle of substance over form and were buttressed by profound concern that the IRS's position would work an injustice on same-sex couples and contravene the spirit of the Supreme Court's marriage-equality decisions. But the IRS did not relent. Standing firm, the IRS declined to employ substance-over-form principles to rewrite the past in an effort to correct the injustice that the federal government had perpetrated against same-sex couples when it refused (unconstitutionally) to recognize their relationships. In place of imaginatively bending the fabric of time to make the tax system fairer by retroactively recognizing same-sex couples' domestic partnerships and civil unions as marriages, the IRS chose to bend time in other ways that disturbingly and disquietingly supported a position that perpetuated past injustice.

When it began discussing the comments received regarding the proposed regulations, the IRS immediately conveyed its lack of interest in altering its post-*Windsor* position by putting its own peculiar gloss on the past—exaggerating the support for its decision to deny recognition to marriage alternatives.[41] Sticking to its guns, the IRS pronounced the critiques leveled at its position "not persuasive."[42] In reaching this determination, the IRS put great weight on the fact that the states had chosen and maintained different labels for marriages, civil unions, and domestic partnerships.[43] The IRS further suggested that asking it to look to the substance of an alternative relationship status to determine whether that status is equivalent to marriage would be "unduly burdensome."[44] What the IRS failed to mention, however, was why states had chosen labels such as "civil union" and "domestic partnership" in the first place—or, for that matter, how the IRS had, without complaint, grappled for decades with complicated and thorny questions regarding the marital status of different-sex couples.[45] The IRS thus ignored the comments pointing out that these marriage alternatives had been created to relegate same-sex couples to "a second-class, separate-but-equal status"[46] and that the IRS was perpetuating discrimination by codifying that second-class tax status in regulations. The IRS acted as if a century of discrimination suffered by same-sex couples under the federal income tax had simply never occurred, instead focusing on the "burden" that it would be required to shoulder if it were asked to evaluate the legal status of a handful of marriage alternatives.

The IRS engaged in a similar temporal sleight of hand when it addressed comments regarding the possibility that taxpayer expectations might be frustrated by recognizing marriage alternatives. The IRS ignored its own pre-*Windsor* position that these relationships should be recognized for federal tax purposes—notwithstanding that this position was well known within the tax bar, publicly disseminated by at least one state tax authority, and cited in the comments submitted in response to the proposed regulations. Reinforcing its truncated view of the past, the IRS stated: "While not all same-sex couples in registered domestic partnerships, civil unions, or similar relationships had an opportunity to marry when they entered into their relationship, after *Obergefell*, same-sex couples now have the option to marry under state law."[47] In this single sentence, the IRS not only succeeded in diminishing past discrimination against same-sex couples to the point of vanishing but also sanitized the post-*Obergefell* world through its disregard of comments explaining that the option to marry is not always meaningful for same-sex couples because of the fear that marrying might result in acts of sexual orientation–based discrimination.

Rendering its erasure of difference and discrimination complete, the IRS reaffirmed the importance to its decision-making of allowing couples (read: different-sex couples) to retain the federal benefits they expected to reap from choosing a civil union or domestic partnership instead of a marriage.[48] The IRS dismissed the suggestion that couples in marriage alternatives were being relegated to the tax wilderness that all same-sex couples inhabited pre-*Windsor*, with little guidance as to how their relationships should be treated for federal tax purposes.[49] Indeed, further accentuating the benefits of its position, the IRS actually contended that it was helping couples who had chosen an alternative relationship status out of principled opposition to marriage "because [its position] ensures that these couples do not risk having their relationship characterized as marriage." Yet the IRS, in making this argument for the first time, failed to consider either (1) that, despite their distaste for the label, these couples had chosen to enter into relationships with legal rights and obligations equivalent to marriage—and that are often explicitly equated with marriage under state law; or (2) that the IRS itself is free to reword its forms and publications to eschew the "marriage" label while still affording equal treatment to marriage alternatives.[50]

Twisting time to its advantage, the IRS persisted in omitting mention of its past guidance indicating that different-sex couples' civil unions and domestic partnerships should be recognized for federal tax purposes. Nonetheless, the IRS continued to find support for its current position in Congress's failure to pass legislation recognizing different-sex couples' civil unions and domestic partnerships in the years following DOMA's passage. The IRS relied on this past congressional inaction to justify the present abdication of its own statutory duty to act in ways that fulfill taxpayers' "right to pay no more than the correct amount of tax" and "right to a fair and just tax system."[51] Notwithstanding the Supreme Court's admonition that "congressional inaction is generally a poor measure of congressional intent,"[52] the IRS seemed so eager to shirk its duties that it failed to consider why Congress might not have acted. In particular, the IRS failed to consider that its earlier position recognizing different-sex couples' civil unions and domestic partnerships—underpinned by long-standing substance-over-form principles that would have dictated the same result even without an IRS pronouncement—might have obviated the need for congressional action, thereby justifying the IRS's adherence to its past position rather than supporting its current one.

In this myriad of ways, the IRS managed to simultaneously wipe clean the pre-*Windsor* slate of history and to sanitize the post-*Windsor* world of the stain of discrimination. Then, like an aficionado of contemporary art, the IRS managed to find great meaning in the resulting, apparently blank slate of linear time.[53]

Rigidly Pliable Time

In its dogged resistance to applying substance-over-form principles to recognize marriage alternatives post-*Windsor*, the IRS took a strikingly different path from the one traveled in chapter 1. There, we watched a variety of tax actors—including the IRS—employ substance-over-form principles to creatively reimagine the past with the aim of furthering the fairness and integrity of the tax system in the present and future. But when implementing the Supreme Court's marriage-equality decisions, the IRS refused to similarly engage the power of the tax imagination in an effort not only to rectify past and present tax injustices but also to prevent future injustices from being visited upon same-sex couples. The IRS could have chosen to travel back in time to elevate what had been a "second-class, separate-but-equal status" for civil unions and domestic partnerships to an unadornedly "equal" tax status with marriage—but it pointedly did not. To the contrary, the IRS added insult to injury by permitting different-sex couples to travel back in time and apply its new position regarding marriage alternatives retroactively if it would provide them a tax advantage (e.g., if they wished to recoup the marriage penalty paid on a prior married-filing-jointly return). Of course, different-sex couples who had entered into civil unions and domestic partnerships and who had reaped tax benefits from filing jointly in the past (e.g., by being the lucky recipients of marriage bonuses) were not required to repay any of those tax benefits—for them, the past was past and the IRS's new position would only prospectively be applied to them.

What's more, the IRS was cognizant of the impact of its decision. After all, commenters had laid out the harm that the IRS was doing in specific terms and using strong language. Faced with a specific description of how its position would perpetrate the very type of injustice that the Supreme Court sought to remedy in *Windsor* and *Obergefell* and for which substance-over-form principles have historically served as a corrective, the IRS made a conscious decision *not* to avail itself of substance-over-form principles and instead appeared to embrace a rigidly linear conceptualization of time. But in embracing temporal rigidity, the IRS actually engaged in a highly creative manipulation of tax time that simultaneously relegated same-sex couples to a subordinated status and reinforced the privileging of heterosexuality and marriage in tax law.

Evoking Bruno Latour's work demonstrating how "moderns" have used time both to cut themselves off from their premodern past and to "other" their premodern contemporaries,[54] the IRS created its own peculiar version of the past when rationalizing its decision to embrace linear time. The IRS seemed to fold time upon itself so that only a certain fragment of the past was visible.[55] In this way, the IRS created something akin to what Máiréad Enright refers to as a "homogeneous national time"[56]—here with a pointedly heterosexual cast. Building on Latour's work, Enright has explained how, in the context of national efforts to address Ireland's history of religious institutional abuse, such "[h]omogeneity enables a radical break with the past—there are no important stragglers. . . . There is little attempt to examine the ongoing impacts of past abuse or to consider whether the motivations and system that enabled that abuse have persisted . . . ."[57] In its post-*Windsor* posturing, the IRS similarly avoided consideration of the ongoing impact of past sexual orientation–based discrimination and showed no inclination to address the persistence of that discrimination, especially in its own decision-making process.

But the IRS did not do this by seeking "closure" and creating bounded segments of time that are sealed off from each other, as Ireland did.[58] Instead, the IRS created a shared, national time in which past instances of discrimination against the LGBTQ+ community—including those perpetrated by Congress and the IRS—are hidden from view by being folded beneath a heterosexual surface reflecting the experience and expectations of different-sex couples. For the IRS, the privileged position of different-sex couples—who were able to enter into civil unions and domestic partnerships in an attempt to reap personal benefit from discrimination against same-sex couples—is to be honored and given priority by being placed above any recognition of, or remedy for, past sexual orientation–based discrimination.

And with past discrimination tucked neatly beneath a sanitized and acceptable surface of heterosexual privilege, the IRS continued its project of folding linear time upon itself in ways that further relegated the LGBTQ+ community to invisibility. By wiping the pre-*Windsor* slate of history clean, the IRS signaled that same-sex couples became worthy subjects for inclusion in national time only following the *Windsor* and *Obergefell* decisions, when they gained access to the institution of marriage and homonormativity could truly complement heteronormativity. Nonetheless, even then, the IRS still managed to fold time in a way that hides the experience of married same-sex couples below a heterosexual surface.

In a comment not discussed earlier, Mark Wojcik, a professor at the John Marshall Law School, stated:

> I would also support an additional phase [*sic*] in the proposed rule, stat-ing expressly that the interpretation will "apply to same-sex marriages" and that "these definitions apply regardless of gender." Although the proposed rule clearly intends to include same-sex marriages, including that under-standing expressly in the proposed rule itself may avoid any problems of interpretation. Additionally, as various IRS and Treasury Department regu-lations using the terms "husband" and "wife" are updated in future years, I also urge the drafters to replace those terms with the term "spouse."[59]

The IRS flatly rejected Wojcik's suggestion to acknowledge the events that occasioned the proposed regulations:

> Treasury and the IRS believe that the definitions in the proposed regula-tions apply equally to same-sex couples and opposite-sex couples, and that no clarification is needed. Proposed § 301.7701-18(a) states, without quali-fication, that, "[f]or federal tax purposes, the terms *spouse, husband*, and *wife* mean an individual lawfully married to another individual," and that the "term *husband and wife* means two individuals lawfully married to each other." The language is specifically gender neutral, which reflects the hold-ings in *Windsor* and *Obergefell*. . . . Similarly, the language in proposed § 301.7701-18(b) refers to a marriage of two individuals, without specifying gender. Amending the regulations to specifically address a marriage of two individuals of the same sex would undermine the goal of these regulations to eliminate distinctions in federal tax law based on gender. For these rea-sons, the final regulations do not adopt this comment.[60]

The IRS then punted Wojcik's suggestion that it embrace a more inclu-sive approach to drafting guidance for taxpayers. The IRS stated that this suggestion "relates to forms and is therefore outside the scope of these final regulations. Nevertheless, Treasury and IRS will consider the com-menter's recommendation when updating IRS forms and publications."[61]

In reality, the IRS did nothing to eliminate gender-based distinctions through these regulations. After all, how could one eliminate gender-based distinctions through a project that revolved around defining the gendered terms *husband* and *wife*? Any interest in eliminating gender-based distinctions is belied by the IRS's persistent embrace of these terms in publications targeted at taxpayers, which continue to use "husband" and "wife" (rather than "spouse") and often do so in an explicitly heterosexual context.[62] Likewise, more formal guidance continues to refer to "husband" and "wife" rather than paraphrasing unconstitutionally gendered pre-*Windsor* statutes in gender-neutral terms.[63]

In drafting these regulations and essentially rejecting Wojcik's comments, what the IRS did was to fold the decades-long battle for marriage equality, the historic victories in *Windsor* and *Obergefell*, and the issues associated with past (and persistent) sexual orientation–based discrimination in the United States deeply below a sanitized heterosexual surface. In a move reminiscent of DOMA—which defined *marriage* for purposes of federal law in a way that branded same-sex couples inferior without so much as mentioning them—the IRS created definitions of *marriage, husband, wife,* and *spouse* that eschewed any mention of sexual orientation and layered the separate existence and experience of the LGBTQ+ community below the visible (and visibly heterosexual) national timeline that it had created.

Though at first blush it may have seemed as if the IRS chose to hold fast to a rigid, linear representation of time when it refused to apply substance-over-form principles to determine the tax treatment of marriage alternatives, what the IRS actually did was to provide a further demonstration of the pliability of time in tax law. There is no lack of imagination in the IRS's regulations defining terms relating to marital status. To the contrary, these regulations represent a powerful—even if profoundly misdirected—exercise of the tax imagination that both reifies and worsens existing injustice. In implementing *Windsor* and *Obergefell,* the IRS did not merely bring same-sex couples into the marital fold. The IRS creatively manipulated time by folding and layering it in ways that further entrenched the privileging of marriage and heterosexuality in and through US federal tax law.[64]

We will next consider an example that provides some hope—however slim—that this misguided use of the tax imagination might someday be recognized and rectified.

Racial Discrimination by Tax-Exempt Entities

In 1954, the United States Supreme Court issued its landmark decision in *Brown v. Board of Education*.[65] In *Brown*, the Court found that segregation in public education violated the constitutional guarantee of equal protection of the laws, holding "that in the field of public education the doctrine of 'separate but equal' has no place. Separate educational facilities are inherently unequal."[66] Nevertheless, as Olatunde Johnson has explained:

> The end of formal, *de jure* segregation . . . did not spell the end to informal, *de facto* school segregation. One strategy white parents used to resist integration was to flee the public school system. In the years immediately following *Brown*, thousands of white children flocked to newly created private schools, leaving a minority of white students in many public school districts. In some communities, the white student body moved en masse to a new private school, taking the indicia of the old schools, such as the school colors, symbols, and mascots. Pledging massive resistance, many southern state governments encouraged establishment of private schools, enacting legislation mandating or allowing the closing of public schools to resist desegregation or providing state tax credits and tuition grants to students attending private schools.[67]

In addition to the financial assistance provided by state governments, segregated private schools received aid and approval from the federal government because they were recognized as tax-exempt under Internal Revenue Code § 501(c)(3) and were eligible to receive tax-deductible charitable contributions.[68] The legal debate over whether the federal government could confer the benefits of tax-exempt status on segregated private schools, like the more recent debate over the recognition of marriage alternatives, squarely raised the choice whether or not to apply substance-over-form principles in a way that would advance tax justice. And as with marriage alternatives, the IRS's refusal to apply substance-over-form principles represented not a lack of imagination but rather the misuse of the tax imagination to preserve power and privilege.

Shift in Policy

In 1965, the IRS "suspended rulings to private schools while considering the question of the effect of racial discrimination on their tax-exempt status."[69] Some two years later, on August 2, 1967, the IRS announced that it would resume issuing rulings to schools but "that exemption will be denied and contributions will not be deductible if the operation of the school is on a segregated basis and its involvement with the state or political subdivision is such as to make the operation unconstitutional or a violation of the laws of the United States."[70] A *New York Times* article reporting on this change highlighted the limited impact of the policy, under which "[a]ll or nearly all of the private schools that have been organized in the South in an effort to maintain segregation will be entitled to tax exemption, at least for the present."[71] The only segregated private schools that would fail to qualify for exemption after the 1967 policy change were (1) those that received "direct financial aid from any state or local government unit" and (2) those whose students received tuition assistance from a governmental unit that "constitute[d] more than half of the total financial support for the schools."[72]

Notably, as the *Times* pointed out, the policy change and the accompanying approval of forty-two southern schools' pending applications for tax exemption were announced at an unusual time—eight o'clock in the evening—on the same day that the IRS had come under pressure from the chair of the Senate Finance Committee, who had just announced hearings later in the week "to determine why the ruling on the tax status of the private schools had been delayed."[73]

Changing Definition of Charitable

The legal justification underpinning the agency's policy shift appears in an IRS legal memorandum dated August 1, 1967 (i.e., the day before the announced change in position).[74] As described later, the analysis in that memorandum revolves around interpretation of the word "charitable" in § 501(c)(3). Prior to discussing that analysis, it is necessary to briefly describe the legal background against which that word would be interpreted by the IRS.

Though the core text of § 501(c)(3) has not undergone dramatic change over the decades,[75] how the IRS interprets the word "charitable" has changed significantly.[76] Early IRS interpretations of "charitable" embraced the "popular and ordinary sense" of the word by confining its meaning to "relief of the poor."[77] This interpretation persisted until the end of the 1950s.[78] Then, in 1959, the IRS proposed new regulations under § 501(c)(3) that would shift the interpretation of the word from its then-prevailing popular sense to its legal sense: "The term 'charitable' is used in section 501(c)(3) in its generally accepted legal sense and is, therefore, not to be construed as limited by the separate enumeration in section 501(c)(3) of other tax-exempt purposes which may fall within the broad outlines of 'charity' as developed in judicial decisions."[79] The IRS provided no explanation for this shift in interpretation; however, the lack of explanation was not unusual for the time.[80] The new interpretation was finalized within a few months[81] and applied at the time that the IRS's 1967 memorandum regarding the tax-exempt status of segregated private schools was drafted—and still persists today.[82]

1967 Legal Memorandum

Legal support for the IRS's shift in position regarding the tax-exempt status of segregated private schools can be found in a memorandum prepared by the IRS Chief Counsel's Office.[83] That office began its memorandum by recapitulating the "basic legal propositions" regarding what constitutes a charitable purpose under § 501(c)(3).[84] First, in keeping with the regulations described earlier, the Chief Counsel's Office reaffirmed that the word "charitable" in § 501(c)(3) was used in its "generally accepted legal sense."[85] Second, the Chief Counsel's Office drew a distinction between activities that might be classified as *charitable* when provided only to a discrete class of beneficiaries and those that might be classified as *charitable* only if open to all members of the community. As an example of the former, the Chief Counsel's Office noted that "it is commonly accepted in the general law of charity that advancement of education may constitute a valid charitable purpose although beneficiaries are limited to a particular class on the basis of race, religion, sex, social class, geographical location, etc., provided the class is not so small that the purpose is not of benefit to the community."[86] As an example of the latter, the Chief Counsel's Office pointed to recreational facilities, which must be open to the general public to qualify as tax-exempt.[87] Finally, the Chief Counsel's Office added that "[a] charitable trust cannot be created for a purpose which is illegal or whose accomplishment would tend to frustrate some well-settled public policy."[88]

EDUCATIONAL ACTIVITY

In view of these basic legal propositions, the Chief Counsel's Office started from the premise "that under accepted principles of law, an otherwise qualified nonprofit private school cannot be denied exemption or qualification for deductible charitable contributions under Federal income, estate or gift tax statutes *solely* by reason of the fact that it limits its students to members of a particular race or religion."[89] It rejected the suggestion that "the change in the legal climate in recent years concerning racial segregation has been such as to invalidate prior concepts of tax law and charitable trust law."[90] As explained in an appendix to the memorandum, the Chief Counsel's Office saw this suggestion as implicating the last of its enumerated list of basic legal propositions: "The proposal is sometimes advanced that the practice of racial discrimination in any form of formal schooling is now so contrary to clearly defined national policy and so manifestly detrimental to community interest that private segregated schools can no longer qualify as organizations 'organized and operated exclusively for ... charitable ... or educational purposes' within the meaning of sections 501(c)(3) or 170(c)(2) of the Code."[91]

Adopting a narrow focus, the Chief Counsel's Office framed the question in a way that directed attention squarely toward the schools themselves and their activities. In the eyes of the Chief Counsel's Office, the schools' "teaching and training functions ... clearly qualif[ied] as educational by any standards heretofore applied" and, accordingly, were presumed to provide a community benefit.[92] The question then became whether "the element of racial discrimination [was] so detrimental to the community that its presence outweigh[ed] any community benefit deriving from the educational functions."[93] In other words, had the legislative, judicial, and executive actions taken since *Brown* come to "evidence not only a national policy against racial discrimination in any function that is touched with public interest; but also a recognition of the fact that community and public interest is not served by racially segregated schooling"?[94]

Reviewing a litany of legislative, judicial, and executive actions regarding racial discrimination, the Chief Counsel's Office concluded that "none of the national action thus far taken in the general area of civil rights law and policy has purported to deal with educational activities outside the public sector."[95] Lacking "some sharply defined expression of policy against racial discrimination in private education embodied in specific national legislation," the Chief Counsel's Office advised against denying tax-exempt status to segregated private schools on public policy grounds.[96]

STATE AID

The Chief Counsel's Office admitted of only one possible exception to its tax absolution of discrimination by private schools—when the aid received from a state unequivocally turned the private school into an arm of the state. According to the Chief Counsel's Office, to negate the general conclusion that segregated private schools qualified for tax-exempt status would require "a clearly expressed and controlling judicial determination that a particular kind of action on the part of a state in connection with the operation of a private segregated school constitutes state involvement of a character which is illegal in the sense of being an action which is subject to judicial restraint as a violation of the Constitution."[97] Referring to the Supreme Court's decision in *Cooper v. Aaron* and a lower court's decision in *Griffin v. State Board of Education*, the Chief Counsel's Office suggested: "From these two court decisions it may be argued that there is a clear public policy against state support of segregated schooling, private or public, through either direct financial support of such institutions by the state or indirect support through the device of tuition grants where such grants constitute the predominant financial support of such schools."[98] If a private school were to accept such aid from the state, "it could then be argued that the school's operations partake of the same illegality as the state action."[99] Consequently, it might be argued that the school was operating either "illegally or at least contrary to clearly defined public policy" in a way that contravenes the prohibition against creating a charity for purposes that are illegal or that violate public policy.[100]

Instances of direct or significant indirect state financial support were the only situations that the Chief Counsel's Office identified in its memorandum as implicating a sufficiently "sharply defined" public policy that might furnish the basis for denying or revoking a segregated private school's tax-exempt status.[101] In fact, these were also the only bases for denial of an exemption that made their way into the IRS's August 1967 announcement on the tax-exempt status of segregated private schools.[102]

FEDERAL AID

If public policy was violated by direct or indirect state financial support for segregated private schools, what about the financial support that the federal government provided to those schools through the grant of tax-exempt status and the ability to accept tax-deductible charitable contributions? Does that financial support "constitute a form of Federal involvement in racial discrimination . . . contrary to the limitations of the Fifth Amendment"?[103] Although the Chief Counsel's Office acknowledged that such an "[a]rgument also has been advanced," it rejected the argument out of hand because it "found no legal support" for this proposition.[104]

Yet, it seems odd to assert—and without explanation in an otherwise lengthy memorandum—that there is no legal support for viewing tax-exempt status and the charitable contribution deduction as forms of federal financial assistance to segregated private schools. As explored in chapter 1, substance-over-form principles were embraced in the early years of the US federal income tax and, just a few years before the Chief Counsel's Office drafted its memorandum, had been called the "cornerstone of sound taxation" by the United States Court of Appeals for the Fifth Circuit.[105] Absolving an organization of the need to pay tax provides an obvious and direct financial benefit, and the ability to accept deductible charitable contributions operates as an indirect financial benefit through what is tantamount to a federal matching program for contributions made to the organization.

This assertion seems even stranger considering that around the same time—in November 1967—then–Assistant Secretary of the Treasury for Tax Policy Stanley Surrey "called for a 'tax expenditure budget' that would report the revenue cost of 'deliberate departures from accepted concepts of net income . . . [through which] our tax system does operate to affect the private economy in ways that are usually accomplished by expenditures—in effect to produce an expenditure system described in tax language.'"[106] What Surrey called for then—and, following his styling, what is referred to now as "tax-expenditure analysis"—applies substance-over-form principles to the very structure of the federal tax laws. Looking past the formal inclusion of provisions within the Internal Revenue Code, tax-expenditure analysis attempts to separate tax provisions that are part of the necessary structure of an income tax from those that are tax preferences or penalties. Although Surrey claimed to have invented this application of substance-over-form principles—identifying and uncovering what are in substance direct spending programs hidden away in the tax laws—the notion that the government can spend through the tax code was neither a new idea nor one that was original to Surrey.[107]

It should thus have taken little imagination on the part of the Chief Counsel's Office to accept the notion that the tax-exempt status of segregated private schools and their ability to accept tax-deductible charitable contributions was, in substance, a form of federal financial assistance whose constitutionality merited sustained legal consideration rather than summary dismissal.[108] Instead, the legal memorandum leaves the impression that the Chief Counsel's Office refused to exercise the power of the tax imagination because it worried about disturbing the status quo and becoming enmeshed in the civil rights struggles of the time—that is, in social, political, and cultural matters that tax law ostensibly stands above. As explored in the coming pages, this temporally charged move—coupled with the earlier shift in the interpretation of the word "charitable"—has had a long-lasting, detrimental impact on the ability to consider the social justice implications of granting tax-exempt status to organizations that discriminate. In these ways, the legal memorandum's analysis foreshadows the IRS's treatment of marriage alternatives that was examined earlier in this chapter. In both cases, the IRS declined to apply the same robust standards of tax fairness to issues affecting minority groups fighting for civil rights and social justice as are applied for the benefit of others while, at the same time, imaginatively manipulating time in troubling ways that have served only to solidify and strengthen the position of those with power and privilege.

Enter the Courts

Before long, aggrieved taxpayers and the courts brought their legal imaginations to bear where the Chief Counsel's Office failed to do so. The same arguments that were summarily dismissed by the Chief Counsel's Office in 1967 were raised by African American taxpayers from Mississippi and their children in a class-action suit brought just two years later. In *Green v. Kennedy*, the taxpayers and their children sought an injunction that would (1) prevent the IRS from conferring tax-exempt status on segregated private schools in Mississippi in the future and (2) require the IRS to revoke the tax-exempt status that it had conferred in the past on segregated private schools in that state.[109] In 1970, a three-judge district court temporarily enjoined the IRS from issuing new tax exemptions to segregated private schools in Mississippi pending the outcome of the litigation.[110]

In reaching its decision, the court rejected the IRS's narrow approach in its 1967 policy announcement: "In our view the scope of constitutional protection cannot be so narrowly defined to disregard the impact of past State action and support, and to ignore the significance of current Federal support and benefits."[111] The court continued: "The Federal Government is not constitutionally free to frustrate the only constitutionally permissible state policy, of a unitary school system, by providing government support for endeavors to continue under private auspices the kind of racially segregated dual school system that the state formerly supported."[112] Recognizing that "the case . . . does not involve outright tuition grants to students by the Government . . . but rather tax benefits to the schools, and to persons contributing to the schools," the court found "this difference to be only a difference of degree that does not negative our essential finding . . . that the tax benefits under the Internal Revenue Code mean a substantial and significant support by the Government to the segregated private school pattern."[113] In seeing through the tax form to the substance of this financial assistance, the court was particularly troubled by the ability of segregated private schools to receive deductible charitable contributions, which the court likened to a federal "matching grant" program for these schools.[114] Given that the segregated private schools created to avoid the impact of the *Brown* decision were operating on the "thinnest financial basis," the court found that contributions were key to constructing school buildings (because tuition was only expected to cover operating expenses) and were necessary to replace state tuition grants that had been declared unconstitutional.[115] Additionally, the grant of tax-exempt status was seen as approval of the schools by the federal government that eased their ability to obtain financing.[116]

In July 1970, while the litigation was still pending but "under increased pressure by some in Congress and by civil rights groups to change its policy on private schools,"[117] the IRS announced its acquiescence with the court's decision. But the IRS did not do this by embracing the notion that the federal government was in substance supporting racial discrimination through the provision of tax benefits. Rather, the IRS indicated that it would deny tax-exempt status to all private schools practicing racial discrimination on the ground that such schools do not qualify as *charitable* within the meaning of § 501(c)(3).[118]

In its final decision ordering a permanent injunction, the district court affirmed the IRS's approach of denying exemption to any school engaging in racial discrimination on the ground that such schools cannot qualify as *charitable* in light of federal policy against racial segregation in education.[119] The court saw merit in this approach because it avoided forcing the court to adjudicate the constitutionality of the federal government's provision of financial support to segregated private schools:

> We are fortified in our view of the correctness of the IRS construction by the consideration that a contrary interpretation of the tax laws would raise serious constitutional questions, such as those we ventilated in our January, 1970, opinion. Clearly the Federal Government could not under the Constitution give direct financial aid to schools practicing racial discrimination. But tax exemptions and deductions certainly constitute a Federal Government benefit and support. While that support is indirect, and is in the nature of a matching grant rather than an unconditional grant, it would be difficult to establish that such support can be provided consistently with the Constitution. The propriety of the interpretation approved by this court is underscored by the fact that it obviates the need to determine such serious constitutional claims.[120]

Indeed, just six months later, another three-judge panel of the same court confronted a similar challenge to the constitutionality of tax benefits conferred on social clubs and fraternal orders that discriminate on the basis of race in their membership.[121] Unable to dodge the constitutional question, the court employed the substance-over-form principles embodied in tax-expenditure analysis to find that fraternal orders' exemption from tax and their ability to accept deductible charitable contributions constituted aid that triggered the application of the Fifth Amendment and rendered the federal government's involvement with the orders' racial discrimination unconstitutional.[122]

A few months following the final decision in *Green*, the IRS formalized its new position in a revenue ruling that required private schools nationwide to have a "racially nondiscriminatory policy as to students" in order to be classified as *charitable* within the meaning of § 501(c)(3) and qualify for tax-exempt status.[123] But neither the *Green* decision nor the revenue ruling ended the controversy over the tax-exempt status of segregated private schools, especially as questions regarding enforcement of the new requirement began to arise.[124] What's more, the *Green* court left open a question that quickly became the focus of litigation: whether a private school that claimed its racial discrimination was rooted in religious belief could qualify as tax-exempt.[125] This litigation involved the separate cases of Goldsboro Christian Schools and Bob Jones University. Those cases wound their way through the courts in the 1970s until they finally reached the Supreme Court in the early 1980s.[126]

The consolidated cases resulted in the landmark decision *Bob Jones University v. United States*.[127] In that decision, the Supreme Court upheld the IRS's interpretation of the word "charitable" in § 501(c)(3).[128] Citing actions by all three branches of the federal government, the Court concluded that it was proper to deny tax-exempt status to private schools that engage in racial discrimination—including private religious schools—because "a firm national policy to prohibit racial segregation and discrimination in public education" existed even before the IRS's 1970 change in position.[129] However, in affirming the denial of tax-exempt status to Bob Jones University and Goldsboro Christian Schools, the Court set a high bar for disqualifying other organizations from tax-exempt status based on violating public policy. The Court confirmed that the IRS has the initial responsibility to make determinations regarding tax-exempt status, including whether an organization's "activities so violate public policy that the entities involved cannot be deemed to provide a public benefit worthy of 'charitable' status."[130] Nevertheless, the Court underscored "that these sensitive determinations should be made only where there is no doubt that the organization's activities violate fundamental public policy."[131]

Temporal Sleight of Hand

In its early treatment of segregated private schools, the IRS chose not to apply substance-over-form principles in an apparent effort to disturb existing power structures in US society as little as possible. While it acted to protect and preserve heterosexual and marital privilege in its post-*Windsor* treatment of marriage alternatives, the IRS acted in 1967 to leave entrenched racial privilege largely intact by sharply limiting the situations in which the tax-exempt status of segregated private schools would be revoked or denied. Nevertheless, aggrieved African American taxpayers and the federal courts quickly stepped in to apply substance-over-form principles where the IRS had refused to do so, nudging the tax system farther along the arc of justice. As employed by these taxpayers and the courts, substance-over-form principles opened the way to reimagining "private" discrimination as being "publicly" approved and financially supported, thereby potentially implicating the federal government in organizations' past, present, and future acts of invidious discrimination and constraining the government to withdraw its support and approval of that discrimination.[132]

EMBRACING STATUTORY OVER CONSTITUTIONAL INTERPRETATION

But the *Green* and *Bob Jones* cases provide no more than a sliver of hope for advancing tax justice—and perhaps even less than that. Though the IRS realized the error in its 1967 policy shift and changed course even before the *Green* court reached a final decision, the IRS nonetheless persisted in its choice *not* to embrace substance-over-form principles. When revising its stance on whether segregated private schools were eligible for tax-exempt status, the IRS stood by its 1967 focus on the schools and concomitant embrace of statutory interpretation—particularly its interpretation of the word "charitable" as incorporating a (newly significant) public policy restriction. The IRS stood fast to its 1967 analytical framework despite having had an injunction issued against it based on the competing framework urged by African American taxpayers and adopted by the *Green* court, which focused on the federal government's role in facilitating discrimination and embraced substance-over-form principles in testing whether the federal tax benefits provided to segregated private schools passed constitutional muster. Ultimately, both the *Green* and *Bob Jones* courts acceded to the IRS's position, with an impact that goes far beyond the question of conferring tax-exempt status on segregated private schools.

The Supreme Court's adoption of the IRS's approach—even while acknowledging that the tax benefits provided to charitable organizations constitute a form of federal financial assistance[133]—has proved pivotal. With its decision in *Bob Jones*, the Court appears to have effectively set in stone the IRS's choice to have questions regarding the impact of discrimination on an organization's eligibility for tax-exempt status play out on the terrain of statutory rather than constitutional interpretation. Commentators analyzing whether tax-exempt status should be denied to organizations that engage in discrimination have, since that decision, focused their attention on the Court's public policy analysis in *Bob Jones*. Scant (if any) attention has been paid to the notion that the federal government might be providing financial support for discrimination that the government is constitutionally prohibited from engaging in itself.

This approach was on full display in the wake of the Supreme Court's marriage-equality decisions discussed earlier in this chapter. Spurred by popular attention and discussion both at oral argument and in the Court's opinions, commentators analyzed the impact of *Windsor* and *Obergefell* on the tax-exempt status of religious and other organizations that engage in sexual orientation–based discrimination.[134] These commentators gave no serious consideration to the constitutional implications stemming from the federal government's past and present provision of financial assistance to organizations that discriminate against same-sex couples—discrimination that the government is now forbidden from engaging in itself. Instead of focusing on the Court's marriage-equality decisions as a possible ground for ending federal assistance to organizations that discriminate, the commentators looked upon those decisions as nothing more than artifacts. In other words, they considered only whether *Windsor* and *Obergefell* provided sufficient evidence of a federal public policy against sexual orientation–based discrimination that might serve as the basis for disqualifying an organization from tax-exempt status because its discriminatory actions now prevent it from qualifying as *charitable* within the meaning of § 501(c)(3).[135]

EXPANDING AND CONTRACTING SPACE AND TIME

More than a simple binary choice between embracing the rigidity of linear time or the temporal flexibility of substance-over-form principles, the choice between a statutory or constitutional analysis predetermines how one imagines and evaluates the propriety of conferring tax-exempt status on organizations that discriminate. The latter assertion—namely, that framing a question as either of constitutional dimension or merely of statutory interpretation will impact how the question is analyzed and answered—should hardly be controversial. But the notion that the choice of framework will likewise determine how one imagines what is at stake in answering the question requires some explanation. This explanation will demonstrate once again how, even when the IRS seems to choose to adhere to a rigidly linear representation of time, its choice can nonetheless serve to manipulate and bend time in other ways—in this case by contracting the temporal *and* spatial frames in which one envisions the question whether or not to confer tax-exempt status as being raised and answered. By contracting the spatiotemporal frame of analysis, the IRS—with the help of the courts—limited the impact of administrative and judicial decisions that otherwise appear to further social justice by attenuating their effect both on those who discriminate and on a federal government that supports them.

Constitutional Analysis

From a spatial perspective, choosing to focus on the constitutional implications of conferring tax-exempt status on an organization broadens the frame to include the federal government and, in reality, all members of the society whom that government represents. Put differently: if the debate over tax-exempt status plays out on constitutional terrain, the IRS and the courts—and all Americans—are forced to consider whether the federal government ought to be permitted to use tax dollars to support organizations that engage in discrimination that the federal government is prohibited from perpetrating itself. In contrast, when the choice is made to relocate the debate over tax-exempt status to statutory terrain, the spatial frame shrinks considerably, allowing us to see only the organization itself. Within that contracted frame, we are asked to consider only whether the organization's actions contravene fundamental public policy and, if so, whether that violation of public policy outweighs all of the good that the organization does. Questions of the federal government's financial entanglement with the organization are pushed outside the frame and, hidden from view, naturally go uninterrogated.

This *spatial* sleight of hand is accompanied by an equally important *temporal* sleight of hand because, as the spatial frame of analysis expands or contracts, so does the temporal frame. Recall that, from a temporal perspective, the choice to analyze tax-exempt status in constitutional terms entails the application of substance-over-form principles because the role of the federal government in fostering discrimination is called into question. In that case, the temporal frame—just like the corresponding spatial frame—becomes broad and encompassing. As explored in chapter 1, substance-over-form principles allow tax actors to travel back in time to rewrite the past in ways that can have repercussions in the tax present and future. Constitutional law's temporal frame is similarly expansive, calling to mind Carol Greenhouse's notion of the "timelessness" or "all-times" of law discussed in the introduction to this book. Thus, when the United States Supreme Court finds government action to be unconstitutional, that unconstitutionality generally exists not only in the present and future but also presumptively extends back in time in seemingly limitless fashion.[136]

The temporal frame of constitutional law thus forces the IRS, the federal courts, and the American people to consider whether the federal government not only *is*, but also whether it *has been*, acting in accordance with the United States Constitution. If the federal government fails to live up to the shared ideals embodied in the Constitution, then it must correct past injustices *and* ensure that it lives up to those shared ideals in the future. Had such "a constitutional commitment to avoiding public subsidization of racism" been embraced in *Bob Jones*,[137] it would have had profound consequences. For instance, in addition to perhaps retroactively revoking organizations' tax-exempt status,[138] the federal government could have been required to end other forms of tax support for racism (e.g., denying the benefits of investment tax credits and accelerated depreciation to businesses that discriminate) as well as its tax support for other types of discrimination.[139] In the broad spatiotemporal frame that constitutional analysis provides, substantial room exists for imagining and fashioning a legal result that comports with notions of social justice.

Statutory Interpretation

In contrast, when the choice is made to shun the application of substance-over-form principles (as it has been by the IRS with the help of the courts), the debate over tax-exempt status instead occurs on the terrain of statutory interpretation, and thus the only relevant question is whether the organization qualifies as *charitable* within the meaning of the statute. In that case, the temporal frame of analysis, just like the corresponding spatial frame, shrinks considerably. The focus is on the organization in the present and boils down to whether the organization engages in discrimination that is so out of step with society that it should be sanctioned through the denial of tax-exempt status.

This inquiry into whether the organization's actions violate public policy takes place in the here and now—using "contemporary standards," to quote the Supreme Court.[140] In other words, the question is whether the organization is currently violating fundamental public policy. As illustrated by *Bob Jones*, the development of public policy accretes over time, and it is only at a certain point in linear time that the weight of policy grows so heavy as to become fundamental—and even then, only from that specific point onward. Until that point, the shrunken temporal frame allows the IRS, the federal courts, and all members of society to ignore the question of whether the organization's activities—which the federal government has financially supported and given its imprimatur—are consistent with the government's constitutional obligations.

Even when a public policy reaches the point of being fundamental, it is only the discriminatory organization that gets punished, and normally only through the prospective revocation of its tax-exempt status.[141] Ironically, no consideration is given to the role that the person meting out punishment (i.e., the federal government) played in perpetrating the discrimination or to whether the government ought to be called upon to redress its past contributions to, and support for, that discrimination. In this way, the past is truly relegated to the past. Taking advantage of the rigidity of linear time, the federal government ensures that both the organization's and its own past acts are fixed at forgotten points on time's arrow that are deemed to be unreachable either from the present or the future toward which we are continually moving. Furthermore, by meting out punishment to the offending organization, the federal government not only cleanses its past but also eliminates any present or future constitutional problems by cutting off its financial entanglement with the organization.

The Supreme Court reduced what, by now, should seem to be only a slim hope that tax injustices might be rectified to just the faintest of glimmers. In *Bob Jones*, the Supreme Court compounded its problematic choice of interpretive terrain by setting the bar to revoke tax-exempt status so high that, in the nearly four decades since that case was decided, no additional fundamental public policy has been identified that justifies revocation of tax-exempt status.[142] In fact, the commentators who opined on the impact of *Windsor* and *Obergefell* on organizations that engage in sexual orientation–based discrimination expressed no fear that those organizations would see their tax-exempt status revoked anytime soon. With the bar set so high, *Bob Jones* has been described as an "anomaly" that does "not establish broad rules that can be applied outside the context of eradicating racism"—and, even then, perhaps only in the limited field of education.[143]

In the end, the IRS's manipulation of the spatiotemporal frame succeeded in cabining the tax imagination—both its own and that of others, and both in the present and the future—so as to short-circuit a full accounting of the federal government's role in perpetuating racial discrimination in education after *Brown v. Board of Education*. And having set a high bar for revoking tax-exempt status and let the federal government off scot-free even in the rare event when an offending organization is (partially) punished, the IRS together with the courts effectively undermined nearly all future efforts to combat (not to mention hold the government accountable for) the furnishing of financial subsidies in the guise of tax benefits to groups that engage in invidious discrimination.

Coming in the context of present, pending, and future battles for civil rights and social justice, it is difficult to conceive of an exercise of the tax imagination—remarkable for its creativity in circumscribing the tax imagination itself—aimed more directly at preserving and protecting power and privilege.

* * *

Substance-over-form principles are typically viewed as an important means of working toward a fairer and more just tax system, as illustrated by the examples in chapter 1. This chapter revealed a less-discussed, darker side of the tax imagination. Both the decision whether to recognize marriage alternatives and the decision whether to confer tax-exempt status on segregated private schools presented the IRS with a distinct choice: whether or not to engage the tax imagination by using substance-over-form principles to travel through time in an effort to correct an injustice. In both cases, the IRS made a conscious choice *not* to employ substance-over-form principles when the power of the tax imagination could have been used to take concrete steps toward creating a better and more just world in the here and now.

But the refusal to deploy the imaginative power of substance-over-form principles in these cases did not represent a failure by the IRS to engage the tax imagination. Both decisions reflect a baleful creativity in manipulating the fabric of time to protect power and privilege and, taken together, raise larger questions about the ends to which the tax imagination is to be put. By becoming attuned to the relationship between tax and time and to the subtle (and not-so-subtle) ways that the tax imagination can be deployed, we can all begin to demand greater transparency in decision-making and greater accountability for— including the revision or reversal of—decisions that misuse the power of the tax imagination by either failing to advance the cause of tax justice or, as here, by actively entrenching existing power and privilege at the expense of the already marginalized.

3

Time as Money

The previous two chapters explored the imaginative power of substance-over-form principles. Chapter 1 considered how these principles engage the tax imagination to travel through time, rewriting the past to produce a more just tax present and future. Then chapter 2 considered how even the choice to avoid substance-over-form principles in favor of rigidly linear representations of time can still be imbued with the power of the tax imagination—but, unfortunately in the cases explored there, in furtherance of insidious ends rather than to advance tax justice.

Chapters 3 and 4 provide a different perspective on the malleability of time by exploring the power of the tax imagination to reify time. This chapter and the next consider examples of how the tax imagination can manipulate the elasticity of time—alternately compressing it and prolonging it—in an effort to solidify time into a thing. In both chapters, the tax imagination is creatively employed to convert time into an exchangeable commodity—currency that can be doled out as a reward to favored taxpayers or used by taxpayers to purchase desired tax benefits.

This idea of time as an exchangeable commodity may call to mind the old adage that "time is money"; however, that proverb fails to capture the ideas explored here. When we colloquially equate time with money, our focus is not on time as such but on how we use our time. For instance, in its entry for "time is money," the *Oxford Dictionary of Proverbs* quotes Benjamin Franklin as saying: "Remember that Time is Money. He that can earn Ten Shillings a Day . . . and . . . sits idle one half of that Day . . . has really . . . thrown away Five Shillings."[1] A more recent quote comes from the *Washington Times*: "When a quarterback is chosen as the Most Valuable Player in the National Football League for the second time in three years, time is money. He can rake in big bucks for appearing in ads, and he can also do his bit for charity by appearing in a United Way commercial."[2] Both examples concern how we use our time: do we devote our time to paid labor, charitable causes, or leisure? What is commodified is thus not time but our labor.

In contrast, chapters 3 and 4 probe examples of how the tax laws are used to commodify time itself. This chapter explores legislative exercises of the tax imagination that compress time and turn it into money. Because the examples in this chapter all involve capital cost recovery, the chapter begins with a brief discussion of the income tax norm of capitalizing and then depreciating the cost of income-producing assets over the time they will generate income. With this background, the chapter then shows how Congress has, both in the past and recently, effectively ceased taxing—and instead become a business partner with—those investing in income-producing assets through the enactment of immediate expensing. Next, underscoring that the United States has no monopoly on the power of the tax imagination, the chapter examines the Spanish legislature's enactment of a deduction for the amortization of "financial goodwill." This deduction provided Spanish companies a financial advantage in bidding on cross-border acquisitions that was later found to constitute unlawful state aid. In both of these examples, the legislature professed to employ the tax imagination to turn time into money for the common good, but closer examination belies those claims.

Chapter 4, which should be read in tandem with this chapter, then expands on the theme of converting time into money by shifting the focus from legislatures to taxpayers and their tax advisers, showing how they turn time into money—not by compressing time but by prolonging it. What all of the taxpayers in both chapters share in common, however, is ownership of property that opens the door to manipulating time in ways that are unavailable to those whose only asset is their labor. In light of the alarming levels of income inequality and wealth inequality in the United States based not only on economic class but also race, gender, and sexual orientation (among other characteristics), chapters 3 and 4 also share an analytical approach that draws together and combines the traditional tax policy analysis of chapter 1 with the critical analysis encountered in chapter 2.

Capitalization and Depreciation

The allowance of a depreciation deduction—that is, a deduction "for the exhaustion, wear and tear (including a reasonable allowance for obsolescence)" of property that is used in business or other income-producing activities[3]—is squarely ensconced among the prosaic tax timing issues discussed in the introduction to this book. This chapter moves beyond the conventional treatment of depreciation, however, to explore how the tax imagination can contort this core tax concept in order to turn time into money for the benefit of select taxpayers. Naturally, the examples of this phenomenon discussed later in this chapter raise questions about which taxpayers receive these benefits and whether the tax imagination is being used to further just ends or not.

Purpose of Depreciation

The basic idea behind depreciation deductions is that an expenditure that is expected to produce income for years to come—for example, a business's purchase of physical plant or equipment—shouldn't be deducted in full immediately. Instead, the cost of the asset is more appropriately spread over the period when the asset will produce income. Capitalization is the mechanism for denying the current deduction, and depreciation is the mechanism for spreading the capitalized cost of the plant or equipment over the asset's income-producing life.

The rationale for capitalizing and then depreciating the cost of income-producing investments is described differently in academic and nonacademic circles. The following sections contain brief descriptions of each of these rationales because understanding them is important to grasping how the legislative exercise of the tax imagination twists this basic tax concept to turn time into money that can be doled out to favored taxpayers.

ACADEMIC JUSTIFICATION

As Deborah Geier has explained, the denial of an immediate deduction for an investment in income-producing assets (what in tax jargon is referred to as "capitalization" of an expense) is justified because it protects the tax base. After all, the purchase of an income-producing asset merely changes the form of a taxpayer's wealth; there is no loss or decrease in wealth that might justify a deduction.[4] Furthermore, denial of the deduction prevents tax from being avoided on the income produced by the asset.[5] As the economist E. Cary Brown long ago demonstrated, immediate deduction of a capital expenditure (so-called immediate or full expensing) is, under certain conditions, equivalent to exempting the income produced by that investment from tax.[6] Although such an exemption is consistent with a consumption tax, it is inconsistent with the notion of imposing a tax on income.[7] Under an income tax, immediate expensing results not in the creation of a taxpayer-government relationship but in a partnership to coinvest in the purchased asset, with the tax savings provided by the immediate deduction constituting the government's contribution to the partnership and the "tax" later collected by the government constituting no more than its return on that investment.[8]

Depreciation, as Geier explained, is consistent with the general income tax realization requirement that gains and losses not be reported until property is sold or otherwise disposed of: "'[T]he concept of a "sustained" loss encompasses events short of disposition. Thus, destruction or abandonment of business or investment property produces a "sustained" loss, as does worthlessness. A "sustained" loss thus means, in a realization-based income tax system, a final or irretrievable loss.' Passage of time losses due to the encroaching end of a finite useful life are final losses and thus appropriately deducted in a realization-based income tax system."[9] Because an asset's value is equal to the present value of the future income the asset is expected to generate, depreciation deductions reflect the annual loss sustained in the value of an asset with a limited useful life because the amount of future receipts expected from the asset irrevocably decreases as each year passes.[10]

Accepting this rationale generally leads to the conclusion that depreciation deductions ought to be smaller in the early years of an asset's useful life and grow larger as that life nears its end.[11] In other words, depreciation deductions should be taken in a decelerated fashion (often referred to as "economic depreciation"), as opposed to the prevailing accelerated and straight-line methods of tax depreciation.[12] Under economic depreciation, the decline in value—and the corresponding depreciation deduction—is smallest in the asset's first year of life (when much future income is still anticipated and the discount to present value is high) and greatest in its final year of life (when all income has been received and no future income is expected).

Not all academics embrace economic depreciation as the ideal baseline method. Douglas Kahn, for instance, has argued that accelerated depreciation methods—which result in larger depreciation deductions in the early years of an asset's useful and decline in size over time—are both sound and appropriate. He maintained that these methods are consistent with allocating the cost of an asset across its useful life based on the amount paid at the time of purchase for the income to be produced in a given year of that life.[13] From this perspective, more is paid for income to be received in the early years of an asset's life because that income is expected soon and the discount to present value is correspondingly small. Conversely, less is paid for income to be received near the end of the asset's life because the discount to present value is much greater. Under this approach, the largest depreciation deduction falls in the first year and the smallest in the last year of the asset's life. This is the opposite of the result under economic depreciation, which is more widely embraced by academics; it is also more generous than the straight-line method (i.e., ratable recovery of an asset's cost over its life) that is sometimes required for tax purposes.

NONACADEMIC JUSTIFICATION

In contrast to the academic concern with protecting the tax base and correctly reflecting the realization of losses due to the passage of time, courts have focused on the effects of capitalization followed by depreciation. With their eyes trained on observable outcomes rather than tidy theoretical explanations, judges see capitalization followed by depreciation as serving a matching function. In other words, by capitalizing the cost of an income-producing asset and then spreading that cost over the time the asset will produce income, the tax laws are said to better measure the taxpayer's net income each year by matching the income produced by the asset with the expenses incurred to produce that income.

Indeed, as early as 1927, the United States Supreme Court described the rationale for allowing depreciation deductions in terms that evoke the notion of matching income and expense.[14] In 1960, the Court more plainly articulated the role of depreciation deductions as producing "an accurate determination of the net income from operations of a given business for a fiscal period."[15] Citing its 1927 opinion, the Court stated that "it is the primary purpose of depreciation accounting to further the integrity of periodic income statements by making a meaningful allocation of the cost entailed in the use . . . of the asset to the periods to which it contributes."[16] The Court has since reaffirmed that the combination of capitalization and depreciation "endeavors to match expenses with the revenues of the taxable period to which they are properly attributable, thereby resulting in a more accurate calculation of net income for tax purposes."[17]

The lower federal courts have naturally echoed these descriptions of the matching function of capitalization and depreciation. For instance, the United States Tax Court has explained: "The primary purpose of allocating depreciation to more than 1 year is to provide a more meaningful matching of the cost of an income-producing asset with the income therefrom; this meaningful match, in turn, bolsters the integrity of the taxpayer's periodic income statements."[18] Similarly, the United States Court of Appeals for the Second Circuit stated: "The original rationale for the depreciation deduction was to allow taxpayers to match accurately, for tax accounting purposes, the cost of an asset to the income stream that the asset produced."[19]

Undermining the Integrity of the Income Tax

Despite their differences, these justifications for capitalizing and then depreciating investments in income-producing assets share a common motivation: they are animated by a desire to maintain the integrity of the income tax. For academics, the integrity of the income tax is maintained by ensuring that the theoretical conceptualization of the tax base is both sound at its core and respected in its application. For the courts, the integrity of the income tax is maintained by ensuring that taxpayers' returns accurately reflect net income.

Though opinions may differ regarding the most accurate method for calculating depreciation (i.e., economic, accelerated, or straight-line), depreciation methods that depart from an accepted baseline distort a taxpayer's net income relative to that baseline. Congress appears to have recognized as much when it liberalized the depreciation rules in 1954.[20] At a time when straight-line depreciation was the norm, Congress defended its adoption of more accelerated methods—a move motivated in part to "increase available working capital and materially aid growing businesses in the financing of their expansion"—on the ground that permitting tax-payers to recover "40 percent of the cost of an asset in the first quarter of its service life and two-thirds of the cost in the first half of its life" was "based on a realistic estimate of useful life" that "conforms to sound accounting principles."[21] Worried that the stimulus might be taken too far, Congress limited the accelerated methods to new property: "The application of the new methods to used property might artificially encourage transfers and exchanges of partially depreciated assets motivated only by tax considerations. The stimulus to investment through liberalized depreciation is most important with respect to the creation of new assets. Moreover, the reality of faster depreciation in the early years is generally greater in the case of new than used property."[22] Congress further limited accelerated depreciation to assets with useful lives of at least three years because the new methods could result in the immediate expensing of shorter-lived assets, which raised concerns about the need "[t]o prevent unrealistic deductions and resulting tax avoidance."[23] Obviously, Congress felt the need to justify this change, which marked a general shift toward using depreciation deductions to stimulate investment, by repeatedly paying lip service to the idea that accelerated depreciation would better reflect net income than the prevailing straight-line method.[24]

Differing from this midcentury congressional perspective, both the United States Department of the Treasury and the congressional Joint Committee on Taxation take account of accelerated depreciation in preparing their annual tax expenditure budgets, although they employ different baselines for measuring the tax subsidy. Since 1974, Congress has required the preparation of these tax expenditure budgets so that it can take account of indirect spending through the tax laws in its annual budgeting process.[25] When measuring the portion of depreciation deductions that constitutes a tax subsidy, the Joint Committee adopts as its baseline the straight-line method required by the Internal Revenue Code's "alternative depreciation system."[26] Using that baseline, the Joint Committee estimated that, from 2018 through 2022, the revenue loss from permitting equipment and buildings to be depreciated on an accelerated basis would total $336.7 billion.[27] In its estimates, the Treasury Department adopts economic depreciation as its baseline.[28] Using that baseline, Treasury estimated that, from 2019 through 2028, the revenue loss from permitting equipment and buildings to be depreciated on an accelerated basis would total $245.6 billion.[29] Given the magnitude of these numbers, it comes as no surprise that a Government Accountability Office report identified accelerated depreciation as by far the largest corporate tax expenditure in 2011.[30]

The United States is not alone in its embrace of accelerated depreciation. Canada, France, and Spain, whose tax systems furnish examples discussed in this book, have similar norms of capitalization coupled with depreciation that are justified on similar grounds to those offered in the United States.[31] And similar to the United States, all three countries have occasionally departed from these norms by permitting taxpayers to use accelerated depreciation methods, including highly accelerated methods that serve as investment incentives.[32]

Immediate Expensing in the United States

Although opinions differ on the appropriate baseline for measuring the tax subsidy embedded in accelerated depreciation, opinions converge when acceleration reaches the extreme of altogether forsaking the income tax norm of capitalization followed by depreciation. Whatever the baseline, permitting taxpayers to immediately expense an income-producing asset (1) distorts a taxpayer's net income by failing to match income with expense and (2) erodes the tax base by effectively exempting the income produced by the asset from tax. Nevertheless, Congress has taken this extreme stance on more than one occasion by imagining a world in which the flow of time can be sped up to the point where its normally unmanageable fluidity can be condensed and hardened into a currency to be distributed to favored taxpayers.

The 1980s: ACRS and the Investment Tax Credit

EFFECTIVE IMMEDIATE EXPENSING
Following the lead of the Reagan administration, Congress created the accelerated cost recovery system (ACRS) in 1981.[33] At the time,

ACRS was described as having "introduced radical changes in business depreciation practices."[34] Through ACRS, Congress abandoned the notion of spreading the cost of an income-producing asset over its useful life and instead opted to spread that cost over one of a few arbitrary—and notably short—periods prescribed by statute.[35] At first blush, Congress appeared to use ACRS to compress time by significantly shortening cost recovery periods, but did not seem to go so far as to adopt immediate expensing. Nonetheless, as part of its efforts to "provide the investment stimulus that is essential for economic expansion," Congress paired ACRS with a substantial revision of the investment tax credit.[36]

No mere lagniappe, the revised investment tax credit permitted taxpayers to take an immediate credit equal to 10 percent (6 percent for the shortest-lived assets) of the purchase price of all new and an increased amount of used property.[37] What's more, despite having given the taxpayer an immediate, dollar-for-dollar reduction in tax liability for a portion of the investment, Congress chose not to require the taxpayer to reduce the cost eligible for depreciation by the amount of the tax credit received.[38] Instead, the taxpayer "double dipped" with respect to that portion of the investment, receiving both a tax credit *and* accelerated depreciation deductions.

It was expected that the combination of ACRS and the investment tax credit would produce artificial tax losses for many corporate taxpayers, which could blunt the legislation's incentive effects because the tax benefits might be usable (if at all) only in future years when the taxpayer had positive taxable income.[39] Consequently, to preserve these incentive effects, Congress "created a 'safe harbor' for a broad class of leasing arrangements to permit firms without taxable income effectively to sell their depreciation allowances and investment credits to corporations with taxable income."[40] These leasing arrangements, which represented "a significant deviation from the traditional dominance of substance over form in determining ownership for tax purposes," were essentially "fictitious" because "the relationship between the parties need have none of the characteristics of a true lessor/lessee relationship" and "[t]he fictional ownership status of the lessor . . . exist[ed] only as a means of transferring tax benefits."[41] As Jeffrey Birnbaum and Alan Murray describe in *Showdown at Gucci Gulch*:

[T]he safe-harbor-leasing arrangement proved to be a political disaster in practice. The new law led to a frenzy of strange tax deals that outraged the public and their representatives in Congress: Global Marine reportedly sold tax benefits on oil rigs worth $135 million to Hilton Hotels. Ford Motor sold IBM the tax breaks on its entire $1 billion 1981 investment program, reportedly for a price of between $100 million and $200 million. Occidental Petroleum sold benefits on $94.8 million in investments, LTV sold breaks on $100 million in equipment, and Chicago & North Western sold tax benefits on $53 million worth of locomotives, freight cars, and other property. In each case, both the buyer and the seller benefited, and all at the taxpayers' expense.

The furor in Congress over the tax-break sales was swift and sharp. The safe-harbor-leasing provision was repealed, but not until after the affair had burned itself well into the public psyche.[42]

The benefits of ACRS and the investment tax credit—which could be further enhanced by borrowing to purchase assets to obtain an interest deduction too—had an effect similar to immediate expensing and, in some cases, was "more generous than immediate write-off."[43] What could be more generous than exempting income generated by an asset from tax? Simple: providing the taxpayer with a *negative* effective tax rate—that is, handing money out to corporate taxpayers rather than collecting it from them.[44] As described earlier, immediate expensing alters the relationship between the taxpayer and the government by converting it into a partnership to coinvest in the asset.[45] The "tax" collected by the government is no longer a tax but really just the return on the government's contribution to the partnership. For those who received benefits even more generous than immediate expensing, ACRS and the investment tax credit did not create a conventional partnership arrangement but instead was "equivalent to government bearing a greater fraction of the initial cost than it receives of the future flows: it is *subsidizing* the project."[46]

THE FALLOUT

These benefits were so generous that the economist Alan Auerbach suggested at the time that "investors who purchase assets in the three-year and five-year recovery classes [covering most personal property] would

prefer ACRS to the abolition of corporation taxation."[47] Indeed, as Auerbach observed: "The changes . . . are expected ultimately to produce a
large revenue loss to the Treasury. Estimates of this projected loss vary
from $54.5 billion to $61.3 billion for fiscal year 1986. In comparison, the
total collection of the corporate income tax amounted to $64.6 billion
in 1980."[48]

Concerned about a growing budget deficit and "counterproductive"
incentives that "create, rather than reduce, economic distortions," Congress reduced the tax benefits provided by ACRS and the investment tax
credit in 1982 with the aim of limiting those benefits to the equivalent of
immediate expensing.[49] Still, the combination of ACRS and the investment tax credit remained "much more valuable than pre-1981 benefits
and quite generous by historical standards."[50] Also in 1982, Congress
prospectively repealed the safe-harbor leasing rules because it was troubled by "the tax avoidance opportunities that safe-harbor leasing had
created, the adverse public reaction to the sale of tax benefits, [and] the
revenue loss."[51] Nevertheless, Congress chose not to "deny interest deductions to firms that benefit from effective expensing, and thus did
not eliminate the possibility of substantial negative marginal tax rates
on debt-financed investments in equipment by profitable companies."[52]

SECTION 179
Congress did make one forthright move toward immediate expensing
in the 1980s. In 1981, Congress enacted § 179 to help small businesses by
permitting a limited amount ($5,000 beginning in 1982, increasing to
$10,000 by 1986) of new or used property to be immediately expensed,
so long as the property was purchased for use in a trade or business.[53]
In 1986, Congress amended § 179 to phase out this assistance for businesses that placed more than $200,000 worth of qualifying property in
service during the taxable year.[54] At the same time, Congress capped the
amount that could be immediately expensed at the amount of taxable
income from business activity.[55]

Early Twenty-First Century: "Bonus" Depreciation

One of the federal government's stock responses to a weakening
economy has been to accelerate depreciation.[56] In fact, "accelerating

depreciation was the primary method by which U.S. tax policy aimed to respond to the recessions beginning in 2001 and late 2007."[57] More recently, the federal government has relied on accelerating depreciation as a form of generalized economic stimulus in times of economic expansion.

ACCELERATING DEPRECIATION IN RECESSION

In the wake of the September 11 terrorist attacks, Congress enacted "bonus" depreciation as part of the Job Creation and Worker Assistance Act of 2002.[58] In enacting this provision, Congress stated its belief "that allowing additional first-year depreciation will accelerate purchases of equipment, promote capital investment, modernization, and growth, and will help to spur an economic recovery."[59] Or, as President George W. Bush put it: "The terrorist attacks of September the 11th were also an attack on our economy, and a lot of people lost their jobs. . . . [T]his new law will provide tax incentives for companies to expand and create jobs by investing in plant and equipment."[60]

Bonus depreciation was generally available with respect to specified categories of new business or investment property acquired between September 2001 and September 2004.[61] Taxpayers were able to deduct 30 percent of the property's basis in the year it was placed in service and then deduct the remaining 70 percent under the regular accelerated depreciation rules beginning in that same year.[62] Making the benefits even more generous, taxpayers could stack bonus depreciation on top of § 179's limited immediate expensing allowance for small businesses, if they qualified for it.[63]

Congress later increased the bonus percentage to 50 percent for property acquired from May 2003 through December 2004.[64] With the economy recovering, Congress let bonus depreciation lapse but resurrected it in 2008 to combat the effects of the Great Recession.[65] A slow recovery led Congress to repeatedly extend bonus depreciation and, "[h]oping to address the sluggish recovery in 2010," even temporarily raised the bonus percentage to 100 percent.[66]

At the same time, § 179's immediate expensing allowance and the group of businesses eligible for it grew significantly. What had been a $10,000 allowance for businesses that placed no more than $200,000 worth of property into service in 1986 grew slowly during the 1990s and early 2000s, with the allowance eventually reaching $24,000 (but the phaseout threshold remaining at $200,000).[67] Then, beginning in 2003, the allowance more than quadrupled to $100,000 for businesses that placed no more than $400,000 worth of qualified property into service.[68] This expansion of § 179, which occurred simultaneously with the increase of the bonus depreciation percentage to 50 percent, was justified on the ground that it would lower the cost of capital—inducing "small business [to] invest in more equipment and employ more workers"— and (counterfactually) reduce recordkeeping burdens.[69] The § 179 expensing allowance further ballooned in response to the Great Recession, jumping in 2008 to $250,000 for businesses that placed no more than $800,000 of qualified property in service and then in 2010 to $500,000 for businesses that placed no more than $2 million of qualified property in service.[70] Although these recession-related expansions of § 179 were ostensibly temporary, they persisted as the economy expanded and were made permanent in 2015.[71]

ACCELERATING DEPRECIATION IN ECONOMIC EXPANSION

After the economy recovered from the Great Recession, bonus depreciation and § 179 immediate expensing did not simply linger but were actively embraced as part of the package of tax cuts enacted in late 2017.[72] The Tax Cuts and Jobs Act (TCJA) extended bonus depreciation through 2026 and increased the bonus percentage to 100 percent for more than five years, authorizing immediate expensing from late 2017 through 2022.[73] Beginning in 2023, the bonus percentage phases down until it reaches zero in 2027.[74] Additionally, the TCJA expanded bonus depreciation to cover used (and not just new) property as well as additional types of property.[75] The TCJA's scant legislative history justified these changes on the ground that they would "lower[] the cost of capital for tangible property used in a trade or business" and encourage businesses "to purchase equipment and other assets, which will promote capital investment and provide economic growth."[76] Additionally, it was asserted (again counterfactually) that "full expensing for certain business assets will eliminate depreciation recordkeeping requirements for such assets."[77]

Beginning in 2018, the TCJA essentially doubled the § 179 immediate expensing allowance to $1 million for businesses that placed no more than $2.5 million of qualified property into service during the year.[78] Both the dollar limitation and the phaseout threshold were indexed for inflation in 2019 and following years.[79] As a point of comparison, had the $10,000 § 179 allowance for 1986 merely been adjusted for inflation, the allowance would have been under $23,000 (not $1 million) in 2018 and the phaseout threshold would have started at slightly over $450,000 (not $2.5 million).[80] Demonstrating the insatiable appetite for tax stimulus dollars, the TCJA's legislative history simply repeated the justifications offered in 2003—nearly verbatim—that even more taxpayers should get access to § 179 because it will spur business investment and reduce recordkeeping burdens.[81]

One might question the need to expand § 179 in light of the TCJA's simultaneous and more generalized expansion of the bonus depreciation rules; however, unlike immediate expensing, the changes made to § 179 were permanent.[82] Accordingly, even though a seemingly junior partner in the immediate expensing world after the TCJA, § 179 nonetheless stands waiting in the wings for the day when the bonus percentage begins to decrease. At that time, § 179 can step in to aid the increasing number of businesses that qualify for its benefits—a group that is now well beyond what might conventionally be thought of as "small" business—to obtain the same or similar results as prevail under 100 percent bonus depreciation.[83]

But, as of this writing, it is unclear whether that day will arrive. While in office, President Donald Trump pitched the entire package of tax cuts, including bonus depreciation and the changes to § 179, as "rocket fuel for our economy."[84] Unfettered by recession-related justifications for this economic stimulus, 100 percent bonus depreciation would have been made permanent, just as the increased § 179 expensing limits were, had it not been necessary to keep the revenue loss from the TCJA and the corresponding growth in the national budget deficit within the confines set in the budget reconciliation process.[85] Indeed, despite inconclusive evidence that the TCJA had a positive impact on business investment,[86] the Trump White House, Republicans in Congress, and conservative think tanks all continued pushing to make immediate expensing permanent; conversely, since taking office, Present Joseph Biden has yet to address bonus depreciation in his administration's tax proposals, despite having released an infrastructure plan that provided a natural opportunity to do so.[87]

Temporal Alchemy

We usually think of time as being in perpetual motion—time runs, flies, or even flows like a river. A fixed image commonly associated with time is the arrow (→), but even this two-dimensional representation of time indicates direction and movement. In contrast, the examples of immediate expensing discussed here embrace a conceptualization of time not as constantly moving and slipping away but as a solid, hard currency that can be grasped and given to those the government favors. Like the time travel that was the subject of chapters 1 and 2, this alchemical transformation of time into money is marked by a high degree of creativity in imagining the relationship between tax and time.

COMPRESSING AND TRANSFORMING TIME

Although we sometimes wish that we could "freeze" time during a precious moment or even feel as if time was "frozen" during a particularly jarring encounter, this common metaphor for turning time from a liquid into a solid to halt its relentless flow fails to capture the complex legislative experience with solidifying time into money. After all, Congress did not stop time when it abandoned the norm of capitalization followed by depreciation in favor of permitting taxpayers to immediately deduct their investments in a wide array of income-producing assets. Instead, Congress compressed and condensed a years-long time span into a single moment—a moment that is alternately described as "immediate" or "full" expensing to convey the instant and complete gratification of taxpayers. But unlike time frozen to preserve enjoyment (or even time frozen in shock or horror), time continues to flow for taxpayers who benefit from the instant gratification of immediate expensing: the benefits these taxpayers receive and the gratification that they feel last well beyond that single moment. The benefits and gratification actually continue throughout the time span that Congress momentarily compressed because the tax savings from immediate expensing extends from the initial moment of expensing throughout the entire life of the asset, during which the income produced by the asset is effectively exempted from tax.

Congress accomplished this compression of time somewhat differently in the two eras discussed here. In its first foray into immediate expensing, Congress was more circumspect in its effort to compress time.

In the 1980s, Congress first pleated time, in the way that a skirt or an accordion is pleated, and then compressed the time span that had been marked with its handiwork. Congress created these pleats when it folded time on itself by allowing the same investment to be recovered twice—once under the investment tax credit, and then again under ACRS. Without any reduction in depreciation deductions for the investment credit taken, these two tax provisions operated wholly independently of each other, as if they existed in parallel temporal planes connected by the crease that Congress had made in the fabric of time.

Just as pleating makes it easier to compress the size of a skirt or an accordion, pleating time made it easier for Congress to compress the span over which depreciation deductions would normally be allowed. Nonetheless, Congress overestimated the amount of force necessary to achieve the desired compression, because the resulting moment of instant gratification turned out to be so condensed and concentrated that the benefits conveyed to taxpayers were in many cases greater than those of immediate expensing. Realizing its mistake, Congress quickly undertook to iron out some of the pleats it had introduced into the fabric of time by requiring coordination between the investment tax credit and ACRS in order to limit the benefit to "just" the tax exemption associated with immediate expensing. The pleats were later fully removed—and generalized immediate expensing abandoned, at least for a time—when Congress repealed the investment tax credit in 1986 and left depreciation alone to do the work of stimulating investment.

In the early twenty-first century, Congress rejected its earlier complicated pleating of time in favor of exerting brute force to compress time from a span of years into a single moment of "immediate" and "full" taxpayer gratification. Congress engaged in early experiments with applying brute force to time when it enacted § 179 in 1981 to provide a limited amount of immediate expensing to small businesses. Congress extended that experimentation as it expanded § 179 as a palliative for the recessions of the 2000s and then through the temporary adoption of 100 percent bonus depreciation in the wake of the Great Recession. This experimentation culminated in the adoption of 100 percent bonus depreciation in 2017—for a longer period and for a far larger swath of property—as immediate expensing became a generalized means of bolstering the economy.

Having shifted its mindset from viewing immediate expensing as a temporary stimulus in recession to considering it as an all-purpose economic stimulus that should become a permanent feature of the income tax, Congress abandoned even the semblance of defending core income tax principles. Recall that when Congress expanded the availability of accelerated depreciation in 1954, it paid lip service to the idea that its changes would more accurately reflect net income, and it even restricted accelerated depreciation to new property out of fear that extending it to used property would stimulate not investment but tax-motivated behavior. In 2017, with its eyes squarely fixed on economic stimulus, Congress made no mention of accurately measuring net income and limited itself to combating only the most blatant abuses of immediate expensing. In lieu of working to preserve the integrity of the income tax, Congress directed its energies toward compressing the normal time span of cost recovery into a single—and very generous—moment for as long as it possibly could.

Thus, through repeated experimentation, Congress harnessed the perpetual motion of time and solidified it into a thing—a currency—that could be handed out to favored taxpayers. But the creativity of its tax imagination did not end there. Congress simultaneously toyed with time in ways that are redolent of chapter 2's discussion of the refusal by the Internal Revenue Service to recognize civil unions and domestic partnerships following the Supreme Court's marriage-equality decisions or to acknowledge that tax-exempt status provided unconstitutional federal financial support to segregated private schools after the landmark *Brown v. Board of Education* decision. Much like the IRS in these situations, Congress consciously chose to exalt form over substance when it created safe-harbor leasing in 1981 to ensure that its largesse reached the intended recipients. Departing from a history of respecting leases only when they had economic substance, Congress decided to treat what was actually a sale of tax benefits as a lease of an income-producing asset. In effect, Congress wrote its own preordained version of future events that would displace and replace actual events that might hinder its targeted commodification of time for the benefit of preferred taxpayers. In doing so, Congress rejected a natural application of substance-over-form principles that would have furthered tax justice, much as the IRS had done before and would do again afterward. But in contrast to the

IRS's experience, Congress opened itself to public opprobrium when it strayed from the path of tax justice, which ultimately led it to repeal safe-harbor leasing.

Similarly raising concerns about tax justice, Congress warped the fabric of time in the process of compressing it. When time reexpanded after being compressed, the nature of the government's relationship with favored taxpayers had changed from one of sovereign/subject to one of partners contributing to a shared enterprise. What had previously been a "tax" was now nothing more than the government's return on the capital (i.e., forgone tax revenue) that it had invested in the shared enterprise. This change in relationship naturally raises questions about who benefited from these investments of forgone tax dollars and in what amounts.

DISPARATE DISTRIBUTION OF BENEFITS

In December 2017, the Joint Committee on Taxation estimated that the TCJA's expansion of bonus depreciation and the § 179 expensing allowance would result in $140.2 billion of lost revenue between 2018 and 2022 (when 100 percent bonus depreciation is in full effect).[88] This is no small amount, as it constitutes 27 percent of the projected revenue loss from the TCJA's business tax reforms and 13 percent of the entire projected revenue loss from the TCJA during that period.[89] A slightly broader view that also encompasses other changes to the depreciation rules provides additional perspective. As discussed earlier, the Joint Committee estimated that the revenue loss from 2018 through 2022 due to accelerated depreciation of equipment and buildings would total $336.7 billion.[90] In its last pre-TCJA report, the Joint Committee estimated that same revenue loss from 2016 through 2020 at only $88.5 billion.[91] In other words, the subsidy is estimated to have increased nearly fourfold after the TCJA.

In 2019, the Institute on Taxation and Economic Policy released a report taking stock of the TCJA's impact on the corporate income tax paid by Fortune 500 companies during the first full year the law was in effect.[92] The report described how sixty highly profitable Fortune 500 companies paid no federal income tax in 2018—and, in some cases, even received refunds from the government—due to a combination of tax breaks, including, significantly, accelerated depreciation.[93] Unsurprisingly in light of this report, the federal government reported "a 31 per-cent drop in corporate tax revenues [in 2018], almost twice the decline official budget forecasters had predicted."[94] The precise cause of the drop was uncertain; however, immediate expensing was listed prominently among the potential culprits.[95] And, of course, this focus on corporate taxes does not account for the dollars handed out to businesses and in-vestors that operate through partnerships or sole proprietorships, be-cause they, too, benefit from immediate expensing and other forms of accelerated depreciation.

Ostensibly, the federal government handed out these large sums of money to businesses and investors to incentivize the purchase of assets with the general aim of bolstering economic growth. Yet, as mentioned earlier, it is far from certain that these incentives are effective in spurring new investment in income-producing assets (as opposed, for instance, to merely altering the timing of already planned investments).[96] What's more, concern has been expressed that these investments—and the tax dollars that they bring to their owners—come at the expense of workers by redirecting dollars away from investments in jobs.[97] In fact, the in-centive provided by bonus depreciation and § 179 expensing to invest in assets (rather than people) has been suggested as an explanation for the "jobless" recoveries of the 2000s.[98] More recently, a 2019 Congressional Research Service report analyzing the TCJA's effects found that "ordi-nary workers had very little growth in wage rates" and further found that wage data for 2018 was consistent with the Congressional Budget Office's projection that the TCJA's significant tax cuts would have only "a modest effect" on workers' wages.[99] Thus, notwithstanding political rhetoric about boosting economic growth and creating jobs, the benefits of immediate expensing seem to favor owners over workers.

But workers are not alone in being passed over in the distribution of this bounty. Not all business owners and investors benefit equally from this government largesse. A report from American University's Kogod Tax Policy Center showed that, "while women-owned firms have grown to number more than one-third of all U.S. firms, the majority are small businesses operating in service industries and continue to have chal-lenges growing their receipts and accessing capital."[100] In assessing the impact on women-owned firms of four small business tax expenditures, the report pointed out how the very design of § 179's expensing allowance could cause it to "effectively bypass women-owned firms . . . who are service firms with few capital-intensive equipment investments altogether."[101] Supporting the notion that § 179 disproportionately excludes women-owned businesses because they are concentrated in the service sector, the Kogod Center's own informal survey of women business owners suggested that they take advantage of § 179 less often than businesses do generally.[102] And if § 179 has a disparate impact along gender lines, it can only be expected that 100 percent bonus depreciation—which likewise provides support only for capital investment—suffers from the same problems. As the report notes, more precise conclusions were not possible because facially neutral US tax law has created a "billion dollar blind spot" that renders the notion that tax law might have disparate impacts along gender (or other) lines out of the bounds of consideration and results in government neither collecting nor maintaining data regarding the demographics of the beneficiaries of tax expenditures like § 179.[103]

TAKING STOCK

In the 1980s and again in the early twenty-first century, Congress employed the tax imagination in a myriad of ways to compress the fabric of time in order to turn time into money. Congress then used this money to fund generous coinvestment programs for owners of capital-intensive businesses—investments that both fail to live up to the promise of providing benefits to workers and suffer from design flaws that likely result in the disproportionate exclusion of women-owned businesses. As a result, we have yet another example of the tax imagination being touted as a force for good—being used here to (purportedly) bolster economic growth for the benefit of all by harnessing and solidifying the raw power of time's flow—but actually operating in ways that disproportionately benefit those who already have power and privilege, thus largely leaving behind those who have historically been disadvantaged.[104]

Next, we turn to another example of this phenomenon—but this time from outside the United States.

Amortization of "Financial Goodwill" in Spain

When I speak with my students about the tax treatment of goodwill, I explain that goodwill is a composite of all of the intangible aspects of a business that keep customers coming back and that make a business's value greater than the sum of its parts. More formally, *Black's Law Dictionary* defines *goodwill* as "[a] business's reputation, patronage, and other intangible assets that are considered when appraising the business, esp. for purchase; the ability to earn income in excess of the income that would be expected from the business viewed as a mere collection of assets."[105] A Spanish business law dictionary similarly defines the Spanish equivalent—*fondo de comercio*—and even includes the English word "goodwill" in its definition of that term.[106]

Tax Treatment of Goodwill

Historically, neither Spain nor the United States permitted the cost of goodwill to be recovered through depreciation deductions because goodwill, unlike a business's plant, equipment, or buildings, lacks a determinable useful life over which its cost can be spread.[107] Beginning in the mid-1990s, however, both countries began to permit goodwill to be amortized.[108] (*Amortization* has the same meaning as *depreciation* but is often used when referring specifically to intangible assets such as goodwill.) The United States and Spain permitted the cost of purchased goodwill to be amortized not because of a sudden recognition that goodwill has a limited useful life, but on other policy grounds.

In the United States, amortization of purchased goodwill was permitted with the aim of reducing disputes between the IRS and taxpayers over (1) the contours of nondepreciable goodwill (as opposed to goodwill-like assets that arguably have a limited useful life); (2) how to properly allocate the purchase price of a business among goodwill and other assets; and (3) the proper period and method for recovering the cost of amortizable intangibles.[109] In Spain, amortization of purchased goodwill was permitted as part of a larger (and somewhat controversial) project of enhancing the corporate tax's neutrality by reducing the number of instances in which tax rules diverged from accounting treatment, because accounting results serve as the starting point for determining the Spanish corporate tax base and differences between tax and accounting treatment could inefficiently skew economic behavior.[110] But even after these changes, goodwill remained ineligible for amortization in both countries if a business was operated in corporate form and the goodwill of the business was indirectly acquired in a stock purchase rather than directly acquired through a purchase of the business's assets or, in Spain, through certain business combinations (e.g., mergers).[111]

Beginning in 2002, however, the Spanish corporate income tax was amended to permit companies resident in Spain for tax purposes to amortize the "financial goodwill" (*fondo de comercio financiero*) attributable to certain stock purchases of foreign companies.[112] If a Spanish company purchased a 5 percent or greater interest in the stock of a foreign company, then the Spanish company was permitted to amortize the portion of the stock price attributable to financial goodwill ratably over a twenty-year period (i.e., at a rate of 5 percent per year), regardless of its accounting treatment.[113] Financial goodwill was calculated using a multistep process. First, the excess of the purchase price for the block of stock over the portion of the foreign company's book value attributable to that stock was calculated. Next, that excess was allocated to the foreign company's assets to account for appreciation in those assets. Finally, any remaining amount of the excess of purchase price over underlying book value was attributed to financial goodwill that could be amortized ratably over the twenty-year period.[114]

To be eligible to amortize this financial goodwill, the Spanish company had to meet several additional conditions: It had to hold its 5 percent or greater interest in the foreign company for more than one year; the foreign company had to be subject to a corporate income tax similar to the Spanish corporate income tax; the foreign company could not be a resident of a tax haven; and the foreign company had to be predominantly engaged in business outside of Spain.[115] It was unclear whether these requirements applied only to the year when the stock was acquired or throughout the amortization period.[116] Nonetheless, the Spanish tax authorities imposed annual information reporting requirements on companies taking the deduction to verify their satisfaction of these requirements.[117]

Little explanation was offered at the time of enactment for the Spanish legislature's decision to permit the amortization of financial goodwill.[118] The explanation accompanying the new law made general reference to the adoption of corporate tax measures that would encourage economic growth; however, the amortization of financial goodwill was not specifically listed among the examples of such measures included in the law.[119] Regardless, commentators have pointed out that the amortization of financial goodwill formed part of broader tax moves by the Spanish government to ensure that Spanish businesses were competitive internationally at a time when the country was opening up to international markets and shifting from being a net importer to a net exporter of capital.[120] In this vein, the amortization of financial goodwill was said to be aimed at reducing domestic tax obstacles to cross-border investment and was described as "an incentive for the internationalization of Spanish companies."[121]

State Aid?

Under the Treaty Establishing the European Community (and, more recently, the Treaty on the Functioning of the European Union), "any aid granted by a Member State or through State resources in any form whatsoever which distorts or threatens to distort competition by favouring certain undertakings or the production of certain goods shall, in so far as it affects trade between Member States, be incompatible with the common market."[122] The European Commission was empowered to investigate state aid cases and, upon concluding that state aid was incompatible with the common market, to order the offending member state to "abolish or alter such aid within a period of time to be determined by the Commission."[123] In addition, the treaty required member states to inform the Commission in advance of plans to grant aid so that the Commission could determine whether to initiate a formal investigation, in which case the proposed aid had to be held in abeyance until a final decision on the state aid question was reached.[124] When a member state failed to notify the Commission in advance and the Commission later found aid to be incompatible with the common market, the Commission generally was required to order the member state to recover the "unlawful" aid (plus interest) from its beneficiaries.[125]

COMMISSION DECISIONS

In light of the obvious incentive effects associated with the amortization of financial goodwill and notwithstanding the threadbare explanation of the deduction's purpose offered by the Spanish legislature, it has been suggested that the Spanish government should have contacted the European Commission in advance so that it could determine whether this tax incentive constituted prohibited state aid before Spanish companies undertook foreign acquisitions in reliance upon it.[126] But the Spanish government did not notify the Commission of this potential case of prohibited state aid before enactment.[127] Instead, after receiving complaints from a number of members of the European Parliament as well as a private actor who asked to remain anonymous—and despite having earlier sent signals that it did not view the amortization of financial goodwill as state aid—the European Commission notified the Spanish government in October 2007 that the Commission had opened a state aid inquiry regarding this tax deduction.[128]

After investigating the complaints, the Commission issued decisions in 2009 and 2011 finding that the amortization of financial goodwill was prohibited state aid.[129] In reaching these decisions, it determined that the amortization of financial goodwill departed from the general Spanish tax system because "the Spanish tax system has never permitted the amortisation of financial goodwill" and, even after the 2002 changes, "no such amortisation is possible for domestic transactions."[130] The Spanish government marshaled a number of arguments in defense of the deduction, including that the amortization of financial goodwill conferred no "true economic advantage since, in the case of sale of the acquired shareholding, the amount deducted is recovered by taxation of the capital gain, thus placing the taxpayer in the same situation as if [the provision] had not been applied."[131] The Commission rejected this argument due to its failure to account for the time value of money. In lieu of mere deferral, the Commission found that the amortization of financial goodwill provided a selective advantage to Spanish companies undertaking foreign acquisitions, because it operated like "an interest-free credit line that allows up to twenty annual withdrawals of a 20th of the financial goodwill for as long as the shareholdings are held on the taxpayer's books."[132] Whether this loan was repaid was left to the corporate taxpayer to decide: "If the investor does not transfer the significant shareholding, the effect is the same as cancellation of the debt by the Spanish authorities. In this case, the measure turns into a permanent tax exemption."[133]

Regarding the question whether this aid distorted competition, the Commission indicated that it had received complaints from companies "that the measure . . . provided a significant advantage fueling the merger appetite of Spanish companies, in particular in the context of auctions."[134] One complainant asserted that "Spanish acquirers, for instance in the banking sector, are able to pay some 7% more than they would otherwise be able to."[135] Consistent with this assertion, the Commission noted that, in one case, it was estimated that an investment bank would receive a €1.7 billion tax benefit from amortizing financial goodwill—an amount equal to 6.5 percent of the offer price in the acquisition.[136] Moreover, "[a]nother report indicated that the Spanish acquirer had been able to bid about 15% more than non-Spanish competitors."[137] The Commission itself calculated that, based on prevailing tax rates and using a 5 percent discount rate, acquisitions made in 2002 (the first year in which the deduction was available) would result in a benefit with a present value equal to more than 20 percent of the financial goodwill inherent in the purchased stock.[138]

THE AFTERMATH

Spanish legal commentary at the time criticized the Commission's decisions and even called into question the Commission's motivation for opening the inquiry, suggesting that it acted due to outside pressure from politicians, the media, and the business community.[139] Nonetheless, the Spanish government chose not to appeal the decisions and instead retroactively terminated the deduction, subject to transitional relief authorized by the Commission for companies that had legitimate expectations that the deduction would not be declared prohibited state aid at the time that they purchased stock in foreign companies.[140] The Spanish government was required to recoup the unlawful state aid (plus interest) from Spanish companies that took the deduction but were not covered by the transitional relief.[141]

Private parties did, however, appeal the Commission's decisions.[142] These appeals have meandered through the courts for years: First, in 2014, the General Court of the European Union overturned the Commission's decisions on the ground that it had not established that the aid provided through the deduction for amortization of financial goodwill was selective in nature (rather than being generally available to all corporate taxpayers).[143] Next, in 2016, the Court of Justice of the European Union set aside the General Court's decision on the ground that it had misconstrued the selectivity requirement and remanded the case for further consideration.[144] Then, in 2018, the General Court, on remand, reconsidered the appeal in light of the Court of Justice's decision, denied the appeal by the private parties, and affirmed the Commission's decisions that the deduction constituted prohibited state aid.[145] As of this writing, the General Court's decision is on appeal back to the Court of Justice of the European Union.[146]

Temporal X-Ray Specs

The earlier examples from the United States showed how Congress converted time into money through a combination of artful manipulation and application of force. The amortization of financial goodwill in Spain demonstrates a different approach to compressing time in order to convert it into currency that can be handed out to favored taxpayers. Before it applied pressure to time, the Spanish legislature neither pleated nor applied brute force to time; rather, the Spanish legislature chose to don a sophisticated and more effective version of the x-ray specs that are a popular novelty among children.

(SEMI)TRANSPARENT STOCK

Where on casual inspection it might have appeared that a Spanish company had merely acquired stock in a foreign company, the Spanish legislature selectively looked through that stock to the underlying assets of the acquired foreign company, almost as if it had taken an x-ray of the stock. Looking through the corporate shell, the Spanish legislature attributed the stock's purchase price to all of the assets visible on the virtual x-ray that is the company's books. Any part of the price that could not be attributed to assets on the books was attributed to the mysterious force of goodwill that bound all the parts of the company together and helped it to function at the level that justified the price paid for the stock. Notwithstanding that many of the company's other assets might likewise be eligible for depreciation, the Spanish legislature chose to focus only on financial goodwill and to confine the purchaser to amortizing only the portion of the purchase price attributable to its cost over a twenty-year period. As a result, one might characterize the stock as being "semitransparent" for depreciation purposes.

The amortization of financial goodwill might alternatively be seen as a bastardized application of substance-over-form principles. Like the virtual x-ray, substance-over-form principles aim to look through the shell of form to the substance of what is occurring. As the European Commission explained: "'Financial goodwill', as used in the Spanish tax system, is the goodwill that would have been booked if the shareholding company and the target company had merged. The concept of financial goodwill . . . therefore introduces into the field of share acquisitions a notion that is usually used in transfer of assets or business combination transactions."[147] In fact, in its response to the Commission's state aid inquiry, the Spanish government argued that the amortization of financial goodwill was not state aid because it merely equalized the treatment of direct (i.e., asset) and indirect (i.e., stock) acquisitions.[148] In essence, the Spanish government argued that it was taking a substance-over-form approach that improved the neutrality of the Spanish tax system as applied to corporate acquisitions.[149]

As the Commission correctly pointed out, however, the acquisition of as little as 5 percent of a corporation's stock without any move to combine the two businesses is hardly comparable, either factually or legally, to the level of control entailed when one corporation purchases another's assets or when two companies merge.[150] In addition, the notion that the choice to permit the amortization of financial goodwill was driven by concerns about equalizing the treatment of corporate acquisitions was belied by the Spanish government's selective application of substance-over-form principles to only certain foreign stock acquisitions and not to all stock acquisitions.[151] Picking up on the earlier discussion of the semitransparency of the acquired corporate stock, one might similarly add that true equalization of treatment would have required all of the corporation's assets (and not just goodwill) to be treated the same as if they had been directly acquired.

Yet, regardless of the logical coherence of the Spanish legislature's approach, the creativity and cunning involved in using the amortization of financial goodwill to incentivize cross-border acquisitions is undeniable. Corporate stock—an asset that is normally nondepreciable because it lacks a limited useful life—was broken into its component parts. Of those components, the Spanish legislature singled out goodwill for special treatment. This might seem an odd choice given that goodwill, like corporate stock, historically had not been depreciable because it, too, lacks a determinable useful life. Nonetheless, just a few years earlier, the Spanish legislature had permitted goodwill to be amortized in the name of increasing the neutrality of the corporate income tax. Piggybacking on this alignment of tax and accounting treatment, the Spanish legislature was able to turn one nondepreciable asset into another that was now arguably entitled to the benefits of this policy-driven relaxation of core tax principles.

In contrast to the push for immediate expensing in the United States, the goal in Spain was not to get already available deductions to taxpayers as quickly as possible; instead, it was to get taxpayers deductions where none had been available before. To do this, the Spanish legislature took an indefinably lengthy expanse of time—the legally unlimited life of a corporation[152]—and condensed it into a comparatively short twenty-year period. No longer having to wait until they finally sold stock to recover its cost, Spanish companies received a tangible and substantial benefit from the government. As the European Commission noted, the amortization of financial goodwill operated much like an interest-free credit line that conferred a benefit with a present value equal to more than 20 percent of the financial goodwill in purchased stock. This government largesse aimed to—and apparently did—give Spanish companies a leg up in bidding on foreign acquisitions. The benefit bestowed on Spanish companies was so great that it generated complaints from members of the European Parliament and eventually led to an inquiry in which the deduction was labeled unlawful state aid. When thinking about the magnitude of the tax benefits, it is worth bearing in mind that de minimis state aid is deemed not to distort competition—with the de minimis threshold having been set at €100,000 in aid or less per beneficiary from 2001 to 2006 and then raised to €200,000 or less per beneficiary beginning in 2007.[153]

DRAWING LINES

As before, it is important to focus not only on the creativity in the legislature's approach to reifying time but also on the recipients of the substantial amount of money produced through that exercise of the tax imagination. The deduction for amortization of financial goodwill was terminated because it constituted unlawful state aid; that is, it was "incompatible with the common market."[154] An important purpose behind the creation of the common market was "to promote . . . economic and social cohesion and solidarity among Member States."[155] The amortization of financial goodwill undermined this purpose because the deduction effectively handed out cash to Spanish businesses to encourage them to undertake cross-border acquisitions and to give them an advantage over foreign competitors in those acquisitions. Thus, far from promoting solidarity and cohesion, the deduction drew lines of division based on economic allegiance, thereby "othering" those whose allegiance lay outside of Spain. Moreover, notwithstanding its ostensible availability to all Spanish companies, the deduction also drew lines of division *within* Spain. As the European Commission and the Court of Justice recognized, the facial neutrality of the provision was misleading because, in practice, the deduction favored companies making cross-border investments over those making domestic investments.[156] Lines were drawn between companies with the financial wherewithal and know-how to make foreign acquisitions and those that were confined to the domestic market.

And these are not the only ways in which the tax benefits from the amortization of financial goodwill were uncommon. There was likewise nothing particularly "common" about the known recipients of this largesse and their competitors. Consider for a moment the names of the private businesses that pursued, or sought to intervene in, the appeals of the Commission's decisions: World Duty Free Group, Banco Santander, Telefónica, Iberdrola, and Deutsche Telekom.[157] These are familiar names—in some cases, not just in Europe but also in the United States. What's more, the market in which they were being given tax dollars to compete was a decidedly "uncommon" one: the market in international corporate acquisitions. This is such a rarefied space that some commentators who defended this tax incentive did so on the ground that no such market exists in which competition might be distorted.[158]

TAKING FURTHER STOCK
This discussion of the amortization of financial goodwill goes to show that the creativity of the tax imagination—and the skewed distribution

of the benefits that creativity can produce—are not unique to the United States. In Spain, too, the legislature imaginatively compressed time to convert it into currency, but it did so through an altogether different method. Eerily echoing the US paean to bolstering economic growth that is so often used to mask handing out benefits to the wealthy and privileged, the Spanish legislature created similarly pernicious effects through its exercise of the tax imagination, sowing division rather than encouraging social and economic cohesion and providing advantages to big businesses in no need of help while leaving behind small businesses without the capacity to expand through cross-border investments.

Chapter 4 continues our consideration of how the tax imagination can convert time into an exchangeable commodity such as money, but it shifts the focus from the compression of time by the legislature to its prolongation by taxpayers and their tax advisers.

4

Bartering with Time

For decades, there has been a lively debate within legal academia regarding the preferability of lawmaking through "rules" (e.g., a fixed speed limit of sixty-five miles per hour) versus "standards" (e.g., requiring cars to be driven at "reasonable" speeds—speeds that cannot be predicted in advance and that will depend on the situation).[1] Some commentators have argued that this debate is pointless or, even if not, is on the verge of becoming obsolete due to technological advances that will merge the two approaches into one.[2] Notwithstanding these critiques, the rules-versus-standards debate has seeped deep into academic tax discourse.[3] What's more, the US federal income tax has, as a practical matter, come to be peppered with rules, standards, and a range of rule/standard hybrids that exist somewhere in between the polar extremes.[4]

Of particular relevance to our exploration of tax time, Congress and the courts have created rules, standards, and rule/standard hybrids that use time as a proxy for the presence or absence of abusive taxpayer behavior. But the United States is not alone in using time as a proxy for the presence or absence of abusive behavior.[5] For instance, paralleling an example discussed later in this chapter, European Union directives aimed at coordinating the taxation of corporate groups permit member states to restrict tax relief to parent-subsidiary relationships that exist for a minimum period of time in order to prevent abuse of that relief.[6] When implementing these directives, France has chosen to restrict its withholding tax exemption for dividends paid by subsidiaries and its so-called participation exemption for dividends received by parent companies to parent-subsidiary relationships that exist for a minimum of two years.[7] In contrast, Spain requires only a minimum one-year holding period before a parent corporation can benefit from withholding tax and participation exemptions.[8]

Yet, in the cat-and-mouse game of tax avoidance, choosing time as a proxy for the presence or absence of abusive behavior merely incentivizes well-heeled taxpayers to imaginatively manipulate time in ways that give their abusive behavior a nonabusive appearance. This chapter examines four US examples of such manipulation along the rule-standard spectrum: (1) the bright-line rule regarding the basis of property gifted to and then inherited back from a decedent; (2) the hybrid rule/standard regarding the tax treatment of like-kind exchanges of property between related persons; (3) the hybrid rule/standard regarding the minimum holding period for a corporation to benefit from the dividends-received deduction; and (4) the pure standard of the step-transaction doctrine, which determines when discrete transactions will be integrated in determining whether a business combination qualifies for tax-free treatment.

In contrast to the examples in chapter 3 (which should be read in tandem with this chapter), where legislatures compressed time to convert it into money, the examples in this chapter demonstrate how taxpayers prolong time to meet the requirements of antiabuse provisions, turning time into a commodity that can be exchanged for valuable tax benefits. Naturally, empowering taxpayers to commodify time for their financial benefit raises questions regarding the distribution of those benefits and whether that distribution furthers or undermines tax justice, an especially important question when, as in all of the examples explored here, the taxpayers being benefited are already a privileged segment of the population—those possessing substantial (and valuable) interests in property.

Gifts in Contemplation of Death

For US federal income tax purposes, a person who inherits property pays no tax on receiving the property and normally takes the property with a tax basis equal to its fair market value on the date of the decedent's death.[9] For property that appreciated in value during the decedent's lifetime, this "stepped-up" basis (to use the argot of tax lawyers) is an extraordinarily generous benefit because it permanently exempts any predeath appreciation from income tax. But it's possible to leverage these rules to even greater advantage. Federal income tax is paid on appreciation in property's value only if the owner sells or otherwise disposes of the property (in tax terminology, when the owner "realizes" the gain).[10] This realization requirement—itself a timing rule—coupled with the stepped-up basis at death form two planks of the tripartite scheme that Edward McCaffery has called "Tax Planning 101: Buy/Borrow/Die. By buying and holding assets that appreciate without producing taxable cash flows, borrowing to finance one's lifestyle, and holding onto their assets until death, the rich—those with capital—can avoid all income taxation."[11]

If inherited property is promptly sold, the inheritance normally results in no income tax liability at all. Receipt of the property is not taxed, and due to the quick sale, there should be no postdeath appreciation to tax either. This treatment stands in stark contrast to the transferred basis rule that applies to gifts of property made while the donor is still living. The recipient of such lifetime gifts takes the same basis in the property as the donor and must pay tax both on the appreciation that accrued while the donor held the property *and* on any appreciation that accrues while the gift recipient holds the property.[12] Death, as explored in the next section, is thus a key player in schemes to avoid tax through gratuitous transfers of property.

Curtailing Abuse

In 1981, Congress added an exception to this generous treatment of inherited property.[13] At the time, Congress had amended the federal gift and estate taxes to (1) greatly increase the amount of property that can be transferred tax-free under the lifetime exclusion available to all taxpayers and (2) create an unlimited marital deduction that effectively exempts all transfers of property between spouses from tax (without the need to tap into the lifetime exclusion, which is reserved for transfers to others).[14] Congress was concerned that these changes would incentivize deathbed transfers of appreciated property to obtain a stepped-up income tax basis at little or no transfer tax cost.

A simple example using a married different-sex couple (who, in 1981, were the only beneficiaries of the unlimited marital deduction) illustrates the concern that motivated this change. If husband and wife were to learn that husband was terminally ill, wife could gift all of her appreciated property to husband without paying any income or gift tax due to a combination of the newly unlimited gift tax marital deduction and the long-standing rule that gifts are not taxable events for income tax purposes.[15] Then, when husband passed away, he could leave that same property to wife in his will. This bequest would generate no estate tax, again because of the unlimited marital deduction, and wife would owe no income tax on receipt of the property either.[16] But because wife would have inherited the property from husband, she would take the property with a stepped-up income tax basis.[17] Thus, at zero tax cost, wife would be able to permanently exempt herself from income tax on the gain that had accrued in all of her property prior to husband's death.

Congress felt that "allowing a stepped-up basis in this situation permits unintended and inappropriate tax benefits."[18] To fend off this abuse, Congress enacted Internal Revenue Code § 1014(e). Section 1014(e) provides that, if a decedent received a gift of appreciated property within one year of death and that property passes on the decedent's death back to the donor, then the donor will be denied a stepped-up basis in the property.[19] Instead, the donor takes the same basis in the reacquired property that the decedent had immediately before death, which typically means that the donor also reacquires the donor's pregift basis in the property.[20] In effect, the donor's property will have taken a round trip—from the donor to the decedent and back—all for naught. To return to the earlier example, § 1014(e) would prevent wife from taking a stepped-up basis in the property if the gift to husband occurred within one year of his death. Wife would instead take the same basis in the property that she had before the gift to husband, and she would still be liable for income tax on *all* of the appreciation in the property when she sells it. If, however, husband's death occurred more than one year after wife's gift, then § 1014(e) would *not* prevent wife from taking a stepped-up basis in the property and she would be able to achieve the sought-after permanent exemption from tax on the appreciation in the property.

Manipulating the Rule

Section 1014(e) is a bright-line rule because it "is applied arithmetically, and cannot be avoided by demonstrating that the decedent's death was unexpected."[21] Consequently, a gift within one year of death will not result in a stepped-up basis—regardless of the surrounding circumstances—because the gift is deemed to be motivated by an abusive desire to obtain "unintended and inappropriate tax benefits."[22] In contrast, a death occurring even a single day after the one-year period expires will result in a stepped-up basis because the gift is deemed free of improper tax motives, even if the gift was actually motivated by the desire to obtain a stepped-up basis.

Bright-line rules such as § 1014(e) can thus be both over- and underinclusive in their targeting. However, with self-interested behavior not only anticipated but also seemingly encouraged among taxpayers,[23] relying on the ostensibly objective, uncontrollable passage of time as a proxy for motive avoids messy, subjective inquiries into taxpayers' motivations for actions that produce tax savings. If enough time has passed between a gift of property and the death of its recipient, the bequest of the property back to its original owner is deemed unrelated to the earlier gift, and the entire course of events is presumed to be motivated by nontax considerations. But how much time must pass before events are considered unrelated is a sticky question. As originally drafted, § 1014(e) would have set the threshold at a lengthy three years, but in conference between the House and Senate over the final version of the law (and with no explanation), the time period was reduced to just one year.[24] With potentially large tax benefits hanging in the balance, this two-thirds reduction in the amount of time that must pass between a gift of property and the recipient's death necessarily reduces § 1014(e)'s scope significantly while correspondingly expanding the possibilities for its manipulation in taxpayers' favor.

As one might expect, tax lawyers responded to the enactment of § 1014(e) by devising legal workarounds using powers of appointment, trusts, and "ricochet" transfers that target the property to an object of the donor's bounty rather than pass it back to the donor (or the donor's spouse, who is treated the same as the donor for this purpose).[25] The creativity of the tax imagination did not, however, end there. Going beyond the typical technical tricks to circumvent § 1014(e), one well-regarded legal commentator has ghoulishly suggested taking the necessary steps to stretch out the dying gift recipient's lifespan just enough to surpass the one-year mark and obtain a stepped-up basis:

> One may question whether a spouse to whom a reverse gift in contemplation of death is made should have a natural death declaration (living

will). Such a document precludes the use of extraordinary measures to keep the client alive. If only a few additional days are needed to satisfy the one-year rule of Section 1014(e), the termination of extraordinary life prolonging measures may be inappropriate. A medical power of attorney, giving the agent the right to decide whether to use extraordinary measures to keep the decedent-to-be alive, might be more appropriate when time-sensitive estate planning has been undertaken.[26]

With only a matter of months, weeks, or even days being the key to permanent forgiveness of tax, suggestions of prolonging someone's life beyond its natural end with the aim of reaping tax benefits—or, to paraphrase the title of a continuing legal education presentation on these issues, finding the tax silver lining in even the blackest of clouds[27]—becomes plausible and predictable (even if morally reprehensible) legal advice. In effect, taxpayers are advised to leverage their tax-avoidance efforts by bartering someone else's borrowed time in exchange for valuable dollars of tax savings.

Distributive (In)Justice

But who, exactly, is best positioned to take advantage of such advice and to barter for tax benefits with this doubly borrowed time? At the outset, it must be recognized that, by design, the benefits of the stepped-up basis rule are limited to taxpayers who own property—and, more particularly, property that has appreciated in value. By now, it should be common knowledge that wealth inequality in the United States has reached alarming levels, with reports of "[t]he 400 richest Americans—the top 0.00025 percent of the population— . . . own[ing] more of the country's riches than the 150 million adults in the bottom 60 percent of the wealth distribution."[28] And this class-based gap between rich and poor also has racial and ethnic dimensions, with Whites owning more wealth than African Americans, Hispanics, and Asian Americans and Pacific Islanders.[29] In fact, applying a tax lens to this data, Beverly Moran and William Whitford showed that African Americans are less likely to benefit from the stepped-up basis at death because they own fewer assets than Whites *and* because they own fewer of the right types of assets (e.g., stocks and bonds that appreciate in value rather than cash or vehicles that do not).[30] A burgeoning line of research has begun to explore and attempt to measure the gender-based wealth gap that likely adds another intersecting line of privilege to this picture.[31] Other lines of privilege may be added in the future as further work is done, for example, undermining the persistent "myth of gay affluence."[32]

Avoiding the antiabuse rule in § 1014(e) further presupposes knowledge of its existence, which implicates the gaps that exist in access to tax advice. Speaking of bright-line rules such as § 1014(e), Emily Cauble has warned:

> In the case of a rule, some taxpayers will find themselves on the wrong side of the line because they failed to receive advice, or received inadequate advice, before acting. As a result, those taxpayers will forgo the opportunity to obtain more favorable tax consequences. Thus, rules can trap unwary taxpayers. This aspect of rules is particularly troubling because unwary, unsophisticated taxpayers may tend to be less wealthy than taxpayers who are sufficiently sophisticated to seek tax advice before acting. As a result, rules can disproportionately benefit wealthy taxpayers while disadvantaging less wealthy taxpayers.[33]

To close Cauble's train of thought in the § 1014(e) context, the class-based gap that exists in access to expert tax advice reinforces the various lines of privilege already embedded in the design of a stepped-up basis rule that benefits only owners of appreciated property.

Even for those who seek tax advice and endeavor to stretch time until the one-year period has passed, the length of the gift recipient's lifespan will be influenced by both current and past access to quality health care. Yet, access to quality health care is not evenly distributed across the US population either. In a 2017 report regarding steps that communities can take toward achieving health equity, the National Academies of Sciences, Engineering, and Medicine stated that "existing evidence on health disparities does reveal differential health outcomes" along lines of race, ethnicity, "gender, sexual orientation, age, disability status, socioeconomic status, and geographic location."[34] Moreover, in a study of wealth inequality, Emmanuel Saez and Gabriel Zucman used tax data to compute mortality rates by age and wealth groups and concluded that, even for those most economically privileged, "there is a clear mortality gradient within the top 10%: the top 10% live less long than the top 1%, who in turn live less long than the top 0.1%."[35] Thus, whether a gift recipient has lived a life of more or less privilege affects the ability to manipulate time by prolonging the recipient's remaining lifespan beyond the all-important one-year mark.

Notwithstanding a bright-line rule keyed to the uncontrollable passage of time and the unpredictable timing of death, some taxpayers can still take steps to prolong the time between a gift of property and the gift recipient's death in order to return the property to its original owner with a stepped-up basis—and, more importantly, with the tax on any appreciation in the property permanently forgone. However, the group of taxpayers best positioned to barter with borrowed time in exchange for these dollars of tax savings is limited by a series of reinforcing lines of privilege. The delimitation of this group begins with the privileging of those who own property that appreciates in value, continues with the privileging of those with access to the best tax advice, and finishes with the privileging of those who enjoy easy access to quality health care—all of which contribute to the disparate distribution of this power to barter with time along lines of class, race, ethnicity, gender, and sexual orientation, among others.

Like-Kind Exchanges

Normally, when property is sold or exchanged, a taxpayer must report (or, in tax parlance, "recognize") the gain or loss realized on that sale or exchange.[36] Code § 1031, however, absolves taxpayers from having to recognize gain or loss when business or investment property is exchanged solely for like-kind business or investment property—for example, when one parcel of real estate is exchanged for a different parcel of real estate.[37] Section 1031 requires the taxpayer to take the new property with the same tax basis that the old property had, thus deferring recognition of gain or loss until the new property is sold for cash or exchanged for property that is not of like kind.[38] The rationale underlying this "nonrecognition" provision is that it is inappropriate to require gain to be taxed or to allow losses to be deducted when the taxpayer has merely continued the same investment in modified form.[39]

Imaginative as they are, taxpayers and their tax advisers came to understand the possibilities for turning § 1031 to their advantage. A simple example from a legal treatise illustrates how taxpayers did this:

> [A]ssume *T* owns Blackacre, which is worth $100 and has a basis of $20, and her wholly owned corporation, *C* Corp., owns like kind property (Whiteacre), which is also worth $100 but has a basis of $140; *T* and *C* swap, and *C* immediately sells Blackacre to an unrelated person. If *T* had sold Blackacre, she would have recognized gain of $80, but *C*, whose $140 basis for Whiteacre becomes its basis for Blackacre, recognizes loss of $40. Without § 1031(f), the presale exchange would have the effect of deferring recognition of *T*'s potential gain and accelerating recognition of *C*'s $40 loss.[40]

Rather than merely postponing gain recognition where the taxpayer continued its investment in modified form (which itself is no mean benefit for owners of business or investment property), "sophisticated"[41] taxpayers such as *T* and *C* were acting in concert to use § 1031 to sell appreciated property for cash without paying tax—and, under the right facts, to simultaneously recognize a loss that could be used to shelter yet other income from tax.[42] This gambit has been likened to "the magician pulling the rabbit out of his hat."[43]

Curtailing Abuse

In 1989, acting on the belief that "it is appropriate to accord nonrecognition treatment only to exchanges . . . where a taxpayer can be viewed as merely continuing his investment," Congress decided "that if a related party exchange is followed shortly thereafter by a disposition of the property, the related parties have, in effect, 'cashed out' of the investment, and the original exchange should not be accorded nonrecognition treatment."[44] Congress thus added § 1031(f) to provide that, if related persons engage in a like-kind exchange that benefits from nonrecognition treatment and within two years either party disposes of the property received in the exchange, then the benefits of nonrecognition treatment will be stripped from the exchange.[45] Any gain that went unrecognized on the related-party exchange must be reported for the year in which the disposition took place.[46]

There are a few exceptions to the application of § 1031(f). Nonrecognition treatment will not be stripped from a related-party exchange if the disposition of property occurs either (1) after the death of one of the related parties or (2) as a result of the property's unanticipated destruction, theft, seizure, or condemnation.[47] In addition, nonrecognition treatment will not be stripped from a related-party exchange if the taxpayer can satisfy the Internal Revenue Service "that neither the exchange nor . . . disposition had as one of its principal purposes the avoidance of Federal income tax."[48]

Other rules add teeth to § 1031(f). Nonrecognition treatment is outright denied to an exchange that "is part of a transaction (or series of transactions) structured to avoid [§ 1031(f)'s] purposes."[49] Furthermore, anticipating that taxpayers might circumvent § 1031(f) by minimizing or eliminating the market risk associated with holding property for two years after an exchange, Congress included a tolling provision that stops the running of the two-year period while the "risk of loss with respect to the property is substantially diminished by—(A) the holding of a put with respect to such property, (B) the holding by another person of a right to acquire such property, or (C) a short sale or any other transaction."[50]

Nevertheless, the IRS has ruled that transfers made after the two-year holding period has expired will not trigger § 1031(f), meaning that the related-party exchange will retain the benefit of nonrecognition treatment even if it was intended all along that the property would be transferred after the expiration of the two-year period.[51] Citing the Supreme Court's opinion in *Gregory v. Helvering* (discussed in chapter 1) and its general blessing of taxpayer efforts to minimize taxes, the IRS concluded that simply waiting for the two-year period to expire did not amount to a plan to circumvent the rules of § 1031(f) because "the parties merely took advantage of what Congress allowed them by enacting the two-year rule."[52] In the IRS's eyes, the two-year rule is a "safe harbor that precludes the application of section 1031(f)(1) to any transaction falling outside that period."[53]

Manipulating the Rule/Standard

Taxpayers and their tax advisers have employed their ingenuity to devise strategies that circumvent § 1031(f)'s hybrid rule/standard. Some have taken advantage of the bright-line definition of who constitutes a related party by, for example, choosing to engage in a like-kind exchange with "an entity with 50 percent or less common ownership or, in the case of an individual, in-laws rather than blood relatives."[54] Others have taken advantage of the standard embedded in § 1031(f) by pressing the case that their exchange and later disposition lack a tax avoidance purpose. They have successfully done so by convincing the IRS that the exchange did not involve the type of basis shifting that motivated the enactment of § 1031(f).[55] Yet, rulings that transactions lack a tax avoidance purpose have not always been met with universal acclaim; indeed, one ruling was heavily criticized not only as flawed but also for opening the door to "mak[ing] gain nontaxable in a broad set of potentially abusive transactions."[56]

Nonetheless, as several commentators have pointed out, the easiest and most straightforward technique for avoiding § 1031(f)'s hybrid rule/standard is far simpler: be patient.[57] In fact, "[t]ax planning in the area of related-party exchanges often focuses on maintaining ownership of the retained and relinquished properties for two years, a time period that the IRS itself has recognized as a safe harbor."[58] Recall that, as a safe harbor, the IRS does not view purposeful delay of a transfer of property beyond the two-year mark as a prohibited plan to circumvent the purposes of § 1031(f).[59]

An IRS private letter ruling provides an interesting example of such planned patience.[60] That ruling concerns a series of like-kind exchanges among a group of related parties to settle a will contest. In the settlement agreement, each of the related parties contractually agreed to be patient—that is to say, they agreed to hold the property received in the like-kind exchange for a minimum of two years and to refrain from taking any action that might toll § 1031(f)'s two-year holding period. Under the agreement, a party could dispose of property received in the exchange if one of the statutory exceptions applied—for example, if the transfer lacked a tax avoidance purpose—however, the party wishing to avail itself of the no-tax-avoidance exception had to pay all of the other parties' costs (including attorneys' fees) incurred in establishing the lack of a tax avoidance purpose to the IRS's satisfaction. If this agreement were breached, the breaching party would be liable for the income tax incurred by the other parties to the exchange (along with any interest owed on those taxes). With the assurance provided by the agreement that there would be no disqualifying disposition of the exchanged properties within two years, the IRS ruled that the exchanges would qualify for nonrecognition treatment under § 1031.

It has been said that "[t]he moral of this story is that patience is truly a virtue, especially under Section 1031(f). Two years may seem like a long time, but it goes by quickly when the related parties consider the tax benefits."[61] But wealth should not be confused with virtue. Unlike taxpayers leveraging borrowed time to circumvent § 1014(e) to obtain a stepped-up basis in property, taxpayers engaging in planned patience to avoid § 1031(f) barter with their own time—time that they obviously can afford to spare. It is, therefore, not virtue that allows them to circumvent § 1031(f) but an abundance of time that does. Coupled with this wealth of time is a wealth of money that both relieves any pressure to make a quick sale and pays for the legal work that goes into standstill agreements such as the one described earlier. As the IRS acknowledged, that agreement was carefully drafted to restrict the parties' actions—choreographing a sequence of property exchanges and then prohibiting disposition of the properties until the required two-year period had passed—all to ensure that a shared plan to circumvent § 1031(f) would not go awry. Far from demonstrating virtue, taxpayers engaging in such strategies demonstrate their profligacy. After all, they barter their surplus time for the far more valuable tax savings resulting from like-kind exchanges that shelter gains on planned sales of property from tax and, under the right circumstances, allow for the recognition of losses in their place.

Distributive (In)Justice

Like § 1014's stepped-up basis rule, like-kind exchanges are, by design, limited to taxpayers who own property and are of particular benefit to those who own appreciated property. The benefits of nonrecognition treatment afforded to like-kind exchanges thus implicate many of the same lines of privilege (e.g., race and gender) explored earlier in the discussion of § 1014. But unlike § 1014, like-kind exchanges are not possible with just any property; instead, both the property relinquished and the property received in the exchange must be held for business or investment purposes to qualify for nonrecognition treatment. Limiting eligible assets in this way—and, since 2018, further limiting like-kind exchanges to only real property held for business or investment purposes—results in even greater skewing of tax benefits to those who are wealthier and White, because they are more likely to own assets eligible for a tax-free like-kind exchange.[62]

The distribution of tax benefits is further skewed when the possibility of using related-party like-kind exchanges to avoid tax is considered. As noted earlier, a prime strategy for circumventing § 1031(f) to obtain the benefits associated with these basis-swapping transactions is simply to be patient.[63] But the patience of those involved in related-party exchanges is not a virtue that all can practice but a luxury good affordable by a very few: § 1031(f) "seems to have a very narrow time horizon, which rewards exchangers and their related parties who have the business plan, financial resources, and patience to wait out the proscribed time."[64] Circumventing § 1031(f) through a strategy of patient waiting is thus limited to those who can afford to plan ahead and wait more than two years after a like-kind exchange before selling the property received in the exchange. Taxpayers in this situation have the luxury of time and the necessary resources to stave off any pressing need to convert property into cash—not to mention the benefit of sophisticated tax planning advice to avoid the potential pitfalls associated with § 1031 and the potential problems associated with counting on the cooperation of others in the execution of one's tax avoidance plans. This all, of course, bespeaks a certain privilege even among the segment of the propertied who are positioned to take advantage of the nonrecognition treatment afforded to like-kind exchanges.

Instead of engaging in distasteful bartering of the borrowed time of dying individuals in exchange for a stepped-up basis, those in the multiply privileged position that allows them to circumvent § 1031(f) are able to prolong time on their own. With the help of money and good tax advice, they feel no haste to complete their transactions. They are able to let those transactions linger for far longer than necessary, waiting for the requisite time to pass in order to reap significant tax savings. For them, it seems that time stretches in a pleasant way, as it does on a lazy Sunday morning reading the newspaper and working on the crossword puzzle. Evoking the luxurious lifestyle of the idle rich, these images are nothing like the statue of the "quiet and diligent" marble lion named Patience who guards the entrance to the New York Public Library.[65]

Dividends-Received Deduction

Because each corporation is a separate taxpayer, ownership of a business through a chain of corporations could result in multiple layers of tax being imposed on the same income as it makes its way up the chain to the ultimate owner. Though double taxation of the same income is an accepted feature of the corporate income tax when a corporation makes a distribution to an individual shareholder, some form of relief from the multiple layers of tax that might be imposed on the same income while it remains within corporate solution has been a feature of the US federal income tax since its early days.[66]

At present, that relief is provided through the dividends-received deduction.[67] When a domestic corporation pays a dividend, corporate shareholders receiving the dividend are entitled to a deduction ranging from 50 percent to 100 percent of the amount of the dividend, depending on the size of their stake in the dividend-paying corporation.[68] By excluding at least half of the dividend from the corporate income tax base, the dividends-received deduction sets the maximum corporate tax rate on dividends at 10.5 percent (i.e., one-half of the current, 21 percent general corporate tax rate).[69]

Curtailing Abuse

Before 1958, corporations leveraged the dividends-received deduction to their advantage by purchasing stock shortly before payment of a dividend and then selling the stock after the dividend was paid.[70] This resulted in the receipt of dividend income and the recognition of a corresponding tax loss of approximately equal amount (because the stock's value would decrease to reflect the payment of the dividend).[71] What at first blush might seem like a wash actually produced a significant tax advantage: The dividends-received deduction sheltered most of the dividend income from tax and left the tax loss to shelter other income from tax. As explained in the Senate report accompanying the new law, this arbitrage resulted in net tax savings because income taxed at higher rates (then, up to 52 percent) was effectively replaced with income taxed at a much lower rate (then, about 7.8 percent).[72]

Corporations similarly turned the dividends-received deduction into a tax shelter by simultaneously holding both "long" and "short" positions in the same stock around a dividend payment date. The corporation would purchase shares of stock (the long position) and borrow shares of the same stock from another shareholder and sell the borrowed shares (the short position).[73] The corporation would receive dividends on the purchased shares of stock, but the dividends-received deduction would shelter most of that income from tax. The corporation would likewise be entitled to a deduction for the dividend-equivalent payment made to the owner of the borrowed stock, which would be "deductible against income taxable at the regular corporate income tax rate."[74] Like the purchase and sale of stock around the dividend payment date, the holding of long and short positions around the dividend payment date had the effect of replacing income taxed at higher rates with dividend income taxed at significantly lower rates due to the dividends-received deduction.

To combat these abuses, Congress enacted Code § 246(c) in 1958.[75] This provision disallowed the dividends-received deduction if (1) a corporation held stock for fifteen days or less (ninety days or less in the case of certain dividends on preferred stock) or (2) a corporation was "under an obligation . . . to make corresponding payments with respect to substantially identical stocks or securities."[76] Anticipating that taxpayers might manipulate the required holding period by minimizing or eliminating the market risk associated with holding the stock, Congress authorized the issuance of regulations reducing a stock's holding period "for any period . . . in which the taxpayer has an option to sell, is under a contractual obligation to sell, or has made (and not closed) a short sale of, substantially identical stock or securities."[77] The Treasury Department promptly issued regulations implementing this tolling provision.[78]

As explained by the New York State Bar Association's Tax Section, these rules aimed to "limit the opportunities for purely tax-motivated transactions around the ex-dividend date by insisting that the tax-payer accept a minimum amount of market risk in order to obtain the [dividends-received deduction]."[79] But Congress came to realize that its efforts to stymie abuse had fallen short when matched against the boundless imaginations of taxpayers and their tax advisers, who, "employing modern hedging techniques[,] were circumventing those limitations."[80] Moving to counteract the persistent abuse, Congress increased the minimum holding period from sixteen to forty-six days in 1984.[81] At the same time, Congress recognized that its limitation of the antiabuse rules in § 246(c) to positions taken in "substantially identical stock or securities" was not comprehensive enough and "should be tightened."[82] Accordingly, Congress amended § 246(c) to disallow the dividends-received deduction "to the extent that the taxpayer is under an obligation . . . to make related payments with respect to positions in substantially similar or related property."[83] Congress also added a new provision authorizing regulations that would reduce a taxpayer's holding period for any period in which the "taxpayer has diminished his risk of loss by holding 1 or more other positions with respect to substantially similar or related property."[84] In both cases, Congress intended "the concept of 'positions in substantially similar property' to be broader than the . . . concept of 'substantially identical stock or securities.'"[85]

In 1997, Congress intervened once again to tighten the holding period requirement in § 246(c) in response to taxpayer manipulation. Prior to this change, the minimum holding period for stock needed to be satisfied only once: "Under present law, dividend-paying stocks can be marketed to corporate investors with accompanying attempts to hedge or relieve the holder from risk for much of the holding period of the stock, after the initial holding period has been satisfied. . . . The Committee believes that no deduction for a distribution on stock should be allowed when the owner of stock does not bear the risk of loss otherwise inherent in the ownership of an equity interest at a time proximate to the time the distribution is made."[86] Accordingly, as altered in 1997, the minimum holding period must now be satisfied separately with respect to *each* dividend paid to qualify for the dividends-received deduction.[87]

Manipulating the Rule/Standard

Through § 246(c), Congress created a hybrid rule/standard. The hold-ing period requirement (i.e., either forty-six or ninety-one days) is a bright-line rule that demands corporations to bear the burdens—and not just reap the benefits—of owning stock for a minimum amount of time before becoming eligible to take the dividends-received deduction. A holding period just one day too short (i.e., forty-five days or ninety days) results in disallowance of the deduction. Before the 1997 changes to § 246(c), taxpayers manipulated this bright-line rule, which then applied only once during the taxpayer's stock ownership, by indefinitely stretching an initial qualifying period of risk-taking to cover all of the dividends received with respect to that stock. By prolonging time in this way, corporate taxpayers were able to continue taking the dividends-received deduction long after they had shifted from bearing both the risks and benefits of owning stock to instead merely "stripping" or "capturing" the dividends—and the accompanying dividends-received deductions—from that stock. In effect, these corporate taxpayers were able to barter the hollowed-out appearance of time exposed to market risk in exchange for valuable tax benefits.

Furnishing additional opportunities for manipulation, the clarity of § 246(c)'s bright-line rule is muddied by standards. For instance, the tolling provision enacted in 1984 reduces a corporation's holding period by the time during which the corporation does not bear the full risk of loss that comes with owning stock. That tolling provision is larded with ambiguous phrases—"diminished risk of loss," "position," and "sub-stantially similar or related property"—whose meaning was not defined by Congress but was to be provided in regulations and that, even after regulations were issued, still depends in important ways on the facts of each case.[88] The same ambiguous phrases (along with others) appear in the provision that denies the dividends-received deduction when a corporation holds both long and short positions in stock around the dividend-payment date—that is to say, when the corporation is under an "obligation" to make "related payments" with respect to "positions" in "substantially similar or related property."[89] Taking advantage of this ambiguity, taxpayers have found imaginative ways to convey an appear-ance of risk-taking where none exists, manufacturing time spent in a hollowed-out semblance of stock ownership that they can then barter in exchange for valuable tax savings.

Itself stretching time to taxpayers' advantage, the IRS waited until 1993 to propose regulations implementing the tolling provision that Congress enacted in 1984.[90] Those regulations were finalized in 1995 but applied largely prospectively, in keeping with a congressional admonition to apply implementing regulations retroactively only with respect to specified transactions.[91] This inordinate delay permitted taxpayers to continue engaging in abusive behavior for more than a decade, as they stretched a few days, several hours, or even just a fleeting moment when they bore both the benefits and burdens of owning stock to create the appearance that they had taken risks in the market for the statutorily required forty-six-day or ninety-one-day period when they had not.[92] Even after regulations were issued, taxpayers have continued their efforts to skirt the application of § 246(c) through innovative approaches to hedging risk of loss.[93]

Distributive (In)Justice

As was the case with § 1014(e) and § 1031(f), not all taxpayers can manufacture time to be bartered in exchange for valuable dividends-received deductions. Most obviously, the dividends-received deduction is limited to corporate taxpayers. But not even all corporations are equally positioned or incentivized to engage in the abusive behaviors targeted by § 246(c). As a legal treatise explains: "The lower effective tax rate (and higher return on investment) provided by the [dividends-received deduction] has spawned an assortment of dividend-capture strategies. *Corporate cash managers want the higher return without market risk that these investments may provide.* To minimize market risk during the required holding periods, aggressive dividend-capture strategies employ a variety of hedging techniques."[94] Naturally, "corporate cash managers" are not a feature of all businesses, especially those of smaller size without a hoard of idle cash for investment. Corporations without employees devoted to managing their investments are also less likely to have access to or knowledge of the variety of hedging techniques mentioned in discussions of dividend-stripping transactions, such as futures or forward contracts, options, short sales, convertible adjustable preferred stock, Dutch auction preferred stock, and forward conversion transactions.[95]

The corporations best positioned to take advantage of these possibilities—not to mention to test their boundaries—are those with cash to spare and the wherewithal to deploy it to actively manage (i.e., artificially reduce) their income tax rate. For instance, in a case that predates the 1984 tightening of § 246(c), the casualty insurance company Progressive Corp. engaged in two different dividend-capture strategies that diminished the risk of loss on its investments in corporate stock.[96] In the first strategy, Progressive purchased stock and simultaneously purchased a put and sold a call with respect to that stock to effectively lock in its sale price.[97] In the second strategy, Progressive purchased stock shortly before a dividend was to be paid and, either at the same time or soon afterward, sold a deep-in-the-money call option with respect to the stock, which the IRS argued was tantamount to a contract to sell the stock.[98] On audit, the IRS denied Progressive the dividends-received deduction on both transactions, alleging that the holding period for the stock should be reduced due to Progressive's diminished risk of loss.[99] Progressive paid the additional taxes owed and sued for a refund.[100] After winning at the trial court level, Progressive was awarded a tax refund of $2,191,595—savings that was generated by more than $4.7 million in dividends-received deductions.[101] Progressive's win was, however, short-lived because the trial court's decision was reversed on appeal, resulting in the disallowance of the dividends-received deduction.[102]

Later in the 1980s—after § 246(c) was tightened in 1984 but before regulations implementing the new tolling provision were issued—Duke Energy Corp. found itself with $100 million to spare after the sale of the Catawba Nuclear Station.[103] Duke decided to invest its surplus cash in preferred stocks while simultaneously hedging the interest-rate risk that those investments entailed.[104] This led to a battle with the IRS over whether Duke was entitled to the dividends-received deduction on investments in a program called the "Preferred Dividend Capture Strategy" that was marketed by 21st Securities Corp.[105]

The dividend-capture strategy involved the purchase of shares of preferred stock and the short sale of other, similar shares of preferred stock, with the two positions largely offsetting each other.[106] As one commentator described it: "[T]he short and long portfolios of high-dividend-paying preferred stocks correlated so closely with each other in the aggregate that there was virtually no net risk in the two positions."[107] With risk of loss nearly eliminated, the program was designed to arbitrage the tax treatment of the dividends received, which would be included in income but largely offset by the dividends-received deduction, and the dividend-equivalent payments, which would be fully deductible for tax purposes and could be used to offset other income.[108] Duke began with an initial investment of $5 million in the program in 1985 but "invested increasing amounts of money in the program (eventually totaling cumulatively more than $400 million) until it withdrew from the program in 1990."[109]

In the program, trades were "entered and exited approximately eight times per year," with each set of trades called a "roll."[110] The timing of the rolls was dictated by 21st Securities's punctilious satisfaction of the forty-six-day minimum holding period for the dividends-received deduction (i.e., 365/46 = 7.9). Maximizing the number of rolls "significantly enhanced Duke's return."[111] Overall, the tax benefits increased Duke's pretax return of under 3 percent to an after-tax return of between 7 and 10 percent.[112]

In contrast to Progressive Corp., Duke managed to dodge disallowance of the dividends-received deduction despite its obligation to make dividend-equivalent payments on the stocks that it sold short, because the trial court found that the two pools of preferred stocks (i.e., those purchased and those sold short) were not "substantially similar" property.[113] The IRS was unable to attack 21st Securities's dividend-capture strategy under the tolling provision enacted in 1984 due to its own failure to promulgate implementing regulations,[114] which were not issued until well after Duke exited the dividend-capture program in 1990. Had regulations been issued in a timely fashion, Duke's claim to the dividends-received deduction would have been jeopardized because the regulations "include[d] an anti-abuse rule that would apply to similar types of portfolios as the ones used in *Duke*."[115] In the end, the court allowed Duke to take both the dividends-received deduction and the deduction for dividend-equivalent payments, which, for 1985 alone, generated tax savings of nearly $860,000.[116]

Both the magnitude of the tax savings at stake in these cases and the sophisticated transactions undertaken to generate those savings illustrate the privileged position occupied by corporations that engage in dividend-stripping transactions. For decades, corporations in this privileged group have—with the assistance of legal and financial advisers—turned taxation into a profit center by carefully minimizing (if not virtually eliminating) the time spent at risk of losing money from their investments in the stock of other corporations and then stretching out this manufactured appearance of stock "ownership" to satisfy § 246(c)'s minimum holding period—all to obtain access to valuable dividends-received deductions. The IRS effectively aided and abetted this privileged group of corporations to creatively manipulate the relationship between tax and time when it delayed promulgating regulations under § 246(c) that could have forestalled these temporal maneuvers. But even after regulations were issued, the flights of the corporate tax imagination have not ceased when it comes to manufacturing time spent in a hollowed-out semblance of stock ownership to be bartered in exchange for dividends-received deductions that enhance the corporate bottom line—not to mention the return to the corporations' equally privileged shareholders.

Step-Transaction Doctrine

In discussing the doctrine of substance over form, chapter 1 briefly introduced us to tax-free corporate reorganizations. This chapter now concludes by returning to the world of tax-free reorganizations to consider how the step-transaction doctrine—a close relative of the doctrine of substance over form—allows taxpayers to barter time in exchange for the tax benefits associated with reorganizations.

Under the step-transaction doctrine, a series of separate transactions may be integrated into a single transaction for tax purposes when doing so better reflects the substance of what the taxpayer aimed to do through the series of separate steps. Or, as the United States Supreme Court has more succinctly put it: "A given result at the end of a straight path is not made a different result because reached by following a devious path."[117] Like the doctrine of substance over form, the step-transaction doctrine is a long-standing judicial creation that has come to be applied throughout the tax laws.[118] Here, however, our consideration of the doctrine will be confined to the corporate reorganization context because of the "special place of importance" that the doctrine occupies in that area.[119]

Tax-Free Corporate Reorganizations

Normally, the acquisition by one corporation of the stock or assets of another corporation would be a taxable event at the corporate level, shareholder level, or both.[120] Nevertheless, as was the case with like-kind exchanges under § 1031, Congress has acted to shield certain corporate acquisitions from tax on the theory "that the new enterprise, the new corporate structure, and the new property are substantially continuations of the old still unliquidated."[121] The key to obtaining this tax-free treatment is meeting Code § 368's definition of *reorganization*, which triggers application of provisions that afford nonrecognition treatment to those involved in corporate acquisitions and, similar to § 1031, operate to defer recognition of gain or loss until a later sale or exchange of the stock or assets.[122]

In a series of lettered paragraphs that provide handy labels for the variety of transactions that qualify as a *reorganization*, § 368 includes within its ambit "mergers, consolidations, recapitalizations, acquisitions by one corporation of the stock or assets of another corporation, and changes in form or place of organization."[123] The requirements applicable to these various types of reorganizations look "primarily to the form rather than the substance of these transactions."[124] For instance, a state law merger of one corporation into another can qualify as a tax-free type A reorganization even if more than half the consideration takes the form of cash.[125] But one corporation's acquisition of the assets of another—a so-called practical merger because, in substance, it is equivalent to an A reorganization—can qualify as a tax-free type C reorganization only if the acquisition is made in exchange for voting stock of the acquirer (or its parent corporation), with very limited ability to use cash or other consideration.[126]

Curtailing Abuse

Formalistic as the definition of *reorganization* is, taxpayers have attempted to use it to their advantage. Early on, the courts "felt called upon to protect the spirit of the legislation against its letter by segregating sales and disguised dividends from 'true' reorganizations."[127] The courts did this by creating a variety of judicial doctrines that must be satisfied, in addition to the literal requirements of § 368, before a transaction can be classified as a *reorganization*. These judge-made requirements include the business-purpose, continuity-of-interest, continuity-of-business-enterprise, and step-transaction doctrines.[128]

Among these judicial requirements, the step-transaction doctrine is particularly nebulous. In fact, Lawrence Zelenak has said that "[n]o one knows the precise contours of the step transaction doctrine, and any attempt at a succinct and comprehensive definition is likely to come to grief."[129] In part, the doctrine's nebulousness is due to the multiplicity of tests used to determine when and how transactions ought to be integrated (or, in tax jargon, "stepped together").[130] A treatise helpfully summarizes the variety of step-transaction tests:

> The courts and the IRS have developed a number of different tests for determining whether two or more steps will be integrated and treated as a single transaction. These include the "binding commitment" test, under which steps will be integrated only if, at the time the first step is taken, there is a legally binding obligation to effect subsequent steps; the "mutual interdependence" test, under which steps will be integrated if "the legal relations created by one transaction would have been fruitless without a completion of the series"; and the "end result" test, under which steps will be "amalgamated into a single transaction when it appears that they were really component parts of a single transaction intended from the outset to be taken for the purpose of reaching the ultimate result."[131]

Compounding the confusion created by having multiple tests is the "confusion as to which test applies when."[132]

Time is a key element both in determining whether to integrate nominally separate steps into a single transaction and in determining which of the several step-transaction tests ought to be applied.[133] As a leading corporate tax treatise observes: "A business transaction often has no sharp beginning or clearly defined end, but it is often necessary in practice to cut it, usually chronologically, into constituent elements for tax purposes."[134] But deciding how and where to carve up a transaction along time's arrow is more art than science: "If the segments are sliced too thin . . . , the tax results may be unfair to the government, the taxpayer, or both. As a consequence, a series of formally separate steps may be amalgamated and treated as a single transaction if the steps are, in substance, integrated, interdependent, and focused toward a particular end result."[135] While a few bright lines do provide some clarity for taxpayers,[136] meaningful guidance on when and how to carve up a transaction chronologically is sparing, which should come as no surprise given that the step-transaction tests have been described as "poorly defined" and critiqued for their lack of predictability.[137] Indeed, it has been said that "the very vagueness of the scope of the step-transaction doctrine may be a virtue in restraining overly ambitious taxpayers and their advisers."[138]

To illustrate, let's consider when a multistep (or "creeping") stock acquisition can qualify as a tax-free type B reorganization. For one corporation's acquisition of another corporation as a controlled subsidiary to qualify as a B reorganization, the acquiring corporation may use only its voting stock as consideration.[139] If the acquiring corporation provides even one dollar of cash to the target corporation's shareholders in exchange for their stock, the acquisition will be disqualified from treatment as a B reorganization.[140] Because an acquisition can qualify as a B reorganization even if the acquiring corporation already owns target stock, thorny step-transaction questions can arise when the acquiring corporation purchased its existing block of stock using cash rather than voting stock.[141] Regulations provide only the broadest of parameters for applying the step-transaction doctrine in this situation, merely restating guidance that Congress provided when it clarified that creeping B reorganizations are possible.[142] Echoing the legislative history, the regulations state that transactions occurring "over a relatively short period of time such as 12 months" will be integrated and considered together.[143] In contrast, the regulations include an example of a cash purchase of stock in 1939 followed by the acquisition of control in exchange solely for voting stock in 1955, summarily concluding that the 1955 acquisition would qualify as a *B* reorganization.[144] This guidance led one legal treatise to observe, tongue firmly implanted in cheek: "Presumably, 16 years does not represent the minimum amount of time that must pass for purchased stock to become old and cold!"[145]

Manipulating the Standard

Given its vagueness and sensitivity to legal and factual context, the step-transaction doctrine lies on the "pure standard" end of the rule-standard spectrum. Indeed, it has been said that application of the doctrine requires "Solomonic judgment calls" on the part of tax planners.[146] Although the step-transaction doctrine looms large over taxpayers and their tax advisers as they plan corporate acquisitions, its amorphousness—sometimes even in the face of specific guidance—leaves ample space for argument and manipulation.

For instance, in *American Potash & Chemical Corp. v. United States*, the United States Court of Claims first decided that a creeping stock acquisition that occurred over a fourteen-month period could not qualify as a *B* reorganization because the requisite level of control was not acquired in a single twelve-month period, taking the regulations' mention of "a relatively short period of time such as 12 months" as a bright-line rule.[147] On reconsideration, however, the court appeared to embrace the government's view that the reference to twelve months was no more than a guideline. The court then remanded the case for trial to determine whether two stock-for-stock acquisitions over a fourteen-month period were part of a continuous offer to acquire the target or were instead discreet offers that would not be stepped together.[148]

American Potash demonstrates that, just as there is no talismanic length of time that renders an earlier transaction "old and cold," close proximity in time does not ineluctably lead to integrating transactions together. In the end, the regulations' guidance merely tracks the conventional wisdom that the likelihood of integrating transactions varies inversely with the length of time separating them (i.e., the longer the period, the less likely the doctrine will apply).[149] Accordingly, even faced with mentions of specific time frames in regulations, tax planners continue to benefit from significant leeway in taking positions about how little time must pass before transactions are deemed separate and, conversely, about how much time can pass before it is no longer possible to step transactions together. As a matter of fact, "the doctrine has been applied to events that are as far apart in time as five years, and courts have declined to apply the doctrine to events spanning only 30 minutes apart."[150]

The ability of sophisticated tax planners to manipulate the standard appears to be amplified rather than diminished by the IRS audit process. In 2019, the Treasury Inspector General for Tax Administration issued a report detailing the results of an audit to determine whether "the IRS had established and implemented an effective strategy to ensure that large corporations meet their tax obligations" with regard to mergers and acquisitions (M&A).[151] The report concluded that "the IRS does not have an overall strategy or systematic approach to identify and address potential noncompliance of M&A transactions."[152] Tellingly, the report found that proposed adjustments were significant when auditors did identify noncompliance, averaging "approximately $15.2 million per issue" in fiscal years 2015 through 2018.[153]

Distributive (In)Justice

In the corporate reorganization context, as in the earlier examples in this chapter, the ability to take advantage of the nebulousness of the step-transaction doctrine redounds to the benefit of taxpayers with property (i.e., corporate shareholders and the corporations themselves). Also like those earlier examples, the ability to manipulate the step-transaction doctrine is not evenly distributed even among this privileged group, because it depends on access to sophisticated tax advisers who are willing to take sometimes aggressive positions for taxpayers' benefit. A ready example of this is found in *J. E. Seagram Corp. v. Commissioner*, a case concerning the tax consequences of Seagram's failed attempt to acquire Conoco, Inc. in the early 1980s.[154]

After selling its stake in Texas Pacific Co. for $2.3 billion in 1980, Seagram was "[f]lush with cash" and "looked around for something to buy."[155] In late May 1981, Seagram had its eye on Conoco and approached Conoco's management with an offer to purchase a significant stake in the company; however, that offer was rebuffed by Conoco's board of directors.[156] Seagram then made a cash tender offer directly to

Conoco's shareholders with the aim of purchasing at least one-third of Conoco's stock, which would have effectively given it control of the company.[157] In response, Conoco urged its shareholders to decline Seagram's "unfriendly" tender offer and entered into talks with E. I. DuPont de Nemours & Co. about the possibility of Conoco merging with DuPont in order to stave off Seagram's attempted acquisition.[158]

After reaching agreement with Conoco, DuPont made its own tender offer, which was conditioned on obtaining 51 percent of Conoco's stock and, as part of the contractual agreement with Conoco, was to be promptly followed by Conoco's merger into a DuPont subsidiary.[159] Before its tender offer opened, DuPont received an opinion from its tax lawyers that the two-step transaction (i.e., the tender offer for a mix of stock and cash followed by a merger) would be integrated into a single transaction for tax purposes and qualify as a tax-free reorganization.[160] A battle ensued between Seagram and DuPont to obtain control of Conoco, with a third company entering the fray and all three potential acquirers repeatedly upping the ante.[161]

When the dust settled at the beginning of August 1981, DuPont emerged victorious.[162] About ten days later, Seagram—whose goal had shifted from acquiring Conoco to obtaining a significant stake in DuPont—exchanged its own block of Conoco stock for DuPont stock as part of DuPont's tender offer.[163] On the same day, DuPont's shareholders approved the merger with Conoco, and that merger was consummated at the end of September 1981—just four months after the battle for Conoco began.[164] DuPont reported the acquisition of Conoco as a tax-free reorganization on its US federal income tax return, and it advised the former Conoco shareholders who received DuPont stock in exchange for their Conoco stock that they would not recognize gain or loss on the exchange either.[165] Contrary to DuPont's position, however, Seagram claimed a capital loss of slightly more than $530 million as a result of the exchange of its Conoco stock for DuPont stock.[166]

In support of the claimed loss, Seagram's attorneys, who hailed from a well-regarded New York law firm, made two distinct arguments that revolved around the step-transaction doctrine. Seagram's attorneys first argued that "DuPont's tender offer and the subsequent merger squeezing out the remaining Conoco shareholders were separate and independent transactions. Consequently, [Seagram] argue[d] that the exchange of Conoco stock for DuPont stock pursuant to DuPont's tender offer rather than pursuant to the merger could not have been in pursuance of a plan of reorganization . . . ."[167] The Tax Court "easily rejected" this position, finding that the step-transaction doctrine would apply to integrate the tender offer with the subsequent merger because DuPont was contractually committed to complete the merger following the tender offer.[168] Moreover, the court noted that Seagram had undercut its own position when: (1) Seagram's chairman and CEO was quoted in a company press release, issued at the time of its exchange of Conoco stock for DuPont stock, "as saying that Seagram was pleased at the prospect of becoming 'a large stockholder of the *combined DuPont and Conoco*'"; and (2) Seagram inconsistently reported no loss for financial accounting purposes and instead "ascribed its carrying cost for its Conoco stock to the DuPont stock."[169]

The argument that DuPont's tender offer and the Conoco-DuPont merger were separate transactions was remarkable because "Du Pont's tax counsel had been sufficiently confident on this point that it had written an opinion letter to that effect. The validity of such 'creeping multi-step mergers' was not generally considered controversial at the time of the Seagram litigation. Such mergers had been blessed judicially, and by the leading treatise on corporate taxation."[170] In addition, the fact that the two steps "were connected by a binding agreement . . . would seem to demolish Seagram's argument that the steps should not be integrated."[171]

The second argument made by Seagram's attorneys was equally aggressive in its attempt to integrate Seagram's tender offer with DuPont's tender offer/merger:

> In its first argument, Seagram contended that the step transaction doctrine *should not* apply even though the tender offer and merger were linked by a binding commitment. In its [second] argument, however, Seagram claimed that Seagram's acquisition of Conoco stock and Du Pont's acquisition *should* be stepped together merely because they were proximate in time. Far from being connected by a binding commitment, the Seagram and Du Pont acquisitions were not even pursuant to the same overall plan—in fact, they were pursuant to competing plans.
>
> Perhaps recognizing the tension (if not outright contradiction) between its two arguments, and hoping to shield that tension from the

> judicial gaze, Seagram's attorneys made a special effort *not* to identify
> their [second argument] as a step transaction argument . . . .[172]

The aim of the second argument was to disqualify the merger from being classified as a *reorganization* on the ground that, counting Seagram's and DuPont's cash purchases together, insufficient stock consideration had been provided to Conoco's "historic" shareholders.[173] With too much cash and too little stock, the merger would resemble a sale more than a continuation of the shareholders' investment in modified form.

In taking these seemingly inconsistent positions, Seagram's attorneys creatively—and rather aggressively—stretched time for their client's benefit. The creativity in their approach lay in treating time's arrow like a rubber band that can be stretched and elongated. By stretching time like a rubber band, Seagram's attorneys were first able to argue that the distance between DuPont's tender offer and the merger, which occurred at different points along time's arrow, grew longer in much the same way that a rubber band grows longer when stretched. Increasing the distance between these events opened the way for disregarding the step-transaction doctrine, which is conventionally seen as less likely to be applied the more distance there is separating events in time. Simultaneously, Seagram's attorneys were able to argue that the competing Seagram and DuPont tender offers, which occurred in parallel along time's arrow, grew closer together in much the same way that the two sides of a rubber band grow closer together when the band is stretched. By closing the space between the tender offers, Seagram's attorneys took advantage of the conventional view that the closer in time events occur, the more likely they are to be stepped together. Through this elongation of time's arrow, Seagram's attorneys attempted to barter not an appearance of time's having passed, as corporations have done to avoid § 246(c) and obtain the dividends-received deduction, but merely the altered appearance of time itself in exchange for a large tax loss.

In the end, imaginative manipulation of time by Seagram's attorneys sufficiently muddied the waters on appeal that the IRS decided to preserve its win in the Tax Court by settling the case "on what appear to have been rather favorable terms for Seagram."[174] Seagram thus benefited greatly from its multiply privileged position: it was a large company sitting on a "cash hoard"[175] that was able to turn tax lemons (i.e., a loss that should have gone unrecognized on a tax-free corporate reorganization) into lemonade through its access to well-respected, sophisticated tax attorneys who on its behalf were willing to take aggressive positions manipulating time and the step-transaction doctrine. This worked to Seagram's financial advantage after its failed attempt to acquire Conoco, and this financial advantage only grew over time. After all, when Seagram sold its stake in DuPont in 1995, it reaped a "multi-billion dollar gain."[176]

Temporal Elasticity

Exploring the reification of time, chapters 3 and 4 illustrate the malleability of time in new and different ways from those encountered in the examination of substance-over-form principles in chapters 1 and 2. The examples in chapters 3 and 4 show how the tax imagination can manipulate the elasticity of time—alternately compressing or prolonging time—in an effort to solidify it into a valuable commodity. Despairingly, however, bouncing back and forth as it has between its compressed and elongated states, time seems ever to be the servant of those possessing wealth, power, and privilege—and, in all of the examples considered in chapters 3 and 4, property.

In chapter 3, it was elected representatives who deliberately compressed time so that capital cost recovery deductions might be converted into money to be doled out to favored taxpayers. In both the United States and Spain, this largesse was cloaked in gauzy talk of encouraging economic growth or bolstering the competitiveness of business for the (presumed) benefit of all. The examples from chapter 3 raise questions about why it is that working to advance society too often seems to involve handing tax dollars out to those who need those dollars least in the vain hope that help will trickle down to those who need it most—and need it now.

In chapter 4, it was taxpayers who helped themselves to tax dollars by bartering time in exchange for access to tax benefits. Reinforcing the lesson from chapter 2 that tools for curtailing abusive behavior and working toward a more just tax system do not always operate as advertised, chapter 4 examined how taxpayers have attempted to circumvent congressional and judicial efforts to stymie tax abuse—sometimes successfully, sometimes not—by prolonging time to make it seem as if their behavior were not tax motivated. Demonstrating the breadth and depth of the tax imagination, taxpayers have employed a variety of strategies to commodify time: from bartering the borrowed time of the terminally ill to avoid paying tax on the appreciation in their own assets; to bartering their surplus time and money to shelter gain from tax (and possibly even to accelerate losses) through like-kind exchanges; to employing innovative hedging techniques to manufacture time spent in a hollowed-out semblance of stock ownership that can be bartered for dividends-received deductions; to, finally, altering the appearance of time to avoid the recognition of gain or trigger the deduction of losses on corporate acquisitions by exploiting the nebulous step-transaction doctrine. Using the passage of time as a marker for distinguishing abusive from nonabusive tax behavior has obviously proved no match for the boundless imaginations of a highly privileged set of taxpayers and their well-heeled tax advisers who, rather than devoting themselves to more socially productive endeavors, spend their time and energy finding new and inventive ways for shirking tax obligations and shifting them onto others.

All of these examples share a disturbing furtiveness. The relevant tax actors seem to hope that their machinations to convert time into money will escape either unnoticed or unappreciated by the public at large, whether because those machinations are masked with gauzy promises of promoting the country's economic growth (as in chapter 3) or because they are buried in the intricate details of arcane tax laws (as in this chapter). Chapter 5 turns to considering ways in which the general public does seem to grasp the power of the tax imagination and the potential impact that its exercise may have—both on them individually and on society more generally. This intuitive awareness that tax time is neither rigid nor fixed nor outside human control bespeaks an openness to recognizing—and, more importantly, to questioning and challenging— how and for whom the raw power of the legal imagination has been used to shape and reshape tax time in less visible ways like those explored in this and the previous chapters of this book.

5

Fearing the Power of Tax Time

Chapters 1 through 4 examined instances in which different tax actors—from taxpayers and their tax advisers to the Internal Revenue Service, the federal courts, Congress, and the Spanish legislature—all creatively manipulated the relationship between tax and time to achieve specific ends, sometimes doing so plainly and at others surreptitiously. Each of these examples demonstrated the unconventional, decidedly non-linear nature of tax time as well as its deep connection with the legal imagination.

This chapter takes a different perspective on tax time: instead of concentrating on those engaging the legal imagination to manipulate tax time, it focuses on the fallout from exercises of the tax imagination. In other words, this chapter looks at those who fear that others' imagining and reimagining of tax time will negatively affect them. For illustrations of such fears of the power of tax time, this chapter turns to choices made regarding income tax collection, specifically through withholding.

Withholding, at its core, is a timing mechanism—it does not impact final tax liability but determines whether taxes are to be paid contemporaneously (e.g., when wages are received) or at some later point (e.g., when wages are reported on a tax return after the close of the tax year).[1] Reactions to two recent experiences with income tax withholding are used as examples. First, the chapter describes reactions to withholding changes made in the United States following enactment of the Tax Cuts and Jobs Act. There were early charges from Democrats that the changes were politically motivated and designed to provide an advantage for Republicans in the 2018 midterm elections. During the spring 2019 tax filing season, those fears morphed into a public backlash when widespread attention was drawn to a drop in the overall number and size of the annual tax refunds that so many US taxpayers have come to expect. Second, again demonstrating that issues of tax time are not unique to the United States, the chapter explores the constellation of worries voiced by politicians, taxpayers, and even successive governments when France replaced its long-standing delayed-payment regime with a withholding regime. Fears were expressed regarding government and taxpayer manipulation of the change; political gamesmanship to advance hidden policy goals; and the risk that politicians might be endangering their careers, relations between employers and employees, and/or the French economy more broadly.

Whether borne out or not, these fears underscore the examples in earlier chapters of how the illimitable inventiveness of the tax imagination can shape time to achieve desired ends. Yet, the more important contribution of this chapter lies in its demonstration of how easily we all recognize exercises of this power when the effects appear on the tax system's surface in ways that directly impact us. It is but a few small steps from such open experience and acknowledgment of the power of the tax imagination to seeing and questioning manipulations of tax time in less visible aspects of the tax laws too.

Withholding in the United States

Despite a checkered past, withholding has been a mainstay of tax collection since the US federal income tax was converted from a class tax on the wealthy to a mass tax during World War II.[2] Following ratification of the Sixteenth Amendment to the United States Constitution, which paved the way for the modern federal income tax, the drafters of the Revenue Act of 1913 built on earlier American and foreign experiences and embraced withholding in an effort to ensure compliance with the new income tax.[3] Withholding was, however, repealed only four years later, largely due to a combination of its limited application and "the way in which the many difficulties of administering withholding on interest income—attributable largely to the prevalence of bond interest coupons payable to bearer—came to dominate public discussions of withholding."[4] Nevertheless, in the midst of World War II, Congress reinstituted withholding with respect to wages (but not investment income) in an effort to combat wartime inflation and to address the cash-flow issues associated with delaying tax collection until the year after income was received—an especially important concern at a time when "millions of financially unsophisticated taxpayers" had been added to the income-tax rolls.[5] Reinstituting income tax withholding was only made easier by Congress's earlier embrace of withholding as the method for collecting Social Security taxes in 1935.[6]

Following its wartime reintroduction, withholding became an "entrenched" part of the tax landscape.[7] Indeed, withholding has persisted mostly unchanged for nearly eighty years, long after wartime inflationary concerns abated and now principally justified by the compliance concerns that originally occasioned its adoption in 1913.[8] One commentator has even recently touted the benefits of withholding, suggesting that withholding should be extended beyond employee salaries to payments made to gig economy workers and other independent contractors.[9]

Tax Cuts and Jobs Act

Others, however, have perceived a more nefarious side to withholding. Prior to enactment of the Tax Cuts and Jobs Act in late 2017, the size of each withholding "exemption" was tied by Congress to the amount of the personal exemption, and the total number of exemptions that an employee could claim was largely governed by statute.[10] With the TCJA's suspension of the personal exemption and increase in the standard deduction, Congress decided to delegate to the Treasury Department the task of determining the amount of each taxpayer's "withholding allowance."[11] Congress provided a list of factors to guide Treasury but granted the department discretion to leave withholding for 2018 the same as it would have been had the TCJA not been enacted.[12] It was Treasury's exercise of discretion in designing the withholding allowance—and, in turn, in updating the withholding tables used by employers when withholding tax from employees' paychecks—that gave rise to concern.

As the acting commissioner of the Internal Revenue Service explained to Congress, the IRS "moved quickly to begin revising the withholding system to take into account various changes made by the statute, such as increasing the standard deduction, removing personal exemptions, increasing the Child Tax Credit, limiting or discontinuing certain deductions, and changing the tax rates and brackets. This issue affects literally every taxpayer who receives a paycheck."[13] The IRS issued new withholding tables on January 11, 2018, not quite three weeks after President Trump signed the TCJA into law.[14] The IRS expected equally quick implementation by employers, who were required to begin using the tables by February 15, 2018.[15]

Reaction to the New Withholding Tables

Notwithstanding a history of being calibrated to overwithhold tax,[16] "[f]or people with simpler tax situations, the new tables [were] designed to produce the correct amount of tax withholding. The revisions [were] also aimed at avoiding over- and under-withholding of tax as much as possible."[17] Even before release of the withholding tables, there were accusations of political pressure on the IRS to manipulate the tables to give Republicans an advantage in the 2018 midterm elections: "The agency is under pressure to take as little as possible so people will see big increases in their take-home pay ahead of this year's midterm elections. But that would come at a cost: smaller or even nonexistent refunds next year, though millions rely on them to plug holes in their family budgets. Democrats are already accusing the Trump administration of plotting 'phantom windfalls' ahead of the November contest that will come back to haunt taxpayers next tax season."[18]

The ranking Democrats on the Senate Finance Committee and House Ways and Means Committee sent a letter to the acting IRS commissioner expressing concern "that Treasury will be under substantial pressure to make good on the promise by the President and various Administration officials that the new tax law will provide households with a $4,000 tax cut . . . [and] may push IRS to incorporate withholding formulas that take insufficient taxes out of workers' paychecks. This will foster the appearance of a larger tax cut in 2018 that then disappears during the 2019 filing season . . . ."[19] Separately, these members of Congress wrote the Government Accountability Office (GAO) to enlist its aid to "review the revised withholding tables and determine whether they provide adequate withholding to protect millions of taxpayers from being surprised during the 2019 filing season."[20]

In late February, the IRS updated its web-based withholding calculator.[21] The IRS then launched a "paycheck checkup" campaign to encourage taxpayers to ensure that the correct amount of tax was being withheld from their paychecks.[22] This campaign included special "tax tips," a series of news releases aimed at "groups most likely to be affected by the withholding changes," YouTube videos educating taxpayers about withholding and the withholding calculator, and use of "social media to spread the word about #PaycheckCheckup."[23] Nonetheless, Democrats continued to press their concerns.[24]

By late May, the acting IRS commissioner expressed his own worry "that not enough taxpayers are using the new withholding calculator to ensure accurate withholding."[25] At the time, tax preparers were warning that "getting an accurate number from the calculator can be difficult for all but the least complicated Form 1040 filers. . . . 'To do it right, you have to put in a lot of information,' said Gil Charney, director of tax law and policy at the H&R Block Tax Institute. 'Your typical taxpayer is not going [to] get into that depth of planning . . . .'"[26] Testifying before Congress, the National Taxpayer Advocate, an internal IRS watchdog, later recounted how it took her three attempts at consulting the online calculator—as well as the withholding tables themselves—to arrive at the correct withholding.[27] Making matters worse, because the withholding calculator was designed to avoid both under- and overwithholding, taxpayers could be in for a surprise whether the calculator was correct or not: "The consequences of getting withholding wrong can be severe," noted T. Keith Fogg, director of the federal tax clinic at Harvard University. Lower-income taxpayers may rely on their tax refund as a kind of enforced savings program, while middle-income people may be unprepared for a tax bill."[28]

In July, the GAO issued its report regarding the changes to the withholding tables.[29] As documented in that report, Treasury anticipated that its revision of the withholding tables would shift 3 percent of taxpayers from being in a position of being overwithheld (and thus entitled to a refund) to a position of being underwithheld (and thus owing tax).[30] As news accounts noted, this translated to approximately 3 million taxpayers who would be shifted from receiving refunds to owing taxes when they filed their returns.[31] Reinforcing the worries earlier expressed by the acting IRS commissioner, the GAO further noted that, even though the online withholding calculator received many more hits in 2018 than it had in the past, most visitors did not successfully complete the calculator because "the step . . . at which users most often exited was the page that required entering paystub information."[32] Unsurprisingly, Democrats renewed their criticism of the Trump administration's handling of the changes to the withholding tables following the GAO report's release.[33] A single Associated Press story relaying those concerns was published in *Yahoo! Finance*, the *Chicago Tribune*, the *Houston Chronicle*, the *Los Angeles Times*, the *Seattle Times*, and newspapers in smaller cities.[34]

As 2018 drew to a close, there were signs of looming problems for the 2019 tax filing season. In an October report, the IRS's Information Reporting Program Advisory Committee (IRPAC) observed: "Despite the IRS's efforts to inform taxpayers to check their withholding and encourage use of the 'calculator' on the IRS website, usage of the 'calculator' through completion has been minimal because of the complexity (per IRS comments)."[35] Concerned that "a significant number of taxpayers [would] be under-withheld when they file their 2018 personal income tax returns," IRPAC recommended that the IRS implement a "onetime waiver of under-withholding penalties" for those taxpayers.[36]

IRPAC's concerns were borne out by a variety of sources. A November story in the *Pittsburgh Post-Gazette* reported: "In a recent poll by the Pennsylvania Institute of Certified Public Accountants, members said three-quarters of their clients were found to need adjustments to their tax withholding this year. Among those clients, 84 percent needed to increase withholdings to avoid running up a tax bill in April of next year."[37] An H&R Block online survey from that same month "show[ed] why so many failed to update their withholding: they don't know how."[38] Finally, it was reported in the tax press that an IRS employee told participants in a December webinar that "'[i]t is estimated that millions of taxpayers could face an unexpected tax bill when they file their 2018 returns' because they didn't update their Form W-4 to reflect changed taxes or income."[39]

At key points in 2018, the idea that the Trump administration might have manipulated the withholding tables surfaced in newspapers—not in sound bites from congressional Democrats but in the words of journalists writing general news stories about withholding[40] and in those of readers and newspaper editors contributing to opinion pages.[41] This trickle of public attention to the problem of underwithholding and "the tax cut that wasn't" (to borrow the title of an editorial in Maine's *Bangor Daily News*) became a groundswell of criticism as 2018 tax returns began to be filed in early 2019.

2019 Tax Filing Season

Even before the 2019 tax filing season officially began—and in the midst of a partial government shutdown—the IRS expanded relief from the underpayment penalty by lowering the threshold of advance tax payments necessary to avoid the penalty.[42] Under pressure from tax professionals and members of Congress,[43] the IRS afforded this relief under a provision that allows the penalty to be waived if "by reason of casualty, disaster, or other unusual circumstances the imposition of such addition to tax would be against equity and good conscience."[44] The IRS noted that, despite its update of the online withholding calculator and release of a new Form W-4 for claiming withholding allowances, "some" taxpayers might not have been able to accurately determine how much tax to have withheld from their paychecks.[45] But to obtain this relief, taxpayers were required to file a form requesting waiver of the penalty.[46]

Early in the 2019 filing season, the IRS indicated that it expected fewer taxpayers to receive refunds and for the average refund to "be 'slightly lower' at the 2019 filing season's end on October 15 than it was last year."[47] This prediction was largely borne out by the end of the spring filing season, when the total number of refunds was down 1 percent (with nearly 1 million fewer refunds issued), the total amount paid in refunds was down 2.7 percent (representing more than $7.5 billion), and the average refund was down 1.7 percent (about $60) as compared to the end of the spring 2018 filing season.[48] Shortly after the April 15, 2019, filing deadline, the Treasury Department "attributed most of the decline in refunds to decreased withholding throughout the year."[49]

More detailed statistics released a few weeks later—when more than 85 percent of returns had been filed[50]—revealed how the weekly filing statistics masked the distribution of the decline among different income groups. By late May 2019, the decline in the total number of refunds from 2018 to 2019 was slightly more than 700,000; however, there was a decline of nearly 2 million in the number of refunds paid to those reporting an adjusted gross income (AGI) of under $25,000 while there was an increase of more than 1.1 million in the number of refunds paid to those with an AGI from $25,000 to under $100,000.[51] Similarly, there was a decline of nearly 220,000 in the number of refunds paid to those reporting an AGI from $100,000 to under $250,000 while there was an

increase of nearly 275,000 in the number of refunds paid to those reporting an AGI of $250,000 or more.[52] Likewise, the overall decline in
the amount of refunds paid, which by late May 2019 was about $5 bil-
lion, was distributed differently among income groups. The amount of
refunds paid to those reporting an AGI under $25,000 was down by
more than $4.2 billion while the amount of refunds paid to those with
an AGI of $250,000 or more increased by more than $4.4 billion.[53] Additionally, the amount of refunds paid to those reporting an AGI from
$25,000 to under $100,000 increased by $1.2 billion while refunds paid
to those reporting an AGI from $100,000 to under $250,000 decreased
by more than $6.5 billion.[54]

Turning to those who did not receive refunds (a group not covered in
the IRS's weekly filing statistics), by late May 2019 the number of returns
filed showing tax due grew by more than 5 percent from 2018 to 2019,
with more than 1.2 million additional returns reflecting a balance due to
the IRS.[55] Most of this increase was concentrated in taxpayers reporting
an AGI of $50,000 or more.[56] Overall, there was an increase in tax due
at time of filing of 2 percent (or more than $2.5 billion) as compared
to 2018.[57] Even before the April tax filing deadline, the IRS estimated
that it had received 1.7 million Forms 2210 (Underpayment of Estimated
Tax by Individuals, Estates, and Trusts), with more than 80 percent of
those forms requesting the IRS's recently expanded penalty relief.[58] Similarly, the number of returns neither showing tax due nor generating a
refund increased by nearly 4 percent from 2018 to 2019, with in excess
of 150,000 additional returns neither receiving a refund nor showing
tax due.[59] The vast majority of this increase was concentrated in returns
reporting an AGI under $30,000.[60]

In sum, the 2019 filing season saw fewer and smaller refunds while
more returns either (1) showed a balance due or (2) showed no tax due
and generated no refund. Notwithstanding oft-repeated advice to stop
providing interest-free loans to the federal government, the picture
painted by these statistics is at odds with the general preference among
US taxpayers to receive an annual tax refund,[61] whether because they
fear penalties, use withholding as a form of forced saving, or for other
reasons.[62] Moreover, it is important to bear in mind the disproportionate impact of these shifts on the lowest-income taxpayers, who experienced a significant drop in the number and size of their refunds and a

significant increase in those neither receiving a refund nor showing tax due. These taxpayers often count on tax refunds to pay for necessities such as health care.[63]

#GOPTaxScam

Cognizant of the preference for and reliance on refunds, politicians are normally loathe to upset taxpayer expectations for fear of risking their wrath.[64] After getting "shellacked" in the 2018 midterm elections[65] and with a presidential election looming on the horizon, Republicans understandably began to fear that the Trump administration's changes to the withholding tables would produce negative fallout for them and their signature tax cuts as the spring 2019 tax filing season got underway. Indeed, the *New York Times* reported at the start of the filing season that "some Republicans in Washington [were] privately worried . . . that smaller refunds [would] cause many Americans to think they were penalized, not helped, by the new tax law."[66]

Bearing out the concerns of these unnamed Republicans, the experience of early filers, who are likely to be counting on the cash infusion from a tax refund,[67] set off a firestorm of criticism that was only fueled by common confusion between a tax refund (i.e., overpayment of a tax bill) and a tax cut (i.e., a reduction in the tax bill).[68] In the first week of the 2019 filing season, the number of refunds was down 24.3 percent, the total amount of refunds was down 30.6 percent, and the average refund was down 8.4 percent.[69] The second week's statistics were somewhat better, with the number of refunds down only 15.8 percent and the total amount of refunds down only 23.2 percent—but the average refund was now down more, by 8.7 percent.[70] While filing season statistics in the past had typically been greeted with a collective yawn,[71] news outlets picked up the story and began reporting about disgruntled taxpayers venting their anger on social media.[72] An article in the *New York Times* even described H&R Block as "prescient" because it had required its tax preparers "to take a new class before their busy season started this year: empathy training."[73]

The hashtags #GOPTaxScam and #TrumpTaxScam, among others, were "full of angry tweeters, complaining that their refunds were either greatly reduced, or that they now owe the IRS."[74] In fact, in early to mid-

February 2019, both hashtags experienced their most significant spikes in usage on Twitter since the period surrounding the enactment of the Tax Cuts and Jobs Act in late 2017 and early 2018—and both hashtags again saw significant (though smaller) spikes around the April tax filing deadline.[75] Naturally, these news reports and Twitter activity caught the attention of Democrats, with Speaker of the House Nancy Pelosi compiling excerpts from several news sources—including quoted taxpayer complaints—in an entry on her blog titled "#GOPTaxScam Promises vs. Reality: Tax Refund Edition."[76] For their part, Republicans found themselves on the defensive, "being forced to grapple with Democrats' general narrative that the Trump administration willfully lowered 2018 paycheck withholding to boost take-home pay—and Republican election prospects last November—resulting in smaller refunds this year."[77]

Even before the filing season had gotten underway, the American Institute of Certified Public Accountants had urged the IRS to expand the group of taxpayers afforded underpayment penalty relief and to make that relief automatic.[78] As the hue and cry over declining refunds erupted, Democrats in Congress jumped on the bandwagon and likewise called for expanded underpayment penalty relief—while taking the opportunity to renew their accusations that the Trump administration had manipulated the withholding tables for political advantage.[79] In late March, as Republicans and the National Taxpayer Advocate added their voices to the call for expanded penalty relief, the IRS relented and lowered the threshold for relief for a second time.[80] Eventually, in August 2019, the IRS announced that it would automatically apply penalty relief to any qualifying taxpayer, rather than requiring taxpayers to request relief.[81] According to the IRS, this move would help more than 400,000 taxpayers who had already filed returns but who did not request penalty relief despite qualifying for it.[82]

Temporal Shell Game

When it updated the withholding tables in early 2018, Treasury appeared to embrace the conventional, linear conceptualization of time. After all, Treasury professed to simply be adjusting paycheck withholding to align it with the TCJA's changes to the individual income tax. It was only a matter of fine-tuning the established rhythm and pattern of the tax collection process, as it mimics the cyclical time experienced in the repetitive passage from day to night or from one tax filing season to the next.

Yet, even before the withholding tables were released, Treasury was accused of misusing its discretion to adjust those tables. Democrats feared that Treasury was actually playing a sophisticated shell game along time's arrow. Having chosen to depart from past practice by calibrating the withholding tables to avoid both underpayments *and* overpayments,[83] Treasury was accused of lowering the withholding from workers' 2018 paychecks to create the appearance of a windfall that would encourage them to vote Republican in the midterm elections. The day of reckoning for the victims of this alleged shell game would not come until early 2019, when they would be asked to repay some or all of their windfall—months after the election was over and after the new Congress had safely been installed. As that day grew nearer, Republicans began to fear that Treasury's tinkering with tax time, in an alleged gamble that failed to pay off, would cause taxpayers' wrath to rain down on them.

When the day of reckoning finally arrived, taxpayers vented their frustration about refunds that had diminished, disappeared, or been replaced with tax bills. Regardless of whether or not Treasury manipulated the withholding tables for political advantage,[84] taxpayers correctly understood that something was amiss with the collection of their taxes. In their reactions, some taxpayers demonstrated awareness that withholding had played a role in the reduction of their refunds.[85] Unsurprisingly, given that withholding long ago receded into the background of everyday life in the United States, others knew something was wrong but required explanation—whether from tax experts, journalists, or others—to understand that their smaller or nonexistent refunds did not depend on whether they had received a tax cut but on how much of their tax bill they had paid in advance.[86]

For all of these taxpayers, Treasury had not simply recalibrated the cyclical rhythm of withholding. Instead, Treasury had taken their refunds—money that they counted on for purchasing expensive durable goods, paying for health care, or paying down bills—and surreptitiously spread those refunds out in small amounts over the course of the prior year, both to their dismay and their disadvantage. For some, Treasury had actually spread out more than just the amount of their expected refund over the prior year, resulting in a surprising tax bill and potential exposure to penalties. In effect, Treasury had seized a single moment in time during the 2019 filing season when taxpayers would have received refunds, forcibly shifted that moment earlier along time's arrow to the end of 2018, and then stretched out that moment (and, in some cases, artificially expanded it as well) over the course of that year. In the guise of a mechanical application of the new law, Treasury borrowed a page from the playbook of taxpayers who, as illustrated in chapter 4, have found ways to creatively prolong tax time and convert it into a commodity that might be bartered in exchange for valuable benefits—here, allegedly, votes in the midterm congressional elections.

Treasury's changes to the withholding tables thus delivered US taxpayers and their political leaders an object lesson in the power of tax time. Taxpayers were reminded that, far from an uncontrollable force that government must adapt to when collecting taxes, time is open to manipulation by those with their hands on the levers of the taxing power in ways that can harm them personally and, for the most economically vulnerable taxpayers, harm them disproportionately. Congressional Democrats, too, were reminded of the power of tax time as they voiced their concern that the Trump administration had engineered widespread underwithholding of tax to disadvantage them in the 2018 midterm elections. Congressional Republicans, in contrast, were reminded that tinkering with tax time—whether for good or for ill—can result in unwelcome consequences even for the ostensible beneficiaries of its manipulation.

To continue exploring public acknowledgment of and appreciation for the plasticity of tax time, we next turn to investigating reactions in France to the possibilities for manipulating tax time that accompanied its adoption of a withholding regime for collecting income tax.

Withholding in France

Coming into line with virtually all other countries in the Organisation for Economic Co-operation and Development,[87] France recently embraced withholding as its primary method for collecting income tax. Echoing the US experience described earlier, France experimented with a few different forms of withholding during a twenty-year period around World War II.[88] Then, in the 1990s, France chose to collect two new social security taxes—the *contribution sociale généralisée* (CSG) and the *contribution pour remboursement de la dette sociale*—through withholding.[89] Yet, for nearly sixty years spanning the second half of the twentieth century and the first two decades of the twenty-first, income tax was generally paid in France during the year *after* income was received.[90]

For some, delayed payment created hardships when income suddenly declined (e.g., due to unemployment or retirement) or tax-relevant personal circumstances changed (e.g., the taxpayer's death or change in marital status).[91] For others, the delay, coupled with uncertainty about their future financial situation, impelled them to inflate precautionary saving to meet future tax bills.[92] To address these problems and more generally "modernize" tax collection, the French legislature approved a move to a combination of withholding and payment of estimated taxes in late 2016, with the measure to take effect in 2018.[93] In 2017, the effective date of the new withholding regime was delayed until 2019.[94] The purpose of the one-year delay was to allow the government to undertake "experimentation and audit" of the new systems.[95] In fact, the government ran two waves of testing and took other steps to better prepare for the transition.[96] The withholding regime entered into force in 2019 without any major problems in its rollout.[97]

The Mechanics

When the idea of withholding resurfaced in 2015, the possibility of abandoning France's long-standing delayed-payment regime for collecting income tax naturally gave rise to questions about how withholding would operate and whether the promised advantages of the new system would withstand scrutiny.[98] Figuring prominently among these concerns were the complexity, burdens, and pitfalls associated with privatizing a government function.[99]

Paramount among these concerns was the question of who would collect taxes, because many feared the possibility of violations of taxpayer privacy.[100] Employers were an obvious choice for withholding tax on wages; however, involving employers would entail sharing tax data with them, which raised the specter of differential treatment of employees based on that data.[101] For instance, there was concern that employers might make salary determinations or decisions about layoffs based on information gleaned from tax data regarding an employee's other sources of income or personal circumstances rather than based on performance.[102] For their part, employers—especially small and medium-sized businesses—worried about the complexity, time, and costs involved in serving as a withholding agent, not to mention the impact it might have on relations with employees.[103]

Ultimately, France opted for a system under which wages, wage replacements (e.g., unemployment benefits or sick pay), and pension payments are subject to withholding by the payer (e.g., the employer in the case of wages).[104] Those working independently—as well as those receiving rental income or certain support or annuity payments—are not subject to withholding but instead make estimated tax payments, which are generally debited monthly (or, at the taxpayer's option, quarterly) from the taxpayer's bank account.[105] The remuneration of those directing or managing business entities is either subject to withholding or the payment of estimated taxes, depending on the type of entity and the individual's role within the business.[106] Various types of investment income either were already subject to contemporaneous payment of tax or were found to be incompatible with the new withholding regime; consequently, the government left their treatment untouched when it moved the income tax more generally from a regime of delayed to one of contemporaneous payment.[107]

The French tax authorities annually calculate the withholding rate for each tax household (*foyer fiscal*) based on the most recently filed tax returns and then communicate that rate to withholding agents and the taxpayer.[108] The rate for January through August is thus based on household income reported and tax paid with respect to the penultimate tax year (e.g., the rate for January through August 2021 was based on information reported on the 2019 tax return that was filed and processed in mid-2020).[109] The rate for September through December is based on household income reported and tax paid with respect to the immediately preceding tax year (e.g., the rate for September through December 2021 was based on information reported on the 2020 tax return that was filed and processed in mid-2021).[110] In situations where a rate cannot be calculated (e.g., for those without a tax filing history) or has yet to be communicated by the tax authorities, withholding agents must apply a default tax rate in accordance with tables prescribed by law.[111] For employees, the relevant withholding rate (whether the calculated or default rate) is applied to wages earned in the current year; however, for those working independently, both the rate and the base for calculating estimated payments is determined by reference to amounts reported in earlier years.[112]

Certain changes in family circumstances that impact the calculation of the rate (e.g., entry into or exit from a marriage or civil union, birth or adoption of a child, or death of a spouse or partner) are to be communicated to the tax authorities within sixty days so that a new rate can be calculated and then communicated to withholding agents and the taxpayer.[113] In addition, taxpayers can request that the tax authorities adjust their rate to take account of other changed circumstances (e.g., an increase or decrease in income). Taxpayers can request an increase in rate at any time; however, taxpayers can request a decrease only if the new rate will reduce advance tax payments by more than 10 percent.[114] If taxpayers who request a decrease in rate prove mistaken in estimating their decline in income and end up being underwithheld, penalties apply to any underwithholding of more than 10 percent unless the error was made in good faith or due to unforeseen circumstances.[115]

To address concerns—both popular and constitutional[116]—about maintaining taxpayer privacy, taxpayers are provided an option to have the default rate applied to their wages.[117] If the default rate is lower than the rate calculated by the tax authorities, the difference must be declared and paid by the taxpayer on a monthly basis; however, if the default rate is more than the rate calculated by the tax authorities, any overwithholding is not returned to the taxpayer until after the return for the taxable year has been filed.[118] A separate option is provided for couples with unequal incomes who are married or joined in a civil union, because these couples are generally required to file and pay taxes on their combined incomes.[119] These couples can request the tax authorities to calculate individualized rates of withholding for their separate incomes, but the household rate continues to apply to shared income (e.g., from rental property).[120]

Timing Concerns

The switch to withholding also raised concerns regarding the imaginative manipulation of time, though very different from those raised when the Trump administration tinkered with an established withholding regime in the United States. In France, the timing issues associated with the move to withholding related to: (1) how to deal with the transition from the old to the new method of tax collection; (2) whether withholding was a subterfuge to achieve other ends; and (3) the risks associated with reducing workers' take-home pay. Each of these concerns will be addressed in turn.

THE TRANSITION

Shifting from delayed to contemporaneous payment would naturally result in an overlap of the two tax collection methods, because the last year under delayed payment would coincide with the first year under the withholding regime. This overlap raised "delicate" questions about how to navigate the transition and who would be burdened with its costs.[121]

Options

One possibility would have been to let the transition play out naturally and to burden taxpayers with its cost. Under this approach, a shift to withholding in 2019 would require payment in that year of both the delayed tax on 2018 income under the old system and current tax on 2019 income under the new system.[122] Given the country's financial situation, there was some concern that the government might adopt this approach, taking advantage of the transition to fill its coffers by saddling taxpayers with a bill for two tax years in one.[123] However, this option implicated the "risk of a fiscal tsunami on household purchasing power as well as on taxpayer morale."[124] Accordingly, there were suggestions that the government could spread the cost by phasing in the new system over several years to mitigate the burden on taxpayers.[125]

Alternatively, the government could choose to bear the burden of the transition by declaring an *année blanche* (a "blank" or lost year).[126] Under this approach, a shift to withholding in 2019 would require payment in 2018 of tax on 2017 income under the old system and payment in 2019 of tax on 2019 income under the new system. The government would continue to be paid taxes each year; however, to avoid a double imposition in a single year, no tax would be collected on 2018 income—either in 2019 or any other year. There was significant concern that wealthy taxpayers might manipulate the timing of their income to take utmost advantage of this fiscal "gift," to the detriment of the public fisc and, more specifically, their less-wealthy compatriots who could not similarly manipulate their income.[127] Moreover, the lost year would, at the end of the wealthy taxpayer's life, redound to the benefit of the decedent's heirs.[128] As one legislator put it, "[t]his is a reform that advantages the dead over the living," because young people would pay tax from their first day of work while a decedent's heirs would no longer pay tax on the decedent's income in the year following death.[129]

Ultimately, the government chose a hybrid approach that treated 2018 as a partially lost year. Taxpayers were provided a special tax credit that was designed to shelter 2018 income from tax in 2019.[130] The credit was, however, limited in two important ways. First, when calculating the credit, only the tax on income covered by the new withholding regime (i.e., salaries, remuneration of those working independently, rental income, etc.) was eligible to be taken into account.[131] Second, "exceptional" amounts of income were excluded from the calculation of the credit. A specific listing of exceptional items was provided for employees, while those working independently were required to compare their 2018 income to income reported in earlier (and, under some circumstances, later) years to determine whether the 2018 income was larger than normal.[132] Thus, the government forgave tax on some but not necessarily all of a taxpayer's 2018 income—not only would exceptional amounts of salary, remuneration, and rental income be taxed but so would investment income falling outside the withholding regime (e.g., interest, dividends, and capital gains).[133]

Fears

Both of the alternative approaches to the transition raised fears of the tax imagination running amok—the only difference lay in who would be plotting to manipulate time for their benefit. On the one hand, there was fear that the government would take advantage of the shift in tax time from delayed to current payment to reap a windfall by burdening taxpayers with two years' worth of taxes in a single year (or, in a less burdensome scenario, spread over a few years). To create this windfall, the government would foreshorten time's arrow by softening its purported rigidity and then folding time on itself so that two years of tax collection would coincide.

On the other hand, if the government were to bear the burden of the transition by forgoing a year's worth of taxes, there were concerns that it would be a boon to the wealthy. This alternative would have the government create a break or disruption in time—a lost year—to obviate the need to collect tax. But any break in time that resulted in permanently forgoing tax revenue would necessarily benefit the wealthy, because fewer than half of French households pay income tax (42–43 percent between 2016 and 2018) and, of those, the wealthiest pay the vast majority of income taxes (in 2016, the wealthiest 10 percent of households paid 70 percent of income taxes).[134] What's more, wealthy taxpayers might themselves creatively manipulate the timing of their income to have as much of it as possible fall through the break in time's arrow, piling one creative manipulation of time atop another in order to maximize the benefit to themselves—and the detriment to everyone else.[135]

In the end, the government's decision to embrace a partially lost year represented a clever solution that deftly quelled fears of abusive manipulation while still leaving space for the tax imagination to work its magic.[136] Rather than either rupturing time or softening its rigid arrow, the government chose to carve a hole in time's arrow. This allowed select types of income to fall outside of time and escape taxation while preserving the government's ability to collect two years' worth of taxes on various other types of income during a single year. Coincidentally, the government left open possibilities for taxpayers to escape tax by manipulating ambiguities and gaps in the category of "nonexceptional" income so that they might nudge more of their income into the hole that the government had created in time's arrow (and the taxing net).

TROJAN HORSE

The move to a withholding regime in France was painted as a technical change—and not true tax reform—because it affected only the collection and not the calculation of the income tax.[137] Yet, just as Democrats expressed concern that the Trump administration had used the cover of technical adjustments to withholding tables to aid Republicans in the

2018 midterm elections, some in France worried that withholding was *le cheval de Troie*—a Trojan horse—for accomplishing other ends.[138]

Prominent among the concerns was the possibility that the progressive income tax might be fused with the flat-rate *contribution sociale généralisée* once the method for their collection was harmonized. Depending on individual policy preferences, the fear was alternatively of: (1) a leveling up through the CSG's conversion into a progressive tax; (2) a leveling down through the income tax's conversion into a flat tax; or (3) an apparent leveling up (that was actually a leveling down) by applying the CSG at progressive rates, but to a limited base consisting of only labor income, thus permitting investment income to escape the tax.[139] Others feared that withholding would be used as a pretext to defamilize the income tax by, for example, eliminating France's complex family income-splitting rules in the name of simplifying operation of the withholding regime.[140] Yet others feared that withholding would make the income tax "painless" for taxpayers and ease the way for legislators to increase the tax burden in the future.[141]

But whatever the surprise contained within the Trojan horse of withholding, these critics' concerns betray fears of the tax imagination at work. Each is fundamentally concerned about political manipulation of tax time to create a subterfuge for attaining a desired end that might not be so easily achieved through more direct means. Whether their concerns were well-founded or not, these critics saw tax time not as a force beyond control but instead as one that can be harnessed and molded to provide the seeds of fiscal and other advantages to be reaped in the future.

PAYCHECK EFFECT

Even with public opinion favoring the switch,[142] some were concerned that the shift to a withholding regime risked triggering a negative reaction among workers once income tax began to be taken out of their paychecks.[143] The fear was that workers would interpret their suddenly smaller take-home pay as reflecting a real reduction in purchasing power that might lead them to: (1) ask their employers for a raise to bring their paychecks back up to prewithholding levels; (2) take their wrath out on politicians who supported the new withholding regime; and/or (3) curtail their spending, with disastrous effects on an economy that already seemed to be slowing.[144] In fact, some speculated that the reform's implementation was set to occur after the 2017 French presidential election to avoid the risk of backlash during the campaign.[145]

At the heart of all these perceived risks—just as in the dawning awareness among Republicans of a looming deluge of taxpayer anger at the start of the spring 2019 US tax filing season—lay fears of the collateral consequences of tinkering with the power of tax time. But to understand these fears and their temporalities, it is necessary to place the change in context by viewing it from the perspective of the affected workers.

Delayed-Payment Status Quo

In practice, French taxpayers did not pay their taxes in a single lump sum under the delayed-payment regime; rather, payments were spread over the course of the year. By default, taxpayers made two estimated payments—one due in mid-February and the other in mid-May—with each equal to one-third of the tax imposed in the prior year on income received two years earlier.[146] For example, the 2018 estimated payments would each be one-third of the tax imposed in 2017 on income reported for 2016. Then, a final payment was due in September equal to any balance assessed by the tax authorities based on the return filed for the prior year (returns are typically due in May).[147] Continuing the earlier example, the September 2018 payment would equal any balance owed on 2017 income reported on the return filed in May 2018, after crediting the February and May 2018 estimated payments against the tax due.

Alternatively, taxpayers could—and a large (though declining) majority did[148]—opt to spread their payments over ten months, with payments made from January to October equal to one-tenth of the tax imposed in the prior year on income received two years earlier.[149] For example, the January to October 2018 estimated payments would each be one-tenth of the tax imposed in 2017 on income reported for 2016. If these payments proved insufficient to cover the tax on 2017 income based on the return filed in May 2018, then any balance would be spread over the last quarter of 2018.[150]

Shift to Withholding

When viewed from the worker's perspective, the withholding regime did not represent a radical departure from the status quo of delayed payment but was more akin to incremental improvement. Even before withholding, taxpayers were accustomed to having their disposable income reduced by regular tax payments—and, for a large majority, these payments were made monthly over at least ten months of the year. The amount of these payments, like the rate of withholding under the new regime, was determined by reference to income reported and tax paid in prior years.[151] Given the overlaps, it was suggested that many taxpayers—particularly those with relatively stable incomes—might hardly notice a difference between delayed payment and withholding.[152]

For the minority whose income declines from one year to the next, the withholding regime represented somewhat of an improvement over delayed payment.[153] For workers, a decline in wages now automatically results in decreased withholding because tax payments are determined by applying the withholding rate to current (rather than historical) wages.[154] But workers still might be overwithheld if decreased wages result in a lower marginal tax rate for the current year, because the withholding rate, unlike the base, is calculated using historical data.[155] To achieve more accurate withholding, workers must submit a request to the tax authorities to recalculate their rate based on projected income for the year. Yet, such a request will be automatically denied if the reduction in advance tax payments is too small, and even if it is granted, taxpayers risk penalties if their income estimate proves incorrect and advance taxes are underpaid.[156] Under delayed payment, taxpayers who experienced a reduction in income could likewise request the adjustment of their estimated payments or an extension of time to make payments, but few actually did so.[157] Tellingly, opponents of the withholding regime tried to replicate its combination of stability and incremental improvement—while achieving their larger goals of allaying taxpayer privacy concerns and eliminating the burden on employers—by urging that the delayed-payment regime be retained but with mandatory monthly payments based on current income.[158]

Given that, for workers, withholding represented no more than incremental improvement over delayed payment, the perceived risk of backlash to this popular "modernization" of tax collection could not lie in the substance of the changes being made. Instead, casting new light on the temporalities of form and substance discussed in chapters 1 and 2, the potential for backlash must lie in the new form that tax collection would take. As explored in the next section, the change in form of tax collection involved temporal shifts that stoked fear in some (or, perhaps, allowed them to stoke fear in others) that the transition to withholding would trigger a backlash among workers with cascading consequences on employer-employee relations, the careers of politicians who backed the move, and the French economy more generally.

Paycheck Shock?
Because the withholding regime would alter only the method of collecting income tax, French taxpayers would pay no more or less tax under the withholding regime than they did before. The big change was *when* they paid tax. Under delayed payment, workers were generally paid at the end of the month, pay was deposited in workers' bank accounts, and tax authorities commonly debited tax payments from those accounts ten times per year in the middle of the month.[159] Under withholding, the intermediate step of depositing pay in workers' bank accounts would be eliminated. Tax payments—divided into twelve smaller installments— would be deducted directly from workers' paychecks, now at the end (rather than the middle) of the month.

The worry was that eliminating the intermediate step would shock workers when the abstract idea of withholding became reality and they received their first paychecks net of income tax. The source of these fears was actually relatively small movements of workers' advance tax payments along time's arrow. Under the withholding regime, workers' advance tax payments would be spread over a longer stretch of time: twelve months instead of the typical ten under delayed payment. The increased number of installments would reduce the size of each payment and afford workers the benefit of some deferral of payments. A further bit of deferral was afforded by shifting tax payments from the middle to the end of the month. The fear seemed to be that workers would not recognize this reshuffling of tax time for what it was, instead interpreting their smaller paychecks as a loss of income that they would attempt to reclaim from their employers, take out on their political leaders, and offset by lowering their spending with detrimental effects on the country's overall economic health. Others, however, had more faith in workers' ability to quickly grasp that their tax payments had merely been shifted around along time's arrow, with the immediate benefit of smaller payments at the end of each month and the longer-term benefit of withholding automatically (if sometimes only partially) adjusting to changes in wages.[160]

Whereas the discussion of form and substance in chapters 1 and 2 revolved around questions of whether and how to travel from the present into the past to rewrite history, the importance of form here arises due to the particular moment in which the shifting of tax payments along time's arrow occurred. Put differently, fear of a backlash was associated with inhabiting a specific position along time's arrow—namely, the moment when the withholding regime began to operate. In countries such as the United States, where withholding has been the norm for decades, smaller take-home pay is such an accepted part of how the tax and working worlds operate that withholding often goes unnoticed.[161] But at its inception, withholding has not yet receded into the background and, indeed, is arguably at its most salient. It is in this moment of transition from settled expectations regarding paycheck size to a new reality of decreased take-home pay that workers might be shocked by an abrupt change, with a host of negative repercussions feared for employers, politicians, and the economy.

Similar questions of form and substance can be detected in the earlier discussion of the displeasure vented by many US taxpayers during the spring 2019 filing season at seeing smaller or nonexistent tax refunds. That backlash was likewise the product of a particular moment. Many US taxpayers had come to expect and count on receiving an annual refund at tax-filing time. But when significant changes to the individual income tax coincided with a high-stakes congressional election, the Trump administration allegedly chose to take advantage of the moment to adjust the withholding tables in a way that shifted overpayments of tax back along time's arrow so that taxpayers would see an increase in take-home pay all year long rather than in a single lump sum after the year had ended. An entirely predictable backlash occurred when taxpayers were surprised to find long-expected refunds had either disappeared, decreased, or been replaced with a tax bill.[162] To the shock of taxpayers, withholding—normally an unnoticed part of the invisible background of working life in the United States—had suddenly rushed to the foreground and claimed their attention. Their actual frustration and discontent—much like the anticipated but ultimately unmanifested shock of French workers at seeing reduced paychecks—could have arisen only because of the existence of this particular moment of rupture when settled expectations were overturned in unanticipated or unappreciated ways.

* * *

Beyond the commonality of being the product of a particular point on time's arrow, the reactions to introducing a new withholding regime in France and to changing an existing withholding regime in the United States bear the mark of popular apprehension at the potential for tax time to be manipulated in inventive—and unwelcome—ways. In their inventiveness and creativity, these examples are a fitting complement to the discussion in earlier chapters of the myriad of ways in which the tax imagination can be used to shape time to serve specific ends. But these examples also add a new dimension to that discussion. They provide evidence of widespread concern about the possibility that tax time might be (or might already have been) leveraged to someone's benefit while visiting harm on others, whether intentionally or unintentionally. This chapter has demonstrated just how easily we can recognize the power of the tax imagination to manipulate time when its effects rise to the surface of the tax system. That includes worries in the United States about taxpayers' disappearing refunds and politicians being disadvantaged come election time. It also includes the multitude of worries in France about government and taxpayer manipulation of the transition to withholding, political gamesmanship to advance hidden policy goals, and a political backlash that might not only endanger politicians' livelihoods and employer-employee relations but also the French economy. This recognition and acknowledgment of the potential for misuse or abuse of the power of the tax imagination suggests that it would take only small steps—with this book hopefully serving as the first such step—to open our collective eyes so that we might see and question manipulations of tax time in other, less visible aspects of the tax laws as well.

Conclusion

Among the revolving cast of tax actors gracing the pages of this book, one of the most frequently recurring roles has been played by tax advisers. They used their expertise to advise taxpayers such as Evelyn Gregory in chapter 1 to facilitate the boundary-pushing abusive behavior of taxpayers described in chapter 4, and drafted the positions taken by the Internal Revenue Service regarding the tax treatment of marriage alternatives and the qualification of private segregated schools for tax-exempt status dissected in chapter 2. At first blush, this prominent role in a story about imagination and creativity may seem odd because tax professionals, as avatars of a dread-inducing tax system, are often portrayed as two-dimensional figures—cardboard cutouts of flesh-and-blood human beings that lack both depth and vibrancy. Indeed, when I was a practicing tax lawyer before entering academia, I would hear the typical lawyer jokes as well as ones specifically aimed at tax lawyers. One common joke was: "What is a tax lawyer? An accountant without the sense of humor." Though aimed at tax lawyers, such nettling casts neither tax lawyers nor accountants in a favorable light. Even within the legal profession, as the tax professor Michael Livingston has noted, "there is the sense that other lawyers look at tax experts the way everyone else looks at lawyers: about as interesting as plumbers, but without the self-confident charm."[1]

Yet, beneath the stereotypical suit and tie, tax lawyers—not to mention other tax professionals—are vibrantly creative people working in and through a complex and multidimensional tax system. Tax law may certainly be "arcane";[2] however, such an interconnected and interdependent web of rules—one that is riddled with exceptions, exceptions to those exceptions, and incentives and disincentives designed to shape and influence taxpayer behavior, all having been enacted at different times and under different circumstances and requiring years of study and practice to master—presents, if anything, more rather than fewer opportunities for creative problem-solving (and sometimes even for the inventive fabrication of tax advantages). If imagination is thought to be a key component of the legal mind,[3] then why would we expect tax lawyers to be less creative and imaginative than other lawyers?

Over the course of chapters 1 through 5, this creativity—what I have described as the "tax imagination"—has been the protagonist of our story. It has sometimes been the hero and at other times the villain, manifesting itself not only in the work of tax professionals but also in the musings and machinations of taxpayers, legislators, judges, and bureaucrats who paradoxically play with and upon time, despite time's normally and conventionally being accepted as a fixed and rigid part of the natural background against which our lives play out. As this story unfolded, we witnessed time itself being pleated, folded, elongated, compressed, commodified, carved up, transcended, and otherwise maneuvered, negotiated, and exploited in various and sundry ways. The ingenuity of taxpayers, tax advisers, bureaucrats, judges, and legislators has proved so multifarious that it tests the observer's well of analogies and the average thesaurus's store of words to adequately describe the power of the tax imagination to manipulate time.

A Brief Recap

We began our exploration of the power of the tax imagination in chapters 1 and 2 with the vehicle that substance-over-form principles provide for traveling backward and forward through time to rewrite the tax past—sometimes repeatedly and sometimes even before the past has become past—with ramifications in the tax present and future. The federal courts embraced the doctrine of substance over form in the early days of the modern federal income tax, as evidenced by our examination of the seminal case *Gregory v. Helvering*. And as evidenced by our exegesis of Internal Revenue Code § 304, Congress has likewise seen fit to codify substance-over-form principles, in that instance with the aim of forestalling abusive tax behavior when decisions coming from the courts failed to stanch that abuse. Through these examples, we witnessed how substance-over-form principles permit taxpayers and their tax advisers, the IRS, the federal courts, and Congress to offer their own reconceptualizations of the past that need not bear the slightest resemblance to even the most carefully choreographed sequences of events—events that nobody contests actually occurred and that are already spaced out along, and otherwise firmly embedded in, time's arrow. In an effort to achieve more just and appropriate tax results, the tax imagination is granted nearly unfettered license to reorder these past events; to invent an entirely new and different path through the tax past to the present; or, as in *Gregory*, even to leave time suspended with no clear indication of what path the taxpayer took to her now indeterminate tax present and future.

Conversely, chapter 2 focused on the IRS's deliberate choice *not* to use the power of the tax imagination to travel through time to correct past tax injustices—and to prevent future ones. First, we examined how, despite specific urging to embrace substance-over-form principles to permit civil unions and domestic partnerships to be treated as marriages following the *Windsor* and *Obergefell* decisions,[4] the IRS chose *not* to engage the tax imagination to correct the injustice of relegating same-sex couples to a "second-class, separate-but-equal" relationship status by elevating them instead to a simply "equal" tax status. In fact, the IRS deftly folded the fabric of time in ways that ensured that implementation of Supreme Court decisions intended to advance LGBTQ+ rights would instead serve to enhance heterosexual and marital privilege. Then, we considered how, decades earlier, the IRS made a similar choice to avoid the application of substance-over-form principles when determining whether segregated private schools should qualify for the benefits of tax-exempt status. This choice eventually—and, it now seems, permanently—shifted the analysis of discriminatory organizations' tax-exempt status from the constitutional plane to the level of statutory interpretation. The effect of this shift was to shrink the spatiotemporal frame of analysis in ways that permit discriminatory organizations to escape punishment for past acts of discrimination while wholly absolving the federal government of blame—notwithstanding its provision of tax dollars to, and its stamp of approval on, prohibited discrimination. In both of these instances, the IRS's choice to adhere to a linear conceptualization of time actually masked its use of the tax imagination to manipulate time in unique and different ways—but ways that served to entrench, rather than to correct, past injustices.

Chapters 3 and 4 aimed the spotlight at the reification of time—that is, efforts to turn time into a valuable commodity. Chapter 3 demonstrated how legislators compress time and turn it into money by departing, sometimes quite radically, from the tax norm of capitalizing investments in income-producing assets and then allowing depreciation deductions that spread the cost of those investments over the asset's useful life. Examples from the United States showed how Congress has used a variety of methods—from a combination of the investment tax credit and accelerated depreciation in the 1980s to more recent and repeated experimentation with bonus depreciation and immediate expensing—to incentivize investments in income-producing assets, sometimes having the federal government effectively partner in those investments and at other times effectively subsidizing them. An example from Spain showed how its legislature creatively looked through one nondepreciable asset (i.e., corporate stock) to single out another previously nondepreciable asset (i.e., goodwill) that it might plausibly contrive to amortize over a compressed time frame in order to provide both an incentive for cross-border business combinations and a leg up to Spanish companies when competing in the market for foreign targets. While the end in each of these examples was the same—handing out tax dollars to favored taxpayers—the means for compressing and reifying time varied widely, including such disparate approaches as pleating and folding time on itself, applying brute force to squeeze and shorten time's arrow, and even taking virtual x-rays to render longer-lived assets transparent in search of shorter-lived assets lurking within them.

Chapter 4 turned the tables by shifting attention away from the activity of legislators handing out money to favored taxpayers and onto the taxpayers themselves, as they used the power of the tax imagination to line their pockets with even more dollars taken from the public fisc. A variety of examples provided from the United States illustrated how taxpayers can elongate time in order to give abusive tax behavior a nonabusive appearance so that they might obtain valuable tax benefits. These examples included instances of taxpayers creatively using (or abusing): (1) the stepped-up basis rules for property acquired from decedents to avoid tax on appreciation in their own assets; (2) the nonrecognition treatment afforded to like-kind exchanges to swap assets with related persons to escape taxation of gains and/or accelerate the deduction of losses; (3) the dividends-received deduction to shelter a corporation's income from tax; and (4) the step-transaction doctrine to selectively (and, again, inappropriately) defer the taxation of gains or accelerate the deduction of losses on business combinations. In each of these examples, taxpayers exchanged time (or, occasionally, just the semblance of time) for valuable tax benefits.

Though with a somewhat different aim, chapter 5 provided additional examples of the workings of the tax imagination—in this case in the context of collecting taxes. Electing to collect taxes through withholding is purely a matter of timing; that is, of *when* taxes are paid, *not how much* in taxes are paid. Nonetheless, as the examples in chapter 5 make clear, this is a procedural choice that can have substantive consequences. In the United States, the Trump administration—in an alleged attempt to gain an advantage for Republicans in the 2018 midterm elections— manipulated the withholding regime in a way that upset expectations, generating a backlash from taxpayers who were shocked to find that their annual refunds were smaller than anticipated, had vanished, or had even been replaced with a tax bill. In France, a move from delayed payment of taxes to a new withholding regime conjured in the popular imagination a host of concerns—some realized, some not—about the possibility that the timing of tax collection might be manipulated for taxpayers' or the government's financial advantage, constitute little more than a subterfuge for covertly achieving other ends, or implicate a host of unintended negative repercussions for French society and the economy. But all of these potential or actual manipulations of tax time— whether feared yet failing to come to fruition, accurately forecasted in advance, or apprehended only after the fact—bespeak the latent power of a tax imagination that stands ready to be activated at any time.

Messages from the Tax Imagination

Because tax law is a reflection of the society that creates it, choices regarding what, whom, and how to tax send clear messages about what and whom a society values.[5] In this way, tax laws act as a mirror that can reveal how society sees itself now as well as how it would like to see itself—and be seen by others—in the future. What, then, do the choices we have seen Americans make in availing themselves of the power of the tax imagination to shape and reshape time tell us about US society?

Taken together, chapters 1 and 2 reveal the Janus-faced character of substance-over-form principles—the supposed "cornerstone of sound taxation" in the United States.[6] On one side, the public face of those principles communicates shared societal aspirations for justice and fairness in application of the tax laws and, in turn, in the distribution of the burden of funding the society that all Americans share together. On the other side, however, the private face of substance-over-form principles shuns those aspirations when doing so serves—however surreptitiously—to reinforce the privilege of those possessing wealth and power in US society at the expense of marginalized groups.

The differing choices illustrated in chapters 1 and 2 belie the sincerity of the messages sent by the doctrine's public face. Bringing the private face of substance-over-form principles into the light for all to see, chapter 2 pointedly forces us to grapple with the general refusal of US society to confront and redress its long and deeply rooted history of division and discrimination along a variety of lines (e.g., race, ethnicity, gender, gender identity and expression, sexual orientation, disability, and immigration status). Chapter 2 demonstrates how, even when discrimination such as refusing to legally recognize same-sex relationships or providing financial support and government approval for race-based discrimination in education are acknowledged in the United States, the priority seems to be disturbing as little as possible both those who benefit from privilege and the legal, social, political, and economic structures that protect and preserve that privilege. Even more appallingly, the federal government seemed to go out of its way in these instances to enhance the very sorts of privilege underpinning the discrimination that it purported to be remedying.

Chapters 3 and 4 add further detail to an already troubling portrait of US society.[7] On the one hand, chapter 3 shows how Congress has repeatedly acted to compress tax time in order to convert it into money that can be distributed to business owners. It has done this in the name of healing an ailing economy by encouraging investment and economic growth and, more recently, to add "rocket fuel" (as President Trump described it) to an already expanding economy. Justifying its exercises of the tax imagination by reference to the economy as a whole, Congress implicitly painted its actions as being taken broadly for the benefit of all Americans. Yet, despite general reverence in the United States for the idea that the tax system should serve as an engine of economic growth, "advancing economic growth is not necessarily and ineluctably an end that serves the good of the public."[8] Indeed, despite the sheer magnitude of the financial benefits provided to business owners through immediate expensing, it appears that workers—whose efforts have garnered renewed appreciation during the disruption caused by the COVID-19 pandemic—saw little increase in their wages due to immediate expensing and the other business tax cuts enacted as part of the 2017 Tax Cuts and Jobs Act. Moreover, workers were not alone in being short-changed by these exercises of the tax imagination. Even among business owners, the benefits of Congress's manipulations of tax time were targeted at capital-intensive businesses that are more likely to be owned by men— and not at the service businesses that women more commonly own. In these ways, chapter 3 revealed congressional action ostensibly designed to benefit all of society as nothing more than cover for adding to the privilege of an already wealthy few.

On the other hand, chapter 4 illustrates the efforts of well-heeled tax-payers to appropriate tax dollars for their own personal benefit—and to the detriment of everyone else. Leveraging layer upon layer of privilege, these taxpayers manipulate time to create the impression that they are acting without any motivation to artificially reduce their tax bills— and thus their contributions to funding the shared societal structures without which their success would not be possible—even when that is precisely what they are doing. Making matters worse, these taxpayers do not accomplish their tax machinations alone; far from it, they are aided in their efforts by an entire industry of well-paid legal and financial advisers[9] and, at times, are even given a leg up by the very government from which they are taking tax dollars. Just as with the examples in chapter 2 illustrating the private face of substance-over-form principles, the examples in chapter 4 belie all of the public talk of creating a fair and just tax system when the wealthy and privileged are permitted (in truth, actively encouraged[10]) to contribute as little as possible to funding the shared society from which they have reaped so many rewards.

Veiled as these messages are—hidden away in an "arcane" tax code—it is no wonder that they are generally left uninterrogated and undisturbed, freely encouraging the entrenchment and perpetuation of the established power and privilege of a few at the expense of so many "others." Nevertheless, by showing that the public can recognize—and react to—temporal exercises of the tax imagination, chapter 5 provides some hope for an eventual measure of accountability and positive change. If the public can grasp the power of the tax imagination to manipulate time when the effects are visible on the surface of the tax system and affect them personally, then it should be equally possible for them to grasp less visible exercises of that power when brought to the surface. That has been the aim of this book and the task that I would encourage other tax scholars to take up in the many areas where time and tax law intersect but that space would not permit to be addressed here.

Using the Tax Imagination to Create a Better World

Through careful excavation of the deeper connections between tax and time, it is possible to expose to the public gaze the far too common phenomenon of the tax imagination being used to bend the arc of the moral universe toward injustice.[11] The power of the tax imagination to manipulate time—to create worlds that exist both inside and outside of time—is a powerful tool that can be used to reflect a society's aspirations for itself as well as to realize those aspirations. All members of society have an interest in understanding and interrogating how and to what end the power of the tax imagination is being used, because it is only with that knowledge that action can be taken to ensure that the tax imagination is being used to shape and control time in ways that further society's own trajectory through time in the direction of greater tax and social justice.

Although, in keeping with my location and training as a US tax scholar, we have focused on the United States, the comparative context provided throughout this book suggests the existence of a shared phenomenon that presents a potential source of problems as well as opportunities. The ability to manipulate tax time is not the province of a single country or legal system. Rather, as might be anticipated from the contributions of non-US scholars to the exploration of the deeper connections between law and time mentioned in the introduction to this book, the ability to manipulate tax time seems to be a matter of tax actors' ingenuity rather than a quirk associated with a peculiar cultural or legal context. What should be taken from this study, therefore, is the need to systematically examine—and then remain ever attentive to—the question of how and to what end the relationship between tax and time is being imagined and reimagined by all of the relevant tax actors. This is a research question worthy of study in all tax systems—not just that of the United States.

If carried out widely, this work can ferret out the similar and different forms that the less visible uses of tax time take in different countries. We witnessed examples of such similarities and differences in the approaches that US and Spanish legislators took in chapter 3 to compressing time and in the imaginative manipulations of withholding in France and the United States explored in chapter 5. In both cases, the similarities and differences that we encountered were influenced by the countries' differing contexts and positions. For instance, the different approaches of the United States and Spain to compressing time were influenced by changes in Spain's legal and economic context as well as its membership in the European Union. In contrast, the differing potential manipulations of withholding depended largely on France's position in transitioning to a new withholding regime as opposed to the Trump administration's position in adjusting an established withholding structure from within.

Exposing and documenting the varied workings of the tax imagination opens the door not only to reactively correcting past injustices but also to expanding the universe of imaginable possibilities for manipulating tax time to actively advance the cause of achieving greater tax and social justice in the present and future. In doing so, this work can simultaneously contribute to a wider understanding that tax belongs not in the invisible background but in the prominent foreground when considering how to address social justice issues. After all, as illustrated by the examples in earlier chapters, the effects of a tax system are not confined to the four corners of a country's tax code. Instead, tax laws are often used to convey valuable financial rewards and incentives or to place a societal stamp of approval (or disapproval) on selected activities or groups of people. In these same ways, the plasticity of tax time can serve as a powerful instrument for shaping and reshaping not only tax worlds but also how we see and experience the "real" world. Shedding the strictures of a linear conceptualization of time, the power of the tax imagination can be deployed to mold time in the service of creating tangible effects and impacts on legal, social, political, and economic contexts with the aim of working toward a more just society for all its inhabitants.

What's more, the systematic examination and reimagination of how society engages with and deploys time in and through tax law has recently taken on renewed relevance and importance that could not have been foreseen when I first embarked on this project. As I conclude my work publishing this book, the COVID-19 pandemic has been disrupting all of our worlds for more than a year—and promises to do so for some time to come. Through the upheaval and damage that it has caused, the pandemic has highlighted, exacerbated, and taken full advantage of the many lines of disadvantage and discrimination that exist in society. Coupled with rising public anger at acts of violence by law enforcement against minorities in the United States and elsewhere following the death of George Floyd at the hands of Minneapolis police, the pandemic has occasioned widespread soul-searching by exposing the structural inequalities that plague society.

Unable to ignore these inequalities any longer, many found themselves asking whether—in the wake of so much shock and upheaval—they truly wished to return to the prepandemic "normal."[12] For example, as Los Angeles mayor Eric Garcetti put it in his April 2020 State of the City Address:

> Before this crisis, on a normal day in the United States, we could see the federal minimum wage stand still for years while executive compensation knew no limit, and hear the slogan of America first elevated above actually putting all Americans first, pushing our immigrant neighbors into the shadows.
>
> We knew some families who could easily pay the full costs of college, while too many others drown in debt.
>
> We had some friends who had better health insurance and better health, and others whose bodies pay the toll of the discrimination in our society and disparities in our medical system.
>
> Long before this, too many Americans had been forgotten by a country that speaks about the many, but too often favors the few.[13]

In light of all this, Garcetti asserted that, "while we set the pace for the nation in so many ways, in innovation, in freedom, in belonging, we must ask of our city and our nation, at this time, is normal really what we want to come back to?"[14]

The challenge placed before us by Garcetti and others is to consider whether and how we can avail ourselves of the silver lining of opportunity within the dark clouds looming all around. Do we have the courage to imagine—and then to work to create—a world that is better and more just than the one that existed in the "before times"? In other words, we must ask ourselves whether we are ready (and I certainly hope that we are) to envision *and* take concrete steps toward a world in which we come together to address and redress structural inequalities while tackling head-on the other problems that face us collectively—most notably, the effects of global warming and climate change caused by past and current human activity that threaten both present and future generations in ways that, much like the COVID-19 pandemic, exploit and exacerbate existing inequalities.[15]

Tax law can play an important role in meeting these challenges.[16] On the one hand, as a reflection of the society that creates it—and as illustrated by so many of the examples explored in this book—tax law is no less permeated by inequalities and discrimination and no less a contributor to our collective problems (e.g., through generous tax subsidies for fossil fuels that contribute to global warming) than any other area of the law or society.[17] But, on the other hand, tax law is not simply a source of problems; it can also be a part of the solution. As we have seen, imagining whole new worlds is part and parcel of the everyday work of creating, interpreting, shaping, and applying the tax laws. The deep connections between time and tax law are evident from the panoply of examples explored throughout this book, which have ranged from cornerstone substance-over-form principles to methods for recovering investments in income-producing property to methods for collecting income tax to policing abusive taxpayer behavior in such varied contexts as the step-up in basis for inherited property, tax-free like-kind exchanges, the dividends-received deduction, and tax-free corporate reorganizations. These and so many other areas of connection between tax and time are the fertile ground of opportunities for imagining and working toward a better world for all.

Unfortunately, when deployed in these areas in the past, the power of the tax imagination to mold time has too often been used to entrench or exacerbate inequality and discrimination rather than to uproot them. But there is room for optimism here because, as we have experienced, the tax past need not dictate the tax future. If dedicated to the pursuit of tax and social justice, the legal imagination—through its ability to creatively manipulate tax time to distribute and redistribute resources and to provide incentives and disincentives that shape behavior—has an important role to play in helping us to conceptualize and realize a future in which all are able to flourish.

NOTES

INTRODUCTION

1 PAUL HORWICH, ASYMMETRIES IN TIME: PROBLEMS IN THE PHILOSO-
PHY OF SCIENCE, at xi (1987).

2 ALBERT EINSTEIN, RELATIVITY: THE SPECIAL AND GENERAL THEORY,
at v (Robert W. Lawson trans., 1920).

3 *See id.*

4 *Id.* at 30–33.

5 JOHN MCCUMBER, TIME AND PHILOSOPHY: A HISTORY OF CONTINEN-
TAL THOUGHT 11 (2011).

6 *Id.* at 11–12.

7 Alan Yuhas, *What Day Is It? No Rhythm and Deepening Blues*, N.Y. TIMES, Apr.
15, 2020, at A4.

8 *E.g.*, MARCEL PROUST, DU CÔTÉ DE CHEZ SWANN (1913).

9 *See* HORWICH, *supra* note 1, at 33–36.

10 Carol J. Greenhouse, *Just in Time: Temporality and the Cultural Legitimation of
Law*, 98 YALE L.J. 1631, 1633–34 (1989) (footnotes omitted); *see* David M. Engel,
Law, Time, and Community, 21 LAW & SOC'Y REV. 605, 606–07 (1987).

11 If, as Carol Greenhouse suggests, law exists in an "all-times," *see infra* text accompanying note 87, tax law combines this "all-times" with an existence in "all-space"
due to its ubiquitous, hovering presence all around us—a presence for US citizens
and residents that exists without borders. I.R.C. § 2031(a); Treas. Reg. §§ 1.1-1(b)
(as amended in 2008), 25.2501-1(a)(1) (as amended in 2020); *see* MARIANA
VALVERDE, CHRONOTOPES OF LAW: JURISDICTION, SCALE AND GOVER-
NANCE (2015). But, as explored in chapter 2, space, like time, is open to manipulation in tax law.

12 JANELLE CAMMENGA, TAX FOUND., FISCAL FACT NO. 686, STATE AND
LOCAL SALES TAX RATES, 2020 (2020). The US Supreme Court has now
eased the way for states to tax sales made over the internet. South Dakota v. Way-
fair, Inc., 138 S. Ct. 2080 (2018).

13 I.R.C. §§ 1, 1401, 3101, 3102, 3402, 6654.

14 Janelle Cammenga, *State Gasoline Tax Rates as of July 2020*, TAX FOUND. (July
29, 2020), https://taxfoundation.org.

15 *Property Taxes*, URB. INST., www.urban.org.

16 *E.g.*, I.R.C. §§ 152, 2001; 72 PA. STAT. AND CONS. STAT. ANN. § 9116 (Westlaw
through 2020 Reg. Sess. Act 95).

17 For an in-depth exploration of this question, see ANTHONY C. INFANTI, OUR
SELFISH TAX LAWS: TOWARD TAX REFORM THAT MIRRORS OUR BET-
TER SELVES (2018).

18 *See, e.g.*, Tessa Davis, *Tax and Social Context: Legal Fictions Within Tax*, 4 SAVAN-
NAH L. REV. 31 (2017); Nancy J. Knauer, *Legal Fictions and Juristic Truth*, 23 ST.
THOMAS L. REV. 1 (2010).

19 Joanna Wheeler, *Double Tax Relief and Time, in* TIME AND TAX: ISSUES IN IN-
TERNATIONAL, EU, AND CONSTITUTIONAL LAW 27, 27 (Werner Haslehner
et al. eds., 2019).

20 ORG. FOR ECON. COOP. & DEV., REVENUE STATISTICS: 1965–2018, at
67 tbl.3.8, 68 tbl.3.9 (2019); *Policy Basics: Where Do Federal Tax Revenues Come
From?*, CTR. ON BUDGET & POL'Y PRIORITIES, www.cbpp.org (last updated
Aug. 6, 2020).

21 *See, e.g.*, INFANTI, *supra* note 17, chs. 3–4.

22 Emily Grabham & Siân M. Beynon-Jones, *Introduction* to LAW AND TIME 1, 21
(Siân M. Beynon-Jones & Emily Grabham eds., 2018).

23 JOEL S. NEWMAN ET AL., FEDERAL INCOME TAXATION: CASES, PROB-
LEMS, AND MATERIALS 271–93 (7th ed. 2019).

24 *Course Descriptions: Timing Issues and the Income Tax*, NYU LAW, www.law.nyu.
edu (last visited Nov. 30, 2020).

25 *See* Grabham & Beynon-Jones, *supra* note 22, at 1.

26 I.R.C. § 441.

27 *See generally* Burnet v. Sanford & Brooks Co., 282 U.S. 359 (1931).

28 BORIS I. BITTKER & LAWRENCE LOKKEN, FEDERAL TAXATION OF IN-
COME, ESTATES & GIFTS ¶ 25.10.1, Westlaw (database updated 2021).

29 *Compare* I.R.C. § 172, *with id.* (prior to amendment by the Tax Cuts and Jobs Act,
Pub. L. No. 115-97, § 13302, 131 Stat. 2054, 2121–23 (2017)).

30 Libson Shops, Inc. v. Koehler, 353 U.S. 382, 386 (1957); *see* BITTKER & LOKKEN,
supra note 28, ¶ 25.10.1.

31 The net operating loss deduction primarily applies to taxpayers engaged in business. BITTKER & LOKKEN, *supra* note 28, ¶ 25.10.1. For an exploration of taxing
individuals more generally based on a longer time horizon, see Lee Anne Fennell
& Kirk J. Stark, *Taxation over Time*, 59 TAX L. REV. 1 (2005).

32 BITTKER & LOKKEN, *supra* note 28, ¶ 47.9.6 (footnote omitted); *see* Arrowsmith
v. Comm'r, 344 U.S. 6 (1952).

33 *See* I.R.C. § 111.

34 Hillsboro Nat'l Bank v. Comm'r, 460 U.S. 370, 383 (1983).

35 *See Arrowsmith*, 344 U.S. at 10 (Jackson, J., dissenting); Alice Phelan Sullivan
Corp. v. United States, 180 Ct. Cl. 659, 665 (1967).

36 I.R.C. § 446(c).

37 Treas. Reg. § 1.446-1(c)(1)(i) (as amended in 2021).

38 I.R.C. § 448.

39 Treas. Reg. § 1.446-1(c)(1)(ii)(A).

40 *Id.* § 1.451-2(a) (as amended in 1979).

41 I.R.C. § 461(h)(2)(C), (D); Treas. Reg. § 1.461-4(g) (as amended in 2004); *see* H.R. REP. NO. 98-861, at 871 (1984) (Conf. Rep.); BITTKER & LOKKEN, *supra* note 28, ¶ 105.6.4.

42 Treas. Reg. § 1.446-1(a)(1).

43 *Id.*

44 I.R.C. § 471(a); *see id.* § 472; Treas. Reg. § 1.471-2(d) (as amended in 1973); BITTKER & LOKKEN, *supra* note 28, ¶ 107.5.1.

45 I.R.C. § 446(b).

46 *Id.* § 1001(a); *see* Cottage Sav. Ass'n v. Comm'r, 499 U.S. 554 (1992).

47 *See* Edward J. McCaffery, *Taxing Wealth Seriously*, 70 TAX L. REV. 305 (2017).

48 *E.g.*, Matthew Frankel, *Time to Enact a Tax Strategy*, USA TODAY, Dec. 28, 2017, at 4B; Melissa Sotudeh, *Tax-Smart Strategies to Help Boost Your Savings*, OREGONIAN, Dec. 25, 2016, at C2; Russ Wiles, *5 Really Last-Minute Tax Tips*, ARIZ. REPUBLIC, Dec. 30, 2016, at A15.

49 Lawrence Lokken, *The Time Value of Money Rules*, 42 TAX L. REV. 1, 9 (1986); *see* Peter C. Canellos & Edward D. Kleinbard, *The Miracle of Compound Interest: Interest Deferral and Discount After 1982*, 38 TAX L. REV. 565 (1983); Daniel I. Halperin, *Interest in Disguise: Taxing the "Time Value of Money,"* 95 YALE L.J. 506, 509–10 (1986); *see also* Mary Louise Fellows, *A Comprehensive Attack on Tax Deferral*, 88 MICH. L. REV. 722, 725 n.11 (1990).

50 I.R.C. §§ 1272–1273, 1275.

51 *Id.* §§ 483, 1274.

52 *Id.* § 7872.

53 *E.g., id.* § 163(d), (j) (before and after amendment by the Tax Cuts and Jobs Act, Pub. L. No. 115-97, § 13301, 131 Stat. 2054, 2117–21 (2017)); *see* Est. of Yaeger v. Comm'r, 889 F.2d 29, 33 (1989); Marie Sapirie, *Questions as the Interest Deduction Limitation Takes Shape*, 159 TAX NOTES 1415 (2018).

54 Fellows, *supra* note 49, at 725–26.

55 Daniel Shaviro, *The Forgotten Henry Simons*, 41 FLA. ST. U. L. REV. 1, 31–32, 33–34 (2013); *see* Fellows, *supra* note 49, at 726.

56 Shaviro, *supra* note 55, at 31 (quoting HENRY C. SIMONS, FEDERAL TAX REFORM 127 (1950) [hereinafter SIMONS, TAX REFORM]); *see also* HENRY C. SIMONS, PERSONAL INCOME TAXATION: THE DEFINITION OF INCOME AS A PROBLEM OF FISCAL POLICY 162, 168–69, 208 & n.1 (1938).

57 SIMONS, TAX REFORM, *supra* note 56, at 127; *see id.* at 59–60.

58 *Id.* at 29, 31, 40–44; *see id.* at 49–52, 78–83, 140–41.

59 *E.g.*, Ford Motor Co. v. Comm'r, 71 F.3d 209 (6th Cir. 1995); *see supra* note 41 and accompanying text.

60 *See* Theodore S. Sims, *Debt, Accelerated Depreciation, and the Tale of a Teakettle: Tax Shelter Abuse Reconsidered*, 42 UCLA L. REV. 263 (1994).

61 *See* CHARLES H. GUSTAFSON ET AL., TAXATION OF INTERNATIONAL TRANSACTIONS: MATERIALS, TEXT AND PROBLEMS 485–93 (4th ed. 2011);

Early Impressions of the New Tax Law: Hearing Before the S. Comm. on Fin., 115th Cong. (2018) (statement of Rebecca M. Kysar, Professor of Law, Brooklyn Law School).

62 BITTKER & LOKKEN, *supra* note 28, ¶ 111.1.8.

63 Badaracco v. Comm'r, 464 U.S. 386, 393 (1984); *see* Klinghamer v. Brodrick, 242 F.2d 563, 564 (10th Cir. 1957); BITTKER & LOKKEN, *supra* note 28, ¶ 111.1.8; *cf.* I.R.C. § 6013(b).

64 Treas. Reg. §§ 1.451-1(a) (as amended in 2021), 1.461-1(a)(3) (as amended in 1999); *see* BITTKER & LOKKEN, *supra* note 28, ¶ 111.1.8.

65 BITTKER & LOKKEN, *supra* note 28, ¶ 111.1.8.

66 I.R.C. § 6072(a).

67 I.R.S. 1040 and 1040-SR Instructions: Tax Year 2019, at 76–77 (2020); I.R.S. Form 1040-X (2020).

68 I.R.S. Instructions for Form 1040-X, at 4 (2020).

69 Badaracco v. Comm'r, 464 U.S. 386 (1984).

70 BITTKER & LOKKEN, *supra* note 28, ¶ 111.1.8.

71 *See, e.g.*, David Hasen, *A Partnership Mark-to-Market Tax Election*, 71 TAX LAW. 93 (2017); Henry Ordower, *The Expatriation Tax, Deferrals, Mark to Market, the Macomber Conundrum and Doubtful Constitutionality*, 15 PITT. TAX REV. 1 (2017); Daniel Shaviro, *The More It Changes, the More It Stays the Same? Automatic Indexing and Current Policy*, *in* THE TIMING OF LAWMAKING 64 (Frank Fagan & Saul Levmore eds., 2017).

72 *See, e.g.*, DAVID G. DUFF ET AL., CANADIAN INCOME TAX LAW 469–87, 757–939 (6th ed. 2018); TIME AND TAX, *supra* note 19; Jacques Buisson, *La portée de la loi fiscale dans le temps*, 2002 REVUE FRANÇAISE DE DROIT ADMINISTRATIF 786; Olivier Fouquet & Philippe Durand, *Le temps fiscal*, REVUE ADMINISTRATIVE, 2000, numéro spécial 1, at 45; Patrick Serlooten, *Le temps et le droit fiscal*, 1997 REVUE TRIMESTRIELLE DE DROIT COMMERCIAL ET DE DROIT ÉCONOMIQUE 177.

73 *See, e.g.*, Rebecca R. French, *Time in the Law*, 72 U. COLO. L. REV. 663 (2001); Liaquat Ali Khan, *Temporality of Law*, 40 MCGEORGE L. REV. 55 (2009).

74 *E.g.*, LAW AND TIME, *supra* note 22; FRANÇOIS OST, LE TEMPS DU DROIT (1999); BENJAMIN J. RICHARDSON, TIME AND ENVIRONMENTAL LAW: TELLING NATURE'S TIME (2017); TEMPORAL BOUNDARIES OF LAW AND POLITICS: TIME OUT OF JOINT (Luigi Corrias & Lyana Francot eds., 2018); TIME, LAW, AND CHANGE: AN INTERDISCIPLINARY STUDY (Sofia Ranchordás & Yaniv Roznai eds., 2020); Christian Djeffal, *International Law and Time: A Reflection of the Temporal Attitudes of International Lawyers Through Three Paradigms*, 2014 NETH. Y.B. INT'L L. 93.

75 Bruce G. Peabody, *Reversing Time's Arrow: Law's Reordering of Chronology, Causality, and History*, 40 AKRON L. REV. 587, 618 (2007); *see id.* at 600–10.

76 *Id.* at 589.

77 *Id.* at 603–04.
78 U.S. CONST. amend. XXII, § 1.
79 Peabody, *supra* note 75, at 603.
80 U.S. CONST. amend. XII.
81 Peabody, *supra* note 75, at 604.
82 *Id.* (footnotes omitted).
83 *Id.* at 589.
84 Greenhouse, *supra* note 10.
85 *Id.* at 1641.
86 *Id.* at 1643.
87 *Id.* at 1642.
88 *Id.* at 1643–44.
89 CAROL J. GREENHOUSE, A MOMENT'S NOTICE: TIME POLITICS ACROSS CULTURES (1996).
90 *Id.* at 214.
91 *Id.* at 183.
92 *Id.* at 183–85.
93 *Id.* at 189–210.
94 *Id.* at 190.
95 *Id.* at 197.
96 *Id.* at 198.
97 *Id.* at 199.
98 *Id.* at 205.
99 *Id.* at 208–09.
100 *Id.* at 209–10; *see* Greenhouse, *supra* note 10, at 1650.
101 GREENHOUSE, *supra* note 89, at 210.
102 Brian M. Stewart, *Chronolawgy: A Study of Law and Temporal Perception*, 67 U. MIAMI L. REV. 303 (2012).
103 Andrew J. Wistrich, *The Evolving Temporality of Lawmaking*, 44 CONN. L. REV. 737, 743, 749 (2012).
104 *Id.* at 752; *see id.* at 777–96.
105 *Id.* at 763–77.
106 *See, e.g., id.* at 821–24, 826.
107 Engel, *supra* note 10, at 635–36.
108 *Id.* at 610–11.
109 *Id.* at 635.
110 *Id.* at 614.
111 Jonathan Goldberg-Hiller & David T. Johnson, *Time and Punishment*, 31 QUINNIPIAC L. REV. 621 (2013).
112 *Id.* at 622.
113 *Id.* at 631–34.
114 *Id.* at 634–37.

115 *Id.* at 643; *see id.* at 643–56.

116 TODD D. RAKOFF, A TIME FOR EVERY PURPOSE: LAW AND THE BAL-
ANCE OF LIFE (2002); *see* Orly Lobel, *The Law of Social Time*, 76 TEMPLE L.
REV. 357, 371–75 (2003) (book review) (raising questions regarding Rakoff's failure
to recognize the role of power relations and inequality between individuals and
groups in the regulation of time).

117 RAKOFF, *supra* note 116, at 127.

118 *Id.* at 128.

119 *Id.* at 184.

120 CHARLES F. WILKINSON, AMERICAN INDIANS, TIME, AND THE LAW:
NATIVE SOCIETIES IN A MODERN CONSTITUTIONAL DEMOCRACY 13
(1987).

121 *Id.* at 14.

122 *Id.*

123 *Id.* at 41.

124 *Id.* at 53.

125 *Id.* at 105.

126 JAMES B. WHITE, THE LEGAL IMAGINATION: STUDIES IN THE NATURE
OF LEGAL THOUGHT AND EXPRESSION 758 (1973). For a discussion of the
current state and past contributions of the law and literature movement, see
GARY MINDA, POSTMODERN LEGAL MOVEMENTS: LAW AND JURISPRU-
DENCE AT CENTURY'S END 149–66 (1995); Julie Stone Peters, *Law, Literature,
and the Vanishing Real: On the Future of an Interdisciplinary Illusion, in* TEACH-
ING LAW AND LITERATURE 71 (Austin Sarat et al. eds., 2011); Richard Weis-
berg, *What Remains "Real" About the Law and Literature Movement: A Global Ap-
praisal*, 66 J. LEGAL EDUC. 37 (2016). *See also* James Boyd White, *The Cultural
Background of* The Legal Imagination, *in* TEACHING LAW AND LITERATURE,
supra, at 29.

127 *See* Anthony C. Infanti, *Tax Equity*, 55 BUFF. L. REV. 1191 (2008).

128 *See* INFANTI, *supra* note 17, at 109–59.

129 GREENHOUSE, *supra* note 89, at 1.

130 *See* INFANTI, *supra* note 17.

1. TIME TRAVEL

1 *See* Joseph Isenbergh, *Musings on Form and Substance in Taxation*, 49 U. CHI. L.
REV. 859, 864–66, 879 (1982) (book review); Robert Willens, *Form and Substance
in Subchapter C*, 84 TAX NOTES 739, 746 (1999).

2 CNT Invs., LLC v. Comm'r, 144 T.C. 161, 198 (2015).

3 Est. of H.H. Weinert v. Comm'r, 294 F.2d 750, 755 (5th Cir. 1961).

4 *See* BORIS I. BITTKER & LAWRENCE LOKKEN, FEDERAL TAXATION OF
INCOME, ESTATES & GIFTS ¶ 4.3.3, Westlaw (database updated 2021); Derek A.
Jones & Jeffrey K. Gurney, Summa Holdings: *Substance-over-Form Does Not Ap-
ply to Congressionally Sanctioned Tax Benefits*, 127 J. TAX'N 116 (2017); Lewis R.

Steinberg, *Form, Substance and Directionality in Subchapter C*, 52 TAX LAW. 457 (1999); Stephen G. Utz, *Partnership Taxation in Transition: Of Form, Substance, and Economic Risk*, 43 TAX LAW. 693 (1990).

5   Heather M. Field, *Fiction, Form, and Substance in Subchapter K: Taxing Partnership Mergers, Divisions, and Incorporations*, 44 SAN DIEGO L. REV. 259 (2007).

6   Saviano v. Comm'r, 765 F.2d 643, 654 (7th Cir. 1985); *see* William W. Chip, *The Economic Substance Doctrine*, 508-2nd TAX MGMT. PORTFOLIO (BNA) § III(A) (2020).

7   I.R.C. § 1031.

8   Treas. Reg. § 1.1002-1(d) (1960).

9   Rev. Rul. 57-469, 1957-2 C.B. 521.

10   *Id.*

11   *See* Emily Cauble, *Reforming the Non-Disavowal Doctrine*, 35 VA. TAX REV. 439 (2016); Chip, *supra* note 6, § III(B); Nickolas J. Kyser, *Substance, Form, and Strong Proof*, 11 AM. J. TAX POL'Y 125 (1994); Robert Thornton Smith, *Substance and Form: A Taxpayer's Right to Assert the Priority of Substance*, 44 TAX LAW. 137 (1990). *But cf.* MARTIN COLLET, DROIT FISCAL 105 (7th ed. 2019); Hervé Lehérissel, *Form and Substance in Tax Law: France*, 87A CAHIERS DE DROIT FISCAL INTERNATIONAL 263, 272–73 (2002).

12   Est. of Rogers v. Comm'r, 29 T.C.M. (CCH) 869, 872 (1970) (citations omitted), *aff'd*, 445 F.2d 1020 (2d Cir. 1971); *see* BITTKER & LOKKEN, *supra* note 4, ¶ 4.3.6.

13   BITTKER & LOKKEN, *supra* note 4, ¶ 4.3.1.

14   Isenbergh, *supra* note 1, at 880 (footnote omitted).

15   *See* Reuven S. Avi-Yonah, *Rodriguez, Tucker, and the Dangers of Textualism*, 167 TAX NOTES FED. 87 (2020); Jonathan H. Choi, *The Substantive Canons of Tax Law*, 72 STAN. L. REV. 195 (2020); Allen D. Madison, *The Tension Between Textualism and Substance-over-Form Doctrines in Tax Law*, 43 SANTA CLARA L. REV. 699 (2003).

16   *See* Peter C. Canellos, *A Tax Practitioner's Perspective on Substance, Form and Business Purpose in Structuring Business Transactions and in Tax Shelters*, 54 SMU L. REV. 47, 57–68 (2001).

17   Frederik Zimmer, *Form and Substance in Tax Law: General Report*, 87A CAHIERS DE DROIT FISCAL INTERNATIONAL 19 (2002).

18   David G. Duff & Benjamin Alarie, *Legislated Interpretation and Tax Avoidance in Canadian Income Tax Law* 4 (2018), https://papers.ssrn.com/; *see id.* at 2–5. *See generally* Guy Masson & Shawn D. Porter, *Form and Substance in Tax Law: Canada*, 87A CAHIERS DE DROIT FISCAL INTERNATIONAL 187 (2002).

19   Duff & Alarie, *supra* note 18, at 5 (quoting Stephen Bowman, *Interpretation of Tax Legislation: The Evolution of Purposive Analysis*, 43 CAN. TAX J. 1167, 1183–84 (1995)); *see* Vokhid Urinov, *General Anti-Avoidance Rule in Canada: History, Scheme, Source, and Enforcement*, *in* THE ROUTLEDGE COMPANION TO TAX

AVOIDANCE RESEARCH 97, 97, 102 (Nigar Hashimzade & Yuliya Epifantseva eds., 2018).

20 Duff & Alarie, *supra* note 18, at 7; *see id.* at 5–10; Urinov, *supra* note 19, at 101–05.

21 Duff & Alarie, *supra* note 18, at 10; Income Tax Act, R.S.C. 1985, c 1 (5th Supp.), § 245.

22 Income Tax Act § 245(2); *see* DAVID G. DUFF ET AL., CANADIAN INCOME TAX LAW 180–92 (6th ed. 2018); Urinov, *supra* note 19, at 105–11.

23 Duff & Alarie, *supra* note 18, at 15–25.

24 *Id.* at 25–29.

25 Lehérissel, *supra* note 11, at 276–82.

26 MAURICE COZIAN ET AL., PRÉCIS DE FISCALITÉ DES ENTREPRISES 122–25, 973–74 (43d ed. 2019); Lise Chatain, *L'usuel et le droit fiscal, in* CUSTOMARY LAW TODAY 75, 77–78 (Laurent Mayali & Pierre Mousseron eds., 2018); Lehérissel, *supra* note 11, at 276–78; Julien Sordet, *L'excès des actes de gestion des entreprises en droit fiscal*, GESTION & FINANCES PUBLIQUES, Jan.–Feb. 2018, at 43, 43; *see* Direction générale des finances publiques, Bulletin officiel des finances publiques-impôts [BOFiP-Impôts], BOI-BIC-CHG-10-10, Frais et charges exposés dans l'intérêt de l'entreprise (2019).

27 Chatain, *supra* note 26, at 78, 81–85; Lehérissel, *supra* note 11, at 276–77.

28 Lehérissel, *supra* note 11, at 276–77; Olivier Fouquet, *Acte anormal de gestion et mauvaise gestion*, 61 REVUE ADMINISTRATIVE 36, 37–38 (2008); Sordet, *supra* note 26, at 46; *see* CE, Oct. 17, 1990, Rec. Lebon 282.

29 Philippe Durand & Marien Seraille, *La théorie du risque manifestement excessif: Le glas a sonné!*, REVUE DE DROIT FISCAL, no. 36, Sept. 8, 2016, act. 489; Fouquet, *supra* note 28, at 37; Sordet, *supra* note 26, at 46–47; *see* CE Sect., July 13, 2016, Rec. Lebon 376.

30 LIVRE DES PROCÉDURES FISCALES [LPF] [Book of Tax Procedure] art. L64.

31 CE, Sept. 27, 2006, Rec. Lebon 401.

32 Loi 2008-1443 du 30 décembre 2008 de finances rectificative pour 2008 [Law 2008-1443 of December 30, 2008 Amending the Budget for 2008], JOURNAL OFFICIEL DE LA RÉPUBLIQUE FRANÇAISE [J.O.] [OFFICIAL GAZETTE OF FRANCE], Dec. 31, 2008, p. 20518; *see* 1 PHILIPPE MARINI, COMMISSION DES FINANCES, RAPPORT SUR LE PROJET DE LOI DE FINANCES RECTIFICATIVE, NO. 135, Sénat Session Ordinaire 2008–2009, at 199–200, 203–05 (2008); GILLES CARREZ, COMMISSION DES FINANCES, RAPPORT SUR LE PROJET DE LOI DE FINANCES RECTIFICATIVE POUR 2008, NO. 1297, Assemblée Nationale, 13ème Législature, at 324–25, 327–31 (2008); *see also* COZIAN ET AL., *supra* note 26, at 959–60; JACQUES GROSCLAUDE & PHILIPPE MARCHESSOU, PROCÉDURES FISCALES 265–66 (9th ed. 2018); Séverine Lauratet & Charlotte Delsol, *Transposition de la nouvelle clause anti-abus générale en droit fiscal français: S'agit-il d'une révolution législative et quelles seront les évolutions jurisprudentielles?*, REVUE DE DROIT FISCAL, no. 47, Nov. 22, 2018, étude 472, at 2–4.

33 LPF art. L64; BOFiP-Impôts, BOI-CF-IOR-30, Procédures de l'abus de droit fiscal (2020); COZIAN ET AL., *supra* note 26, at 961–65; GROSCLAUDE & MARCHES-SOU, *supra* note 32, at 266–68, 271.

34 COZIAN ET AL., *supra* note 26, at 963–64; Lauratet & Delsol, *supra* note 32, at 3.

35 Loi 2018-1317 du 28 décembre 2018 de finances pour 2019 [Law 2018-1317 of December 28, 2018 on the Budget for 2019], art. 109(I)(1°), J.O., Dec. 30, 2018, text no. 1. There is some question about the constitutionality of this provision; however, given that it applies only to transactions taking place beginning January 1, 2020, and may be invoked by the tax authorities only beginning January 1, 2021, a decision regarding its constitutionality is yet to be made. Jean-François Desbuquois & Julien Kozlowski, *Évolutions récentes de l'abus de droit*, REVUE FISCALE DU PATRIMOINE, no. 3, Mar. 2019, étude 8; Frédéric Douet, *Abus de droit pour motif "principalement fiscal,"* SEMAINE JURIDIQUE NOTARIALE ET IMMOBILIÈRE, May 10, 2019, at 44, 45; Olivier Fouquet, *Les deux nouvelles procédures de "mini-abus de droit" instituées par le projet de loi de finances pour 2019 sont-elles constitutionnelles?*, REVUE DE DROIT FISCAL, no. 49, Dec. 6, 2018, act. 519.

36 CODE GÉNÉRAL DES IMPÔTS [Tax Code] art. 205A; *see* Council Directive 2016/1164, art. 6, 2016 O.J. (L 193) 11; Lauratet & Delsol, *supra* note 32, at 4–6; Yves Rutschmann & Pierre-Marie Roch, *Transposition de la clause anti-abus générale en matière d'IS (CGI, art. 205 A) et nouvelle procédure d'abus de droit (LPF, art. L. 64 A): Les paradoxes de la réforme*, SEMAINE JURIDIQUE NOTARIALE ET IMMOBILIÈRE, Jan. 25, 2019, at 122, 123.

37 Jérôme Turot, *La liberté de gestion des entreprises entre enfer et paradis (et plus près de l'enfer)*, REVUE DE DROIT FISCAL, no. 27, July 6, 2017, étude 378.

38 Zimmer, *supra* note 17, at 19, 21.

39 *Id.* at 21.

40 *Id.* at 22.

41 *Id.* at 21.

42 *See* United States v. Phellis, 257 U.S. 156, 168 (1921).

43 Gregory v. Helvering, 293 U.S. 465 (1935), *aff'g* 69 F.2d 809 (2d Cir. 1934), *rev'g* 27 B.T.A. 223 (1932); *see* Isenbergh, *supra* note 1, at 866; Ray A. Knight & Lee G. Knight, *Substance over Form: The Cornerstone of Our Tax System or a Lethal Weapon in the IRS's Arsenal?*, 8 AKRON TAX J. 91, 92 (1991); Madison, *supra* note 15, at 700.

44 Assaf Likhovski, *The Story of* Gregory: *How Are Tax Avoidance Cases Decided?*, *in* BUSINESS TAX STORIES 89, 127 (Steven A. Bank & Kirk J. Stark eds., 2005).

45 Revenue Act of 1942, ch. 619, § 504, 56 Stat. 798, 957.

46 *Gregory*, 27 B.T.A. at 224.

47 *Id.*

48 *Id.*

49 Helvering v. Gregory, 69 F.2d 809, 810 (2d Cir. 1934).

50 Likhovski, *supra* note 44, at 91.

51 *Gregory*, 27 B.T.A. at 224; Brief for the Respondent at 4, Gregory v. Helvering, 293 U.S. 465 (1935) (No. 127).

52 *Gregory*, 69 F.2d at 810.

53 *Id.*; Likhovski, *supra* note 44, at 91–92.

54 *Gregory*, 69 F.2d at 810; Likhovski, *supra* note 44, at 91 n.8, 92.

55 Likhovski, *supra* note 44, at 92.

56 *Gregory*, 69 F.2d at 810; *Gregory*, 27 B.T.A. at 224–25.

57 Brief for the Respondent, *supra* note 51, at 28.

58 *Gregory*, 27 B.T.A. at 224; *see* Gregory v. Helvering, 293 U.S. 465, 467 (1935).

59 *See* Likhovski, *supra* note 44, at 90–91.

60 *Id.* at 91.

61 *Gregory*, 69 F.2d at 810; Brief for the Respondent, *supra* note 51, at 33.

62 *See* Likhovski, *supra* note 44, at 91; *cf.* I.R.C. § 311(b).

63 *Gregory*, 69 F.2d at 811.

64 *Id.*

65 *Id.* at 810.

66 *Id.* at 810–11.

67 *Id.* at 811.

68 *Id.*

69 *Id.*

70 *Id.*

71 Eugene Scott, *In Kavanaugh's Non-answer on Same-Sex Marriage, Many Heard a Troubling Response*, Wash. Post: The Fix (Sept. 7, 2018), www.washington-post.com.

72 Gregory v. Comm'r, 27 B.T.A. 223, 225 (1932).

73 *Id.*

74 *Id.* at 225–26.

75 Gregory v. Helvering, 293 U.S. 465, 467–69 (1935).

76 *Id.* at 469.

77 *Id.* at 469–70.

78 *Id.* at 470.

79 *Id.*

80 Helvering v. Gregory, 69 F.2d 809, 811 (2d Cir. 1934).

81 *See* I.R.C. §§ 108(e)(4), 306, 707(a)(2)(A), 737, 1031(f), 7872.

82 Revenue Act of 1950, Pub. L. No. 81-814, § 208, 64 Stat. 906, 931–32.

83 I.R.C. § 317(b).

84 *See* Boris I. Bittker & James S. Eustice, Federal Income Taxation of Corporations and Shareholders ¶ 9.01[1], Westlaw (database updated 2020).

85 *See* Rev. Rul. 76-385, 1976-2 C.B. 92.

86 *See* United States v. Davis, 397 U.S. 301 (1970).

87 I.R.C. §§ 1001, 1221.

88 *Id.* §§ 1(h), (j); 1222. For an additional tax on net investment income (including both dividends and capital gains) that will be ignored here for the sake of simplicity, see *id.* § 1411.

89 *Id.* §§ 301, 316.

90 *Id.* § 1(h)(11); Jobs and Growth Tax Relief Reconciliation Act of 2003, Pub. L. No. 108-27, § 302, 117 Stat. 752, 760.

91 *Compare* I.R.C. § 301(c), *with id.* § 1001(a).

92 *Id.* § 1001(a).

93 *Id.* § 301(c)(1).

94 *Id.* § 301(c)(2).

95 Wanamaker Trs. v. Comm'r, 11 T.C. 365 (1948), *aff'd per curiam*, 178 F.2d 10 (3d Cir. 1949).

96 S. Rep. No. 81-2375, at 42–43 (1950); H.R. Rep. No. 81-2319, at 53 (1950).

97 S. Rep. No. 83-1622, at 4676 (1954); H.R. Rep. No. 83-1337, at A79 (1954).

98 I.R.C. §§ 1(h), 11.

99 *Id.* §§ 61(a)(3), 1001(a).

100 *Id.* §§ 1(h), 1221, 1222.

101 *See id.* § 302(b), (d) (assuming that ABC is not a regulated investment company).

102 *Id.* § 317(b).

103 *See* Bittker & Eustice, *supra* note 84, ¶ 9.09[4][d]; Treas. Reg. § 1.304-2(c), ex. 1 (as amended in 1968); Prop. Treas. Reg. § 1.304-2(c), ex. 1, 74 Fed. Reg. 3509, 3516 (Jan. 21, 2009), *withdrawn*, 84 Fed. Reg. 11,686 (Mar. 28, 2019).

104 I.R.C. § 304(a)(1)(A).

105 *Id.* § 304(c)(1); Treas. Reg. § 1.304-5(b)(1) (1994).

106 I.R.C. § 304(c)(3).

107 *Id.* § 318.

108 *Id.* § 318(a)(1)(A)(ii).

109 *Id.*

110 *Id.* § 304(a)(1)(B).

111 *Id.* § 317(a).

112 *E.g., id.* §§ 269, 306(b)(4), 357(b), 453(e)(7), 1031(f)(2)(C); Treas. Reg. § 1.881-3(a)(4), (b) (as amended in 2020).

113 *E.g.,* I.R.C. §§ 877A, 1014(e), 1015(a), 7872(c)(1)(A)–(C).

114 *Id.* § 304(a)(1) (flush language).

115 *See id.* § 304(b)(1).

116 Revenue Act of 1928, Pub. L. No. 70-562, § 53(a), 45 Stat. 791, 808.

117 Likhovski, *supra* note 44, at 92.

118 Revenue Act § 275(a).

119 Likhovski, *supra* note 44, at 93.

120 Revenue Act § 272(a).

121 Likhovski, *supra* note 44, at 93.

122 Gregory v. Helvering, 27 B.T.A. 223 (1932).

123 Helvering v. Gregory, 69 F.2d 809 (2d Cir. 1934).

124 Gregory v. Helvering, 293 U.S. 465 (1935).

125 *See* Taxpayer Relief Act of 1997, Pub. L. No. 105-34, § 1013(a), 111 Stat. 788, 918; Tax Reform Act of 1986, Pub. L. No. 99-514, § 1875(b), 100 Stat. 2085, 2894; Deficit Reduction Act of 1984, Pub. L. No. 98-369, § 712(*l*)(1), 98 Stat. 494, 953; Tax Equity and Fiscal Responsibility Act of 1982, Pub. L. No. 97-248, § 226(a)(3), 96 Stat. 324, 491–92; Act of Aug. 31, 1964, Pub. L. No. 88-554, § 4(b)(1), 78 Stat. 761, 763; *see also, e.g.*, H.R. REP. NO. 105-148, at 464–66 (1997); H.R. REP. NO. 98-861, at 1222–23 (1984) (Conf. Rep.).

126 United States v. Davis, 397 U.S. 301, 313 (1970); *see* I.R.C. § 302(b)(1). The remaining paragraphs of § 302(b) are inapplicable to these facts.

127 I.R.C. § 304(b)(1).

128 *Id.* §§ 302(c)(1), 304(b)(1), 318(a)(2)(C).

129 *Id.* §§ 304(a)(1) (flush language), 351(a), 358(a)(1).

130 *Id.* § 304(a)(1) (flush language).

131 *Id.* § 301(c)(1).

132 *Id.* § 301(c)(2); *see* Prop. Treas. Reg. § 1.304-2(c), ex. 2, 74 Fed. Reg. 3509, 3516 (Jan. 21, 2009), *withdrawn*, 84 Fed. Reg. 11,686 (Mar. 28, 2019).

133 Prop. Treas. Reg. § 1.304-2(a)(3), 74 Fed. Reg. at 3515.

134 Treas. Reg. §§ 1.302-2(c) (as amended in 2007), 1.304-2(c), ex. 1 (as amended in 1968).

135 I.R.C. § 304(b)(2)(A).

136 *Id.* § 304(b)(2)(B).

137 *Actor*, MERRIAM-WEBSTER, www.merriam-webster.com (last visited Dec. 1, 2020).

138 *See supra* note 3 and accompanying text.

2. TIME TRAVEL AVOIDED (OR, JUSTICE DENIED)

1 ANTHONY C. INFANTI, OUR SELFISH TAX LAWS: TOWARD TAX REFORM THAT MIRRORS OUR BETTER SELVES (2018).

2 Boyter v. Comm'r, 668 F.2d 1382, 1385 (4th Cir. 1981). This discussion draws from and builds upon my earlier work. *See* Anthony C. Infanti, *Hegemonic Marriage: The Collision of "Transformative" Same-Sex Marriage with Reactionary Tax Law*, 74 TAX LAW. 411 (2021).

3 H.R. REP. NO. 104-664, at 2 (1996); Baehr v. Lewin, 74 Haw. 530 (1993).

4 Pub. L. No. 104-199, § 3(a), 110 Stat. 2419, 2419 (1996) (codified at 1 U.S.C. § 7).

5 Anthony C. Infanti, *The Internal Revenue Code as Sodomy Statute*, 44 SANTA CLARA L. REV. 763 (2004).

6 Ops. of the Justs. to the Senate, 802 N.E.2d 565, 569 (Mass. 2004); Goodridge v. Dep't of Pub. Health, 798 N.E.2d 941, 955–57 (Mass. 2003).

7 *E.g.*, California Domestic Partners Rights and Responsibilities Act, 2003 Cal. Legis. Serv. ch. 421 (West); Act of Oct. 2, 1999, 1999 Cal. Legis. Serv. ch. 588 (West); An Act Concerning Marriage and Civil Unions, 2006 N.J. Sess. Law Serv. ch. 103

(West); Domestic Partnership Act, 2003 N.J. Sess. Law Serv. ch. 246 (West); An Act Relating to Civil Unions, 1999 Vt. Adv. Legis. Serv. 91 (LexisNexis).

8 *E.g.*, 750 ILL. COMP. STAT. ANN. 75/10 (West, Westlaw through P.A. 101-651); Act of Oct. 2, 1999 (codified as amended at CAL. FAM. CODE § 297(b) (West, Westlaw through ch. 372 of 2020 Reg. Sess.)).

9 Letter from Pamela Wilson Fuller, Senior Technician Reviewer, Branch 2, Internal Revenue Serv., to Robert Shair, Senior Tax Advisor, H&R Block (Aug. 30, 2011).

10 Amy S. Elliott, *IRS Memo Indicates Civil Unions Are Marriages for Tax Purposes*, 133 TAX NOTES 794 (2011); *Individuals: Same-Sex Civil Unions*, ILL. REVENUE (2012), www.revenue.state.il.us.

11 570 U.S. 744, 775 (2013).

12 Rev. Rul. 2013-17, 2013-38 I.R.B. 201.

13 *Id.* at 204.

14 *Id.*

15 Anthony C. Infanti, *The Moonscape of Tax Equality: Windsor and Beyond*, 108 NW. U. L. REV. COLLOQUY 110, 124 (2013).

16 Garden State Equal. v. Dow, 82 A.3d 336, 361-68 (N.J. Super. Ct. 2013).

17 576 U.S. 644, 675-76, 680-81 (2015).

18 Definition of Terms Relating to Marital Status, 80 Fed. Reg. 64,378 (proposed Oct. 23, 2015).

19 *Id.* at 64,380. Treasury regulations reflect the views of the IRS as well as other divisions of the Treasury Department; however, the text refers only to the IRS (rather than Treasury and the IRS) both for the sake of brevity and because attorneys within Chief Counsel's Office have primary responsibility for drafting regulations. *See id.*; I.R.S. IRM 32.1.1.3–.4, 32.1.4; MICHAEL SALTZMAN & LESLIE BOOK, IRS PRACTICE AND PROCEDURE ¶ 3.02[3], Westlaw (database updated 2021).

20 Definition of Terms Relating to Marital Status, 80 Fed. Reg. at 64,380.

21 *Id.* at 64,379.

22 *Section of Taxation*, AM. BAR ASS'N, www.americanbar.org (last visited Dec. 2, 2020).

23 Hum. Rts. Campaign, Comment Letter on Proposed Regulations Containing Definition of Terms Relating to Marital Status (Dec. 7, 2015).

24 Donald H. Read, Comment Letter on Proposed Regulations Containing Definition of Terms Relating to Marital Status 2 (Dec. 7, 2015).

25 Section of Tax'n, Am. Bar Ass'n, Comment Letter on Proposed Regulations Containing Definition of Terms Relating to Marital Status (Dec. 3, 2015). I served as the principal author of these comments, working together with members of the Teaching Taxation and Estate & Gift Tax Committees.

26 Donald H. Read, Supplemental Comment Letter on Proposed Regulations Containing Definition of Terms Relating to Marital Status 1–2 (Jan. 29, 2016).

27 *Id.* at 2.

28 *Id.*

29 *Id.*

30 Section of Tax'n, *supra* note 25, at 6–7.

31 *Id.* at 7.

32 Read, *supra* note 26, at 2–3.

33 *Id.*

34 Section of Tax'n, *supra* note 25, at 9.

35 *Id.* at 8–9.

36 *Id.* at 9.

37 *Id.* at 10.

38 Read, *supra* note 26, at 3.

39 *Id.*

40 Section of Tax'n, *supra* note 25, at 11.

41 T.D. 9785, 2016-38 I.R.B. 361, 365; *see* Infanti, *supra* note 2.

42 T.D. 9785, 2016-38 I.R.B. at 368.

43 *Id.* at 365–66.

44 *Id.* at 365.

45 *See* Toni Robinson & Mary Moers Wenig, *Marry in Haste, Repent at Tax Time: Marital Status as a Tax Determinant*, 8 VA. TAX REV. 773, 788–823 (1989).

46 Section of Tax'n, *supra* note 25, at 6.

47 T.D. 9785, 2016-38 I.R.B. at 367.

48 *Id.*

49 *Id.*

50 *See* I.R.C. § 7805(c); Treas. Reg. § 301.7805-1(c) (1967); Treas. Order 111-01 (Mar. 16, 1981).

51 I.R.C. § 7803(a)(3)(C), (J); *see* Leandra Lederman, *Is the Taxpayer Bill of Rights Enforceable?* (Ind. Univ. Maurer Sch. of Law, Working Paper No. 404, 2019).

52 Ark. Best Corp. v. Comm'r, 485 U.S. 212, 222 n.7 (1988); *see* Bostock v. Clayton Cnty., 140 S. Ct. 1731, 1747 (2020).

53 *See* Louis Menand, *How to Look at a Rauschenberg*, NEW YORKER (Aug. 30, 2017), www.newyorker.com; Dean Peterson, *Why These All-White Paintings Are in Museums: And Why Mine Aren't*, VOX (Sept. 8, 2017), www.vox.com.

54 BRUNO LATOUR, NOUS N'AVONS JAMAIS ÉTÉ MODERNES: ESSAI D'ANTHROPOLOGIE SYMÉTRIQUE (1991).

55 *See* Irene van Oorschot, *Doing Times, Doing Truths: The Legal Case File as Folded Object*, *in* LAW AND TIME 229 (Siân M. Beynon-Jones & Emily Grabham eds., 2018).

56 *See* Máiréad Enright, *"No, I Won't Go Back": National Time, Trauma and Legacies of Symphysiotomy in Ireland*, *in* LAW AND TIME, *supra* note 55, at 46, 48.

57 *Id.* (footnote omitted).

58 *Id.*

59 Mark E. Wojcik, Comment Letter on Proposed Regulations Containing Definition of Terms Relating to Marital Status (Dec. 7, 2015).

60 T.D. 9785, 2016-38 I.R.B. 361, 362.

61 *Id.*

62 *E.g.*, I.R.S. Pub. No. 596, Earned Income Credit 12, 13–14, 16–17 (2020); I.R.S. Pub. No. 501, Exemptions, Standard Deduction, and Filing Information 7, 10, 11–12, 14, 16, 18, 23 (2020); I.R.S. Pub. No. 17, Your Federal Income Tax: For Individuals 22, 25, 26, 29, 31, 32–33, 75, 139, 154, 157, 208, 224, 226, 228 (2020).

63 Centralized Partnership Audit Regime, 82 Fed. Reg. 27,334, 27,343 (June 14, 2017); Rev. Proc. 2018-58, 2018-50 I.R.B. 990; I.R.S. Announcement 2020-16, 2020-38 I.R.B. 578; I.R.S. Announcement 2018-10, 2018-26 I.R.B. 776; I.R.S. Announcement 2018-7, 2018-16 I.R.B. 503; I.R.S. Announcement 2017-18, 2017-48 I.R.B. 545; I.R.S. Announcement 2017-17, 2017-46 I.R.B. 515; I.R.S. Announcement 2017-12, 2017-38 I.R.B. 238; I.R.S. Announcement 2017-2, 2017-10 I.R.B. 1009; I.R.S. Announcement 2016-38, 2016-43 I.R.B. 523; I.R.S. Announcement 2016-35, 2016-39 I.R.B. 423; I.R.S. Announcement 2016-31, 2016-38 I.R.B. 379.

64 *See* Infanti, *supra* note 2.

65 347 U.S. 483 (1954).

66 *Id.* at 495.

67 Olatunde Johnson, *The Story of* Bob Jones University v. United States: *Race, Religion, and Congress' Extraordinary Acquiescence, in* STATUTORY INTERPRETATION STORIES 127, 131 (William N. Eskridge Jr. et al. eds., 2011) (footnotes omitted); *see also Tax-Exempt Status of Private Schools: Hearing Before the Subcomm. on Tax'n & Debt Mgmt. Generally of the S. Comm. on Fin.*, 96th Cong. 247, 252 (1979) (Staff of Joint Comm. on Tax'n, Description of S. 103 and S. 449 Relating to Tax-Exempt Status of Private Schools) [hereinafter JCT Report]; CAMILLE WALSH, RACIAL TAXATION: SCHOOLS, SEGREGATION, AND TAXPAYER CITIZENSHIP, 1869–1973, at 85–108 (2018).

68 *Proposed IRS Revenue Procedure Affecting Tax-Exemption of Private Schools: Hearings Before the Subcomm. on Oversight of the H. Comm. on Ways and Means*, 96th Cong. 3–4 (1979) (statement of Jerome Kurtz, Comm'r of Internal Revenue) [hereinafter Kurtz Testimony]; *see* Note, *The Judicial Role in Attacking Racial Discrimination in Tax-Exempt Private Schools*, 93 HARV. L. REV. 378, 379 & n.5 (1979).

69 Kurtz Testimony, *supra* note 68, at 3.

70 I.R.S. News Release, [1967] 7 Stand. Fed. Tax Rep. (CCH) ¶ 6734 (Aug. 2, 1967).

71 Eileen Shanahan, *Schools in South May Avoid Taxes: New Exemption Will Affect Private Classes for Whites*, N.Y. TIMES, Aug. 3, 1967, at 24.

72 *Id.*

73 *Id.*; *see also* Note, *Federal Tax Benefits to Segregated Private Schools*, 68 COLUM. L. REV. 922, 924–25 (1968).

74 I.R.S. Gen. Couns. Mem. 33,585 (Aug. 1, 1967), 1967 WL 16003; *see* I.R.S. Gen. Couns. Mem. 33,752 (Feb. 12, 1968), 1968 WL 15976, *revoked by* I.R.S. Gen. Couns. Mem. 37,462 (Mar. 17, 1978), 1978 WL 43366.

75 *Compare* I.R.C. § 501(c)(3), *with* Revenue Act of 1954, Pub. L. No. 83-591, § 501(c)(3), 68A Stat. 3, 163, *and* Revenue Act of 1913, ch. 16, § II(G)(a), 38 Stat. 114, 172; *see* Bob Jones Univ. v. United States, 461 U.S. 574, 615–17 (1983) (Rehnquist, J., dissenting).

76   E. Ky. Welfare Rts. Org. v. Simon, 506 F.2d 1278, 1286–87 (D.C. Cir. 1974), *vacated and remanded on other grounds*, 426 U.S. 26 (1976).

77   I.T. 1800, II-2 C.B. 152, 153 (1923); *see* Treas. Reg. § 3.101(6)-1 (1938); Johnson, *supra* note 67, at 130.

78   Treas. Reg. § 39.101(6)-1(b) (1953); *see* Prescribing Stopgap Regulations Under the Internal Revenue Code of 1954, 19 Fed. Reg. 5167 (Aug. 17, 1954); Treas. Reg. § 1.501(c)(3)-1(f) (1960).

79   Notice of Proposed Rulemaking, 24 Fed. Reg. 1420, 1423 (Feb. 26, 1959).

80   The requirement of a preamble explaining proposed or final regulations dates only to the 1970s. 1 C.F.R. § 18.12 (2020); Clarity of Rulemaking Documents in the Federal Register, 41 Fed. Reg. 56,623 (Dec. 29, 1976); Clarity of Explanatory Material, 41 Fed. Reg. 32,861 (Aug. 5, 1976); Revision of Regulations, 37 Fed. Reg. 23,602 (Nov. 4, 1972); Regulations Affecting Federal Register, and Special Editions Thereof, 37 Fed. Reg. 6804 (Apr. 4, 1972); Summary Statements and Highlights Listing, 36 Fed. Reg. 5203 (Mar. 18, 1971).

81   T.D. 6391, 24 Fed. Reg. 5217, 5219 (June 26, 1959).

82   Treas. Reg. § 1.501(c)(3)-1(d)(2) (1967); *see id.* (as amended in 2017).

83   Gen. Couns. Mem. 33,585, *supra* note 74.

84   *Id.* at *1.

85   *Id.*

86   *Id.* at *2.

87   *Id.*; *see* Rev. Rul. 67-325, 1967-2 C.B. 113.

88   Gen. Couns. Mem. 33,585, *supra* note 74, at *2.

89   *Id.*

90   *Id.* at *3.

91   *Id.* at *6 (footnote omitted).

92   *Id.* at *7.

93   *Id.*

94   *Id.*

95   *Id.* at *9; *see id.* at *3–4.

96   *Id.* at *11; *see id.* at *9–11.

97   *Id.* at *12.

98   *Id.* at *13; Cooper v. Aaron, 358 U.S. 1 (1958); Griffin v. State Bd. of Educ., 239 F. Supp. 560 (E.D. Va. 1965).

99   Gen. Couns. Mem. 33,585, *supra* note 74, at *12.

100   *Id.*; *see supra* note 88 and accompanying text.

101   Gen. Couns. Mem. 33,585, *supra* note 74, at *13.

102   *See supra* note 72 and accompanying text.

103   Gen. Couns. Mem. 33,585, *supra* note 74, at *6.

104   *Id.*

105   Est. of H.H. Weinert v. Comm'r, 294 F.2d 750, 755 (5th Cir. 1961).

106 Daniel N. Shaviro, *Rethinking Tax Expenditures and Fiscal Language*, 57 TAX L. REV. 187, 200 (2004) (quoting STANLEY S. SURREY, PATHWAYS TO TAX REFORM 3 (1973)).

107 Anthony C. Infanti, *Tax Reform Discourse*, 32 VA. TAX REV. 205, 245–47 (2012); Shaviro, *supra* note 106, at 199–201; *e.g.*, Boris I. Bittker, *A "Comprehensive Tax Base" as a Goal of Income Tax Reform*, 80 HARV. L. REV. 925 (1967).

108 *See* Note, *supra* note 73, at 927–40 (demonstrating how a law student writing at the time saw through the form of these tax benefits to their substance as federal financial assistance and analyzed that assistance in constitutional terms).

109 309 F. Supp. 1127, 1129–31 (D.D.C. 1970).

110 *Id.* at 1138, 1140.

111 *Id.* at 1137.

112 *Id.*

113 *Id.* at 1134.

114 *Id.* at 1134–36.

115 *Id.* at 1135 (quoting Coffey v. State Educ. Fin. Comm'n, 296 F. Supp. 1389, 1392 (S.D. Miss. 1969)).

116 *Id.*

117 Johnson, *supra* note 67, at 132.

118 *Equal Educational Opportunity: Hearings Before the S. Select Comm. on Equal Educ.*, 91st Cong. 1992, 1995–97 (1970) (statement of Randolph W. Thrower, Comm'r of Internal Revenue); *see* Green v. Connally, 330 F. Supp. 1150, 1156 (D.D.C.), *aff'd sub nom.* Coit v. Green, 404 U.S. 997 (1971) (per curiam); JCT Report, *supra* note 67, at 255.

119 *Green*, 330 F. Supp. at 1161–64, 1179–80.

120 *Id.* at 1164–65 (footnote omitted); *see id.* at 1169, 1171.

121 McGlotten v. Connally, 338 F. Supp. 448 (D.D.C. 1972).

122 *Id.* at 456–57, 459, 460. The court found that social clubs' more limited exemption was part of the income tax's structure and not a tax preference that might constitute government aid; moreover, the court found "no mark of Government approval" in the designation of a social club as exempt. *Id.* at 458; *see id.* at 457–59. Congress overruled this portion of the court's decision in 1976 by denying tax-exempt status to social clubs with written discriminatory policies. I.R.C. § 501(i); Act of Oct. 20, 1976, Pub. L. No. 94-568, § 2, 90 Stat. 2697, 2697.

123 Rev. Rul. 71-447, 1971-2 C.B. 230; *see Green*, 330 F. Supp. at 1171–73, 1179; Johnson, *supra* note 67, at 133.

124 *See* Stephen B. Cohen, *"Seg Academies," Taxes, and Judge Ginsburg, in* THE LEGACY OF RUTH BADER GINSBURG 73, 74–75, 78–84 (Scott Dodson ed., 2015); Neal Devins, *Tax Exemptions for Racially Discriminatory Private Schools: A Legislative Proposal*, 20 HARV. J. ON LEGIS. 153, 157–61 (1983); Johnson, *supra* note 67, at 133–38; JCT Report, *supra* note 67, at 255–58, 279–81. *See generally* Paul S. Milich, Note, *Racially Discriminatory Schools and the IRS*, 33 TAX LAW. 571 (1979).

125 *Green*, 330 F. Supp. at 1169.

126 Johnson, *supra* note 67, at 139–48.

127 461 U.S. 574 (1983).

128 *Id.* at 585–92.

129 *Id.* at 593; *see id.* at 593–96, 602–04.

130 *Id.* at 598.

131 *Id.*

132 *Contra id.* at 622 n.4 (Rehnquist, J., dissenting).

133 *Id.* at 591, 599 n.24, 603–04 (majority opinion); *see* Donna D. Adler, *The Internal Revenue Code, the Constitution, and the Courts: The Use of Tax Expenditure Analysis in Judicial Decision Making*, 28 WAKE FOREST L. REV. 855, 875–76 (1993).

134 *E.g.*, Samuel D. Brunson & David J. Herzig, *A Diachronic Approach to* Bob Jones: *Religious Tax Exemptions After* Obergefell, 92 IND. L.J. 1175, 1177–79 (2017); Johnny Rex Buckles, *The Sexual Integrity of Religious Schools and Tax Exemption*, 40 HARV. J.L. & PUB. POL'Y 255, 257–61 (2017).

135 Brunson & Herzig, *supra* note 134; Buckles, *supra* note 134; John R. Dorocak, *How Might a Church's Tax-Exempt Status (and Other Advantages) Be Revoked Procedurally for Opposition to Same-Sex Marriage or Be Defended Possibly as Free Exercise of Religion?*, 53 WILLAMETTE L. REV. 161 (2017); Herman D. Hofman, *For Richer or for Poorer: How* Obergefell v. Hodges *Affects the Tax-Exempt Status of Religious Organizations That Oppose Same-Sex Marriage*, 52 GONZ. L. REV. 21 (2016); Timothy J. Tracey, Bob Jones*ing: Same-Sex Marriage and the Hankering to Strip Religious Institutions of Their Tax-Exempt Status*, 11 FIU L. REV. 85 (2015); Lloyd Hitoshi Mayer & Zachary B. Pohlman, *What Is Caesar's, What Is God's: Fundamental Public Policy for Churches* , 44 HARV. J.L. & PUB. POL'Y 145 (2021); *see also* CYNTHIA BROWN & ERIKA K. LUNDER, CONG. RSCH. SERV., R44244, RECOGNITION OF SAME-SEX MARRIAGE: IMPLICATIONS FOR RELIGIOUS OBJECTIONS 24–30 (2015); Ronald D. Gorsline & Bryson M. Kirksey, *Tax Issues of Educational Organizations*, 482-2nd TAX MGMT. PORTFOLIO (BNA) § III(A) (2020).

136 *See* 1 LAURENCE H. TRIBE, AMERICAN CONSTITUTIONAL LAW 213–35 (3d ed. 2000).

137 Robert M. Cover, *Foreword:* Nomos *and Narrative*, 97 HARV. L. REV. 4, 67 (1983).

138 *Cf.* Cornelius v. Benevolent Protective Ord. of Elks, 382 F. Supp. 1182, 1192–96 (D. Conn. 1974).

139 *See* Cover, *supra* note 137, at 67 n.195; Charles O. Galvin & Neal Devins, *A Tax Policy Analysis of* Bob Jones University v. United States, 36 VAND. L. REV. 1353, 1377–79 (1983).

140 Bob Jones Univ. v. United States, 461 U.S. 574, 593 n.20 (1983); *see* Galvin & Devins, *supra* note 139, at 1362–63, 1366–67; *The Supreme Court: 1982 Term*, 97 HARV. L. REV. 1, 264, 266–67 (1983).

141 Rev. Proc. 2020-5, § 12.03, 2020-1 I.R.B. 241; *see Bob Jones Univ.*, 461 U.S. at 581, 583–84.

142 Brunson & Herzig, *supra* note 134, at 1187.

143 Tracey, *supra* note 135, at 132, 135; *see* DOUGLAS MANCINO & FRANCES HILL, TAXATION OF EXEMPT ORGANIZATIONS ¶ 7.05[1]–[3], Westlaw (database updated 2021).

3. TIME AS MONEY

1 THE OXFORD DICTIONARY OF PROVERBS 310 (Jennifer Speake ed., 2003).

2 *Id.*

3 I.R.C. § 167(a).

4 Deborah A. Geier, *The Myth of the Matching Principle as a Tax Value*, 15 AM. J. TAX POL'Y 17, 42 (1998); *see* Douglas A. Kahn, *Accelerated Depreciation—Tax Expenditure or Proper Allowance for Measuring Net Income?*, 78 MICH. L. REV. 1, 13 (1979).

5 Geier, *supra* note 4, at 45–46; David A. Weisbach, *Measurement and Tax Depreciation Policy: The Case of Short-Term Intangibles*, 33 J. LEGAL STUD. 199, 204 (2004).

6 E. Cary Brown, *Business-Income Taxation and Investment Incentives, in* INCOME, EMPLOYMENT AND PUBLIC POLICY: ESSAYS IN HONOR OF ALVIN H. HANSEN 300, 302–10 (1948); *see* BORIS I. BITTKER & LAWRENCE LOKKEN, FEDERAL TAXATION OF INCOME, ESTATES & GIFTS ¶ 23.1.5, Westlaw (database updated 2021); Geier, *supra* note 4, at 42–43; Christopher H. Hanna, *Demystifying Tax Deferral*, 52 SMU L. REV. 383, 384–88 (1999); Calvin H. Johnson, *Soft Money Investing Under the Income Tax*, 1989 U. ILL. L. REV. 1019, 1022–36; Alvin C. Warren, Jr., *Accelerated Capital Recovery, Debt, and Tax Arbitrage*, 38 TAX LAW. 549, 551–53 (1985).

7 Geier, *supra* note 4, at 45.

8 Hanna, *supra* note 6, at 388–91; Johnson, *supra* note 6, at 1027–30; Rebecca N. Morrow, *Government as Investor: The Case of Immediate Expensing*, 106 KY. L.J. 1, 18–21 (2017–2018).

9 Geier, *supra* note 4, at 59 (footnotes omitted) (quoting Joseph M. Dodge & Deborah A. Geier, Simon *Says: A Liddle* Night Music *with Those Depreciation Deductions, Please*, 69 TAX NOTES 617, 623 (1995)).

10 *Id.* at 59–60; *see* Dodge & Geier, *supra* note 9; Johnson, *supra* note 6, at 1041–42; Weisbach, *supra* note 5, at 204.

11 Geier, *supra* note 4, at 61–62; BITTKER & LOKKEN, *supra* note 6, ¶ 23.1.4; *cf.* Kahn, *supra* note 4, at 12, 30–34.

12 *See* I.R.C. § 168(b); Kahn, *supra* note 4, at 17, 34.

13 Kahn, *supra* note 4, at 35–40. *Contra* Walter J. Blum, *Accelerated Depreciation: A Proper Allowance for Measuring Net Income?!!*, 78 MICH. L. REV. 1172 (1980).

14 United States v. Ludey, 274 U.S. 295, 301 (1927).

15 Massey Motors, Inc. v. United States, 364 U.S. 92, 106 (1960).

16 *Id.* at 104.

17 Indopco, Inc. v. Comm'r, 503 U.S. 79, 84 (1992).

18 Liddle v. Comm'r, 103 T.C. 285, 289 (1994), *aff'd*, 65 F.3d 329 (3d Cir. 1995).

19 Simon v. Comm'r, 68 F.3d 41, 44 (2d Cir. 1995).

20 *See* Internal Revenue Code of 1954, Pub. L. No. 83-591, § 167, 68A Stat. 3, 51–52.

21 S. REP. NO. 83-1622, at 25–26 (1954); *see* H.R. REP. NO. 83-1337, at 22–24 (1954).

22 S. REP. NO. 83-1622, at 25; *see* H.R. REP. NO. 83-1337, at 23.

23 S. REP. NO. 83-1622, at 29.

24 H.R. REP. NO. 83-1337, at 22; *see* MARVIN A. CHIRELSTEIN & LAWRENCE ZELENAK, FEDERAL INCOME TAXATION 185–86 (14th ed. 2018); Yoram Margalioth, *Not a Panacea for Economic Growth: The Case of Accelerated Depreciation*, 26 VA. TAX REV. 493, 509–10 (2007).

25 Congressional Budget and Impoundment Control Act of 1974, Pub. L. No. 93-344, §§ 301(d)(6), 601, 88 Stat. 297, 308, 323; *see* STAFF OF JOINT COMM. ON TAX'N, JCX-81-18, ESTIMATES OF FEDERAL TAX EXPENDITURES FOR FISCAL YEARS 2018-2022, at 1–3 (2018); Bruce Bartlett, *The End of Tax Expenditures as We Know Them?*, 92 TAX NOTES 413, 414 (2001).

26 STAFF OF JOINT COMM. ON TAX'N, *supra* note 25, at 7.

27 *Id.* at 24 tbl.1.

28 OFF. OF TAX ANALYSIS, U.S. DEP'T OF TREASURY, TAX EXPENDITURES 3 (2018). The Treasury Department also provides data using a "reference law baseline." *Id.* at 2–3. That baseline, which does not classify accelerated depreciation as a tax expenditure, is disregarded here because it distinguishes between generally applicable tax rules and exceptions while the normal tax baseline hews more closely to a comprehensive income tax base. *Id.* at 2–3, 10–11.

29 *Id.* at 23 tbl.1.

30 U.S. GOV'T ACCOUNTABILITY OFF., GAO-13-339, CORPORATE TAX EXPENDITURES: INFORMATION ON ESTIMATED REVENUE LOSSES AND RELATED FEDERAL SPENDING PROGRAMS 11 tbl.1 (2013); Rebecca N. Morrow, *Accelerating Depreciation in Recession*, 19 FLA. TAX REV. 465, 468, 487 (2016).

31 *See* MARTIN COLLET, DROIT FISCAL 364–65 (7th ed. 2019); DAVID G. DUFF ET AL., CANADIAN INCOME TAX LAW 830–31, 876–77 (6th ed. 2018); FERNANDO PÉREZ ROYO ET AL., CURSO DE DERECHO TRIBUTARIO: PARTE ESPECIAL 386–87 (12th ed. 2018).

32 *E.g.*, EL ABC DE LOS GASTOS Y DEDUCCIONES FISCALES 29–37, 51–57 (9th ed. 2019); DUFF ET AL., *supra* note 31, at 895–96; CHRISTOPHE DE LA MARDIÈRE, DROIT FISCAL DE L'ENTREPRISE ET FISCALITÉ NOTARIALE 178–82, 184–85 (2018); JUAN CALVO VÉRGEZ ET AL., DERECHO TRIBUTARIO: PARTE ESPECIAL 79–93, 145–47 (7th ed. 2018).

33 Economic Recovery Tax Act of 1981, Pub. L. No. 97-34, § 201, 95 Stat. 172, 203 [hereinafter ERTA]; Randall D. Weiss & James W. Wetzler, *The Evolution of Economics at the Joint Committee on Taxation, Part 1*, 151 TAX NOTES 983, 996 (2016).

34 Alan J. Auerbach, *The New Economics of Accelerated Depreciation*, 23 B.C. L. Rev. 1327, 1327 (1982).

35 *See* H.R. Rep. No. 97-215, at 206 (1981) (Conf. Rep.); S. Rep. No. 97-144, at 48 (1981); Auerbach, *supra* note 34, at 1327–28, 1331–34; Alvin C. Warren, Jr. & Alan J. Auerbach, *Transferability of Tax Incentives and the Fiction of Safe Harbor Leasing*, 95 Harv. L. Rev. 1752, 1754 (1982).

36 S. Rep. No. 97-144, at 47; ERTA §§ 211–214, 95 Stat. at 227–41.

37 I.R.C. §§ 46(a)(2)(B), 46(c)(7), 48(c)(2) (1982); ERTA §§ 211(a), 213, 95 Stat. at 227, 240; *see* Auerbach, *supra* note 34, at 1334–35.

38 Warren & Auerbach, *supra* note 35, at 1758.

39 *Id.* at 1758–61; Auerbach, *supra* note 34, at 1335; Weiss & Wetzler, *supra* note 33, at 996.

40 Auerbach, *supra* note 34, at 1328 (footnotes omitted).

41 Warren & Auerbach, *supra* note 35, at 1762–63; *see* S. Rep. No. 97-494, at 130–37 (1982).

42 Jeffrey H. Birnbaum & Alan S. Murray, Showdown at Gucci Gulch: Lawmakers, Lobbyists, and the Unlikely Triumph of Tax Reform 11 (1987); *see* Weiss & Wetzler, *supra* note 33, at 996.

43 Warren & Auerbach, *supra* note 35, at 1754–57; Auerbach, *supra* note 34, at 1348–49.

44 *See* Auerbach, *supra* note 34, at 1348; Warren & Auerbach, *supra* note 35, at 1754–55.

45 *See supra* text accompanying note 8; *see also* Auerbach, *supra* note 34, at 1348.

46 Auerbach, *supra* note 34, at 1348–49.

47 *Id.* at 1348; *see id.* at 1331–32.

48 *Id.* at 1328.

49 S. Rep. No. 97-494, at 83, 98 (1982); *see id.* at 83–84, 96–98, 122–26, 138–39; Alvin C. Warren & Alan J. Auerbach, *Tax Policy and Equipment Leasing After TEFRA*, 96 Harv. L. Rev. 1579, 1580–83 (1983); Warren, *supra* note 6, at 554–55.

50 Weiss & Wetzler, *supra* note 33, at 987.

51 Staff of Joint Comm. on Tax'n, General Explanation of the Revenue Provisions of the Tax Equity and Fiscal Responsibility Act of 1982, at 53 (1982) (Comm. Print); *see id.* at 54–67; Richard J. Bronstein & Alan S. Waldenberg, *The Short Life and Lingering Death of Safe Harbor Leasing*, 69 A.B.A. J. 1844, 1844, 1846 (1983); James W. Wetzler, *The Not-So-Simple Analytics of Expensing*, 155 Tax Notes 687, 690 (2017).

52 Warren & Auerbach, *supra* note 49, at 1584; *see* Warren, *supra* note 6, at 557–63. *See generally* Calvin H. Johnson, *Tax Shelter Gain: The Mismatch of Debt and Supply Side Depreciation*, 61 Tex. L. Rev. 1013 (1983).

53 Economic Recovery Tax Act of 1981, Pub. L. No. 97-34, § 202, 95 Stat. 172, 219; H.R. Rep. No. 97-215, at 209 (1981) (Conf. Rep.).

54 Tax Reform Act of 1986, Pub. L. No. 99-514, § 202(a), 100 Stat. 2085, 2142–43; Staff of Joint Comm. on Tax'n, General Explanation of the Tax Reform Act of 1986, at 109 (1987) (Comm. Print).

55 Tax Reform Act § 202(a).

56 Morrow, *supra* note 30, at 471.

57 *Id.* (footnotes omitted).

58 Pub. L. No. 107-147, § 101(a), 116 Stat. 21, 22.

59 H.R. Rep. No. 107-251, at 20 (2001).

60 Press Release, Off. of the Press Sec'y, Remarks by the President on Signing Job Creation and Worker Assistance Act of 2002 in Live Radio Address (Mar. 9, 2002); Margalioth, *supra* note 24, at 496.

61 Job Creation and Worker Assistance Act § 101(a).

62 Staff of Joint Comm. on Tax'n, General Explanation of Tax Legislation Enacted in the 107th Congress, at 220 (2003) (Comm. Print).

63 *Id.*

64 Jobs and Growth Tax Relief Reconciliation Act of 2003, Pub. L. No. 108-27, § 201(a), 117 Stat. 752, 756.

65 Economic Stimulus Act of 2008, Pub. L. No. 110-185, § 103, 122 Stat. 613, 618; Gary Guenther, Cong. Rsch. Serv., RL31852, The Section 179 and Section 168(k) Expensing Allowances: Current Law and Economic Effects 3 (2018).

66 Morrow, *supra* note 30, at 481; *see* Guenther, *supra* note 65, at 8–9.

67 I.R.C. § 179(a), (b)(1)–(2) (1986); Small Business Job Protection Act of 1996, Pub. L. No. 104-188, § 1111(a), 110 Stat. 1755, 1758; Omnibus Budget Reconciliation Act of 1993, Pub. L. No. 103-66, § 13116, 107 Stat. 312, 432.

68 Jobs and Growth Tax Relief Reconciliation Act § 202.

69 H.R. Rep. No. 108-94, at 25 (2003); *see* I.R.C. § 312(k)(3)(B) (2003); Treas. Reg. § 1.312-15(d) (1972).

70 Small Business Jobs Act of 2010, Pub. L. No. 111-240, § 2021, 124 Stat. 2504, 2556; Economic Stimulus Act § 102; *see* Guenther, *supra* note 65, at 2–3 tbl.I, 6–8.

71 Morrow, *supra* note 30, at 477–79.

72 *E.g.*, Don Lee, *Tax Bill Looks Risky in Long Term*, L.A. Times, Dec. 26, 2017, at C1; Tory Newmyer, *Trump and GOP Speeding Past Scrutiny on Their Way to a Massive Tax Overhaul*, Wash. Post, Dec. 1, 2017, at A18; Jim Tankersley & Binyamin Appelbaum, *"Rocket Fuel" Plan for an Economy That Is Already Moving Fast*, N.Y. Times, Nov. 30, 2017, at A21.

73 Tax Cuts and Jobs Act, Pub. L. No. 115-97, § 13201(a), 131 Stat. 2054, 2105 (2017).

74 *Id.* § 13201(a), (b)(1).

75 *Id.* § 13201(c), (g); Richard M. Nugent et al., *Bonus Questions on the New Bonus Depreciation Rules*, 160 Tax Notes 457, 466–67 (2018).

76 H.R. Rep. No. 115-409, at 232 (2017).

77 *Id.*; *see* I.R.C. § 312(k)(3)(B); Treas. Reg. §§ 1.168(k)-1(f)(7) (as amended in 2007), 1.168(k)-2(g)(7) (2020), 1.312-15(d) (as amended in 2019).

78 I.R.C. § 179(a), (b)(1)–(2).

79 *Id.* § 179(b)(6).

80 *CPI Inflation Calculator*, https://data.bls.gov.

81 H.R. REP. NO. 115-409, at 235–36.

82 Tax Cuts and Jobs Act, Pub. L. No. 115-97, § 13101(d), 131 Stat. 2054, 2102 (2017); GUENTHER, *supra* note 65, at 1; Nugent et al., *supra* note 75, at 467.

83 *See* Treas. Reg. § 1.168(k)-2(e)(3)(ii) (2020); GUENTHER, *supra* note 65, at 5.

84 Peter Baker, *Trump Pitches His Tax Cut Proposal as "Rocket Fuel" for the Economy*, N.Y. TIMES, Sept. 30, 2017, at A17; Rebecca Ballhaus, *Trump Says Tax Cuts Will Supercharge Economic Growth*, WALL ST. J. (Sept. 29, 2017), www.wsj.com.

85 COUNCIL OF ECON. ADVISORS, ECONOMIC REPORT OF THE PRESIDENT 50 (2019).

86 JANE G. GRAVELLE & DONALD J. MARPLES, CONG. RSCH. SERV., R45736, THE ECONOMIC EFFECTS OF THE 2017 TAX REVISION: PRE-LIMINARY OBSERVATIONS 5–7 (2019); Emanuel Kopp et al., *U.S. Investment Since the Tax Cuts and Jobs Act of 2017*, at 4, 7–8, 10, 15–16, 17 (Int'l Monetary Fund, Working Paper No. WP/19/120, 2019); Philip Bump, *A New Report Further Undermines Trump's Claim That the Tax Cuts Were Economic "Rocket Fuel,"* WASH. POST (May 28, 2019), www.washingtonpost.com.

87 S. 3296, 116th Cong. (2020); *see, e.g.*, *Expanding Opportunities for Small Businesses Through the Tax Code: Hearing Before the S. Comm. on Small Bus. & Entrepreneurship*, 115th Cong. 2 (2018) (statement of Sen. Marco Rubio); *Growth, Opportunity, and Change in the U.S. Labor Market and the American Workforce: A Review of Current Developments, Trends, and Statistics: Hearing Before the Subcomm. on Health, Emp't, Lab., & Pensions of the H. Comm. on Educ. & the Workforce*, 115th Cong. 17, 28 (2018) (testimony of Stephen Moore, Senior Fellow in Economics, Heritage Foundation); COUNCIL OF ECON. ADVISORS, *supra* note 85, at 38; Jad Chamseddine, *GOP Seeks to Make Full Expensing Permanent*, 166 TAX NOTES FED. 1210 (2020); Nathan J. Richman, *Infrastructure Plan Notably Omits Depreciation and Amortization*, 171 TAX NOTES FED. 269 (2021).

88 JOINT COMM. ON TAX'N, JCX-67-17, ESTIMATED BUDGET EFFECTS OF THE CONFERENCE AGREEMENT FOR H.R. 1, THE "TAX CUTS AND JOBS ACT" 3 (2017).

89 *Id.* at 6, 8.

90 *See supra* note 27.

91 STAFF OF JOINT COMM. ON TAX'N, JCX-3-17, ESTIMATES OF FEDERAL TAX EXPENDITURES FOR FISCAL YEARS 2016–2020, at 32, 34 tbl.1 (2017).

92 INST. ON TAX'N & ECON. POL'Y, CORPORATE TAX AVOIDANCE REMAINS RAMPANT UNDER NEW TAX LAW (2019).

93 *Id.* at 2–4; Stephanie Saul & Patricia Cohen, *$0 Corporate Tax Bills Kindle Voter Resentment*, N.Y. TIMES, Apr. 30, 2019, at A1.

94 Brian Faler, *Big Businesses Paying Even Less Than Expected Under GOP Tax Law*, POLITICO (June 13, 2019), www.politico.com; *see* Asha Glover, *Groups Want Answers on Lower-Than-Expected Corporate Tax Receipts*, 164 TAX NOTES 243 (2019).

95 Faler, *supra* note 94.
96 *See supra* note 86 and accompanying text.
97 Morrow, *supra* note 8, at 47; Theodore P. Seto, *The Problem with Bonus Depreciation*, 126 TAX NOTES 782 (2010).
98 Seto, *supra* note 97, at 783.
99 GRAVELLE & MARPLES, *supra* note 86, at 9–11.
100 CAROLINE BRUCKNER, KOGOD SCH. OF BUS. TAX POL'Y CTR., BILLION DOLLAR BLIND SPOT: HOW THE U.S. TAX CODE'S SMALL BUSINESS EXPENDITURES IMPACT WOMEN BUSINESS OWNERS 7 (2017).
101 *Id.*
102 *Id.* at 19–20.
103 *Id.* at 20; *see id.* at 6–7, 9, 19–20, 22.
104 For more on the use of promises of economic growth to mask the funneling of tax benefits to the wealthy and privileged, see ANTHONY C. INFANTI, OUR SELFISH TAX LAWS: TOWARD TAX REFORM THAT MIRRORS OUR BETTER SELVES 135–59 (2018).
105 *Goodwill*, BLACK'S LAW DICTIONARY (11th ed. 2019).
106 LUIS RIBÓ DURÁN & JOAQUÍN FERNÁNDEZ FERNÁNDEZ, DICCIONARIO DE DERECHO EMPRESARIAL 410 (1998).
107 Treas. Reg. § 1.167(a)-3(a) (as amended in 2004); ENRIQUE ORTIZ CALLE, EL RÉGIMEN JURÍDICO TRIBUTARIO DE LAS AMORTIZACIONES EN EL IMPUESTO SOBRE SOCIEDADES 160–67 (2001).
108 Omnibus Budget Reconciliation Act of 1993, Pub. L. No. 103-66, § 13261, 107 Stat. 312, 532; Corporate Income Tax Law arts. 11(4), 12(3) (B.O.E. 1995, 43) [hereinafter Ley 43/1995]; *see* Anibal Caro, *Amortización de fondo de comercio financiero*, CARTA TRIBUTARIA: MONOGRAFÍAS, no. 327, 2000, at 2; Julián Ibáñez Casado, *Análisis de la reforma del Impuesto sobre Sociedades*, 11 ANALES DE ESTUDIOS ECONÓMICOS Y EMPRESARIALES 259, 264 (1996); Constancio Zamora Ramírez, *Una propuesta para el análisis de las relaciones entre la contabilidad y la fiscalidad: Estudio del caso español*, CUADERNOS DE CIENCIAS ECONÓMICAS Y EMPRESARIALES, no. 39, 2000, at 115, 128.
109 H.R. REP. NO. 103-111, at 760 (1993).
110 Ley 43/1995 pmbl., art. 10(3); *see* Ibáñez Casado, *supra* note 108, at 262–63, 264; Zamora Ramírez, *supra* note 108, at 115–16, 134.
111 I.R.C. § 197(e)(1)(A); Law Consolidating the Corporate Income Tax Law arts. 11(4), 89(3) (B.O.E. 2004, 4) [hereinafter Ley 4/2004]; Caro, *supra* note 108, at 5–6, 8; Juan Manuel Contreras Delgado de Cos, *Amortización fiscal del fondo de comercio financiero: ¿Política fiscal o ayuda de Estado?*, ANUARIO DE LA COMPETENCIA, no. 1, 2007, at 341, 351; Begoña Pérez Bernabeu, *La consideración por la comisión como ayuda de estado del régimen de amortización del fondo de comercio previsto en el artículo 12.5 LIS*, CRÓNICA TRIBUTARIA, no. extraordinario 4, 2010, at 19, 19.

112 Jordi de Juan Casadevall, *Bruselas contra España: La calificación de la amortización fiscal del fondo de comercio financiero como ayuda ilegal*, GACETA FISCAL, no. 284, 2009, at 80, 88; Eduardo Gracia Espinar & Ana Martínez Gutiérrez, *La nueva amortización fiscal del fondo de comercio financiero*, ESTRATEGIA FINANCIERA, June 2003, at 68, 68; Hugo López López, *El régimen jurídico de las ayudas de Estado y su incidencia en el sistema tributario español: La amortización fiscal del fondo de comercio financiero para la adquisición de participaciones en entidades extranjeras*, QUINCENA FISCAL, no. 15–16, 2010, at 85, 88.

113 Law on Fiscal, Administrative, and Social Measures art. 2(5) (B.O.E. 2001, 24) [hereinafter Ley 24/2001]; *see* Dirección General de Tributos, Consulta no. V0135-03 (Nov. 28, 2003); Dirección General de Tributos, Consulta no. 1490-02 (Oct. 4, 2002); Gracia Espinar & Martínez Gutiérrez, *supra* note 112, at 69; Ignacio Luis Gómez Jiménez, *Deducibilidad fiscal del fondo de comercio financiero por la adquisición de participaciones en entidades no residentes*, CARTA TRIBUTARIA: MONOGRAFÍAS, no. 1, 2005, at 11–14.

114 Ley 4/2004 art. 12(5); Contreras Delgado de Cos, *supra* note 111, at 350–51; Gracia Espinar & Martínez Gutiérrez, *supra* note 112, at 68–69; Gómez Jiménez, *supra* note 113, at 3; Manuel Gutiérrez Lousa & José Antonio Rodríguez Ondarza, *Los incentivos fiscales a la internacionalización de la empresa española*, NUEVAS TENDENCIAS EN ECONOMÍA Y FISCALIDAD INTERNACIONAL, no. 825, 2005, at 49, 66.

115 Ley 4/2004 arts. 12(5), 21(1); *see* Dirección General de Tributos, Consulta no. 0109-05 (Mar. 17, 2005); Dirección General de Tributos, Consulta no. 0065-04 (Jan. 22, 2004); Dirección General de Tributos, Consulta no. 1855-02 (Nov. 27, 2002).

116 Gómez Jiménez, *supra* note 113, at 7–11, 22–23.

117 Modification of the Corporate Tax Regulations art. 1(2) (B.O.E. 2003, 252).

118 Miguel Cruz Amorós, *El controvertido tratamiento fiscal del fondo de comercio financiero derivado de la adquisición de participaciones en entidades no residentes*, *in* JUSTICIA Y DERECHO TRIBUTARIO: LIBRO HOMENAJE AL PROFESOR JULIO BANACLOCHE PÉREZ 355, 356 (Carmen Banacloche et al. eds., 2008).

119 Ley 24/2001 pmbl.; Cruz Amorós, *supra* note 118, at 356; López López, *supra* note 112, at 104.

120 Gutiérrez Lousa & Rodríguez Ondarza, *supra* note 114, *passim*; *see* Cruz Amorós, *supra* note 118, at 357; López López, *supra* note 112, at 104.

121 Josep Piñol, *Fondo de comercio financiero: La historia interminable*, LEGAL TODAY (Mar. 15, 2017), www.legaltoday.com; *see* Casadevall, *supra* note 112, at 88, 95.

122 EC Treaty art. 87(1) (now TFEU art. 107(1)).

123 *Id.* art. 88(2) (now TFEU art. 108(2)).

124 *Id.* art. 88(3) (now TFEU art. 108(3)); Council Regulation (EC) No. 659/1999, art. 4, 1999 O.J. (L 83) 1, 4.

125 Council Regulation No. 659/1999, art. 14, 1999 O.J. at 6.

126 López López, *supra* note 112, at 109.

127 *Id.*

128 State Aid C45/2007, 2007 O.J. (C 311) 21, 21–22, 27; Pérez Bernabeu, *supra* note 111, at 20.

129 Commission Decision 2011/282/EU, 2011 O.J. (L 135) 1; Commission Decision 2011/5/EC, 2011 O.J. (L 7) 48.

130 Commission Decision 2011/5/EC, 2011 O.J. at 62.

131 *Id.* at 53.

132 *Id.* at 62.

133 *Id.* at 57; *see* López López, *supra* note 112, at 93–94.

134 Commission Decision 2011/5/EC, 2011 O.J. at 65.

135 *Id.* at 57.

136 *Id.* at 58.

137 *Id.*

138 *Id.* at 62.

139 *E.g.*, Pérez Bernabeu, *supra* note 111, at 22, 25; Rafael Calvo & Salvador Pastoriza, *Procedimiento de investigación formal de ayudas de Estado vs deducibilidad fiscal del fondo de comercio financiero*, ESTRATEGIA FINANCIERA, Jan. 2008, at 69, 71–74; Cruz Amorós, *supra* note 118, at 372; Begoña Pérez Bernabeu, *El requisito de la selectividad en las ayudas de estado de carácter fiscal y su incidencia en el ordenamiento español: Dos ejemplos recientes*, REVISTA DE INFORMACIÓN FISCAL, no. 95, 2009, at 45, 56–62; Casadevall, *supra* note 112, at 84–95; Marta Villar Ezcurra, *La amortización del fondo de comercio financiero en España y su problemática jurídico-comunitaria: ¿Un nuevo caso de ayuda de estado?*, REVISTA DE CONTABILIDAD Y TRIBUTACIÓN, no. 298, 2008, at 73, 89–90; López López, *supra* note 112, at 90–91; *cf.* Contreras Delgado de Cos, *supra* note 111, at 350.

140 Amendments to the Law on Collective Investment Vehicles, at disposición final sexta (B.O.E. 2011, 31); General Budget for 2011 art. 74 (B.O.E. 2010, 39); *see* Iratxe Celaya Acordarrementería & Maite Urruticoechea Uriarte, *El fondo de comercio financiero desde una perspectiva fiscal*, ACTUALIDAD JURÍDICA URÍA MENÉNDEZ, no. 29, 2011, at 98, 101; Begoña Pérez Bernabeu, *El régimen de amortización del fondo de comercio*, CRÓNICA TRIBUTARIA, no. extraordinario 3, 2011, at 25, 27, 30.

141 Commission Decision 2011/282/EU, 2011 O.J. (L 135) 1, 35; Commission Decision 2011/5/EC, 2011 O.J. at 73–74; *see* Lilo Piña Garrido, *Recuperación de ayudas de Estado consistentes en medidas fiscales contrarias a Derecho Comunitario (I)*, CRÓNICA TRIBUTARIA, no. 148, 2013, at 171, 186–87.

142 Celaya Acordarrementería & Urruticoechea Uriarte, *supra* note 140, at 101–02.

143 Case T-399/11, Banco Santander, S.A. v. Comm'n, ECLI:EU:T:2014:938 (Nov. 7, 2014); Case T-219/10, Autogrill España, S.A. v. Comm'n, ECLI:EU:T:2014:939 (Nov. 7, 2014).

144 Cases C-20/15 P & C-21/15 P, Comm'n v. World Duty Free Group, S.A., ECLI:EU:C:2016:981 (Dec. 21, 2016).

145 Case T-399/11 RENV, Banco Santander, S.A. v. Comm'n, ECLI:EU:T:2018:787 (Nov. 15, 2018); Case T-219/10 RENV, World Duty Free Group, S.A. v. Comm'n, ECLI:EU:T:2018:784 (Nov. 15, 2018).

146 Case C-53/19 P, Banco Santander, S.A. v. Comm'n, 2019 O.J. (C 112) 32; Case C-51/19 P, World Duty Free Group, S.A. v. Comm'n, 2019 O.J. (C 112) 30.

147 Commission Decision 2011/5/EC, 2011 O.J. (L 7) 48, 50.

148 *Id.* at 54–55.

149 Contreras Delgado de Cos, *supra* note 111, at 356–57.

150 Commission Decision 2011/5/EC, 2011 O.J. at 62, 64.

151 *Id.* at 63.

152 Consolidated Text of the Law on Capital Stock Companies art. 25 (B.O.E. 2010, 1).

153 Commission Regulation (EC) No. 1998/2006, art. 2, 2006 O.J. (L 379) 5, 8; Commission Regulation (EC) No. 69/2001, art. 2, 2001 O.J. (L 10) 30, 31.

154 EC Treaty art. 87(1) (now TFEU art. 107(1)).

155 *Id.* art. 2.

156 *See* María del Carmen Cámara Barroso, *Un nuevo episodio sobre la amortización del fondo de comercio financiero español*, REVISTA DE CONTABILIDAD Y TRIBUTACIÓN, no. 408, 2017, at 139; *¿Punto y final del paso de nuestro régimen de amortización del fondo de comercio financiero por las instancias europeas?*, CENTRO DE ESTUDIOS FINANCIEROS: FISCAL IMPUESTOS (Nov. 15, 2018), www.fiscal-impuestos.com.

157 *See* Case T-207/10, Deutsche Telekom, A.G. v. Comm'n, ECLI:EU:T:2018:786 (Nov. 15 2018); Cases C-20/15 P & C-21/15 P, Comm'n v. World Duty Free Group, S.A., ECLI:EU:C:2016:981 (Dec. 21, 2016).

158 Casadevall, *supra* note 112, at 93; López López, *supra* note 112, at 106.

4. BARTERING WITH TIME

1 Frank Cross et al., *A Positive Political Theory of Rules and Standards*, 2012 U. ILL. L. REV. 1, 16; *see, e.g.*, Louis Kaplow, *Rules Versus Standards: An Economic Analysis*, 42 DUKE L.J. 557 (1992); Russell B. Korobkin, *Behavioral Analysis and Legal Form: Rules vs. Standards Revisited*, 79 OR. L. REV. 23 (2000).

2 Anthony J. Casey & Anthony Niblett, *The Death of Rules and Standards*, 92 IND. L.J. 1401 (2017); Pierre Schlag, *Rules and Standards*, 33 UCLA L. REV. 379 (1985).

3 *E.g.*, Emily Cauble, *Safe Harbors in Tax Law*, 47 CONN. L. REV. 1385 (2015); Philip T. Hackney, *Charitable Organization Oversight: Rules v. Standards*, 13 PITT. TAX REV. 83 (2015); David A. Weisbach, *Formalism in the Tax Law*, 66 U. CHI. L. REV. 860 (1999).

4 *See* Susan C. Morse, *Safe Harbors, Sure Shipwrecks*, 49 U.C. DAVIS L. REV. 1385, 1387 (2016).

5 *E.g.*, Income Tax Act, R.S.C. 1985, c 1 (5th Supp.), §§ 15(2), 15(2.6), 78 (Can.); *see* DAVID G. DUFF ET AL., CANADIAN INCOME TAX LAW 471–77 (6th ed. 2018); DAVID G. DUFF & GEOFFREY LOOMER, TAXATION OF BUSINESS ORGANIZATIONS IN CANADA 742–47 (2015).

6 Council Directive 2011/96, art. 3(2)(b), 2011 O.J. (L 345) 8, 10; *see* Charles M. Harris, Jr., *The European Community's Parent-Subsidiary Directive*, 9 FLA. J. INT'L L. 111, 134–36, 150–51 (1994).

7 CODE GÉNÉRAL DES IMPÔTS [TAX CODE] arts. 119 ter, 145; Direction générale des finances publiques, Bulletin officiel des finances publiques-impôts [BOFiP-Impôts], BOI-RPPM-RCM-30-30-20-10, Régime de droit commun pour les dividendes distribués aux sociétés mères européennes (2019); BOFiP-Impôts, BOI-IS-BASE-10-10-10-20, Conditions relatives aux participations éligibles au régime spécial (2020).

8 Nonresident Income Tax Law arts. 14(1)(h), 31(4)(a) (B.O.E. 2004, 5).

9 I.R.C. §§ 102(a), 1014(a)–(b).

10 *Id.* § 1001(a).

11 Edward J. McCaffery, *Taxing Wealth Seriously*, 70 TAX L. REV. 305, 306 (2017).

12 I.R.C. § 1015(a).

13 Economic Recovery Tax Act of 1981, Pub. L. No. 97-34, § 425, 95 Stat. 172, 318.

14 *Id.* §§ 401, 403.

15 *See* I.R.C. § 2523; BORIS I. BITTKER & LAWRENCE LOKKEN, FEDERAL TAXATION OF INCOME, ESTATES & GIFTS ¶ 40.3, Westlaw (database updated 2021).

16 I.R.C. §§ 102, 2056.

17 *Id.* § 1014(a)–(b).

18 H.R. REP. NO. 97-201, at 188 (1981).

19 I.R.C. § 1014(e)(1).

20 *Id.*; *see id.* § 1015(a).

21 Barbara A. Sloan & T. Randolph Harris, *Estate Planning for the Terminally Ill Client: Even the Blackest Cloud Has a Silver Lining*, 2007 ABATAX-CLE 0511039 (Westlaw).

22 *See supra* note 18 and accompanying text.

23 ANTHONY C. INFANTI, OUR SELFISH TAX LAWS: TOWARD TAX REFORM THAT MIRRORS OUR BETTER SELVES 3–6 (2018).

24 H.R. REP. NO. 97-215, at 256 (1981) (Conf. Rep.).

25 *E.g.*, HOWARD M. ZARITSKY, TAX PLANNING FOR FAMILY WEALTH TRANSFERS: ANALYSIS WITH FORMS ¶ 8.07[5]–[6] Westlaw (database updated 2021); John J. Scroggin, *Income Tax Planning for Clients with Shorter Life Expectancies*, 92 PRAC. TAX STRATEGIES 197, 200–01 (2014); Sloan & Harris, *supra* note 21.

26 Howard M. Zaritsky, *Adapt Gift-Giving Strategies to Fit Special Circumstances*, 62 PRAC. TAX STRATEGIES 348, 356–57 (1999); *see* ZARITSKY, *supra* note 25, ¶ 8.07[5][a].

27 Sloan & Harris, *supra* note 21.

28 Christopher Ingraham, *Wealth Concentration Returning to Levels Unseen Since '20s*, WASH. POST, Feb. 9, 2019, at A17; *see* THOMAS PIKETTY, CAPITAL IN THE TWENTY-FIRST CENTURY 347–50 (2014); EMMANUEL SAEZ & GA-

BRIEL ZUCMAN, THE TRIUMPH OF INJUSTICE: HOW THE RICH DODGE TAXES AND HOW TO MAKE THEM PAY 6–7 (2019); Emmanuel Saez & Gabriel Zucman, *Wealth Inequality in the United States Since 1913: Evidence from Capitalized Income Tax Data*, 131 Q.J. ECON. 519, 551–59 (2016); Eric Levitz, *The One Percent Got $21 Trillion Richer Since 1989. The Bottom 50 Got Poorer*, N.Y. MAG., June 16, 2019; Andrew Van Dam, *Wealth Inequality: A New Look at the Rich-Poor Gulf*, L.A. TIMES, Nov. 26, 2018, at A14.

29 CTR. FOR GLOB. POL'Y SOLS., THE RACIAL WEALTH GAP: ASIAN AMERICANS AND PACIFIC ISLANDERS (2014); SIGNE-MARY MCKERNAN ET AL., URB. INST., LESS THAN EQUAL: RACIAL DISPARITIES IN WEALTH ACCUMULATION (2013); Cedric Herring & Loren Henderson, *Wealth Inequality in Black and White: Cultural and Structural Sources of the Racial Wealth Gap*, 8 RACE & SOC. PROBS. 4, 14–16 (2016); Calvin Schermerhorn, *Why the Racial Wealth Gap Persists, More Than 150 Years After Emancipation*, WASH. POST: MADE BY HIST. (June 19, 2019), www.washingtonpost.com.

30 Beverly I. Moran & William Whitford, *A Black Critique of the Internal Revenue Code*, 1996 WIS. L. REV. 751, 759–72, 779–80.

31 *E.g.*, Carmen Diana Deere & Cheryl R. Doss, *The Gender Asset Gap: What Do We Know and Why Does It Matter?*, 12 FEMINIST ECON. 1 (2006); Erin Ruel & Robert M. Hauser, *Explaining the Gender Wealth Gap*, 50 DEMOGRAPHY 1155 (2013).

32 Nathan McDermott, *The Myth of Gay Affluence*, ATL. (Mar. 21, 2014), www.theatlantic.com; *see, e.g.*, Kerith J. Conron et al., *Sexual Orientation and Sex Difference in Socioeconomic Status: A Population-Based Investigation in the National Longitudinal Study of Adolescent to Adult Health*, 72 J. EPIDEMIOLOGY & CMTY. HEALTH 1016 (2018); Marieka Klawitter, *Meta-Analysis of the Effects of Sexual Orientation on Earnings*, 54 INDUS. REL. 4 (2015).

33 Cauble, *supra* note 3, at 1414 (footnote omitted).

34 NAT'L ACADS. OF SCI., ENG'G, & MED., COMMUNITIES IN ACTION: PATHWAYS TO HEALTH EQUITY 58 (2017); *see id.* at 57–76, 79–85.

35 Saez & Zucman, *supra* note 28, at 571–72; *see* U.S. GOV'T ACCOUNTABILITY OFF., GAO-19-587, RETIREMENT SECURITY: INCOME AND WEALTH DISPARITIES CONTINUE THROUGH OLD AGE 34–41 (2019).

36 I.R.C. § 1001(a), (c).

37 *Id.* § 1031(a). Before 2018, both real and personal property qualified for the benefits of § 1031. Beginning in 2018, only real property can benefit from § 1031's nonrecognition treatment. Tax Cuts and Jobs Act, Pub. L. No. 115-97, § 13303, 131 Stat. 2054, 2123 (2017).

38 I.R.C. § 1031(d).

39 BITTKER & LOKKEN, *supra* note 15, ¶ 44.2.1; Kelly E. Alton et al., *Related-Party Like-Kind Exchanges*, 115 TAX NOTES 467, 468 (2007).

40 BITTKER & LOKKEN, *supra* note 15, ¶ 44.2.8.

41 N. Cent. Rental & Leasing, LLC v. United States, 779 F.3d 738, 741 (8th Cir. 2015).

42 *See* Alton et al., *supra* note 39, at 469–70.

43 Terence Floyd Cuff, Teruya Brothers *and Related-Party Exchanges—How Much More Do We Know Now?*, 102 J. TAX'N 220, 220 (2005).

44 H.R. REP. NO. 101-247, at 1340 (1989); *see* Omnibus Budget Reconciliation Act of 1989, Pub. L. No. 101-239, § 7601, 103 Stat. 2106, 2370.

45 I.R.C. § 1031(f)(1).

46 *Id.*

47 *Id.* § 1031(f)(2)(A)–(B).

48 *Id.* § 1031(f)(2)(C).

49 *Id.* § 1031(f)(4).

50 *Id.* § 1031(g).

51 I.R.S. Field Serv. Adv. 2001-37-003 (May 10, 2001); *see* Alton et al., *supra* note 39, at 474.

52 Field Serv. Adv. 2001-37-003, *supra* note 51.

53 *Id.*

54 Alton et al., *supra* note 39, at 493; *see* Kelly E. Alton et al., *Related Party Like-Kind Exchanges:* Teruya Brothers *and Beyond*, 111 J. TAX'N 324, 330–32 (2009); Terence Floyd Cuff, *How Marital Status Affects (and Does Not Affect) Like-Kind Exchanges*, 31 REAL EST. TAX'N 4, 16–17 (2003); Cuff, *supra* note 43, at 228.

55 *E.g., Deferral Under Section 1031 Allowed Where Related-Party Transaction Not Designed for Tax Avoidance*, 107 J. TAX'N 246 (2007); Richard M. Lipton, *Favorable IRS Rulings on Related-Party Exchanges Implicitly Clarify Some Issues*, 106 J. TAX'N 265 (2007).

56 Terence Floyd Cuff, *Some Observations on Related Party Exchanges Under Section 1031(f): Part 1*, 9 BUS. ENTITIES, no. 4, 2007, at 16, 23.

57 Alton et al., *supra* note 54, at 330; Cuff, *supra* note 43, at 221.

58 Alton et al., *supra* note 39, at 493; *see* William P. Wasserman, *Mr. Mogul's Perpetual Search for Tax Deferral: Techniques and Questions in Section 1031 Like-Kind Exchanges in a World of Changing Tax Alternatives*, C551 ALI-ABA 851, 956 (1990) (Westlaw).

59 *See supra* note 52 and accompanying text.

60 *E.g.*, I.R.S. Priv. Ltr. Rul. 95-17-005 (Jan. 18, 1995); *see* Louis S. Weller, *Hot Issues in Like-Kind Exchanges*, SE30 ALI-ABA 761, 779, 792 (1999) (Westlaw).

61 Weller, *supra* note 60, at 794.

62 *See* Dionissi Aliprantis & Daniel Carroll, *What Is Behind the Persistence of the Racial Wealth Gap?*, ECON. COMMENT., Feb. 2019, at 1, 3 tbls.1 & 2; Su Hyun Shin & Sherman D. Hanna, *Decomposition Analyses of Racial/Ethnic Differences in High Return Investment Ownership After the Great Recession*, 26 J. FIN. COUNSELING & PLAN. 43, 45 tbl.1, 52, 53 tbls.4 & 5 (2015); Edward N. Wolff, *Deconstructing Household Wealth Trends in the United States, 1983–2013*, at 11–12, 43 tbl.3 (Nat'l Bureau of Econ. Rsch., Working Paper No. 22704, 2016).

63 *See* Cuff, *supra* note 43, at 221.

64 Alton et al., *supra* note 54, at 329.

65 Colleen Gibson, *Quiz: Are You Patience or Fortitude?*, N.Y. PUB. LIBR. (Aug. 10, 2018), https://nypl.org.

66 BITTKER & LOKKEN, *supra* note 15, ¶ 90.4.1; Todd Reinstein & Howard S. Goldberg, *Dividends—Cash and Property*, 764-4th TAX MGMT. PORTFOLIO (BNA) § VI(A) (2020).

67 Reinstein & Goldberg, *supra* note 66.

68 I.R.C. § 243.

69 STAFF OF JOINT COMM. ON TAX'N, JCS-1-18, GENERAL EXPLANATION OF PUBLIC LAW 115-97, at 103 n.398 (2018) (Comm. Print).

70 S. REP. NO. 85-1983, at 28 (1958).

71 *Id.*

72 *Id.* at 29.

73 *Id.*

74 H.R. REP. NO. 85-775, at 14 (1957); *see* S. REP. NO. 85-1983, at 29.

75 Technical Amendments Act of 1958, Pub. L. No. 85-866, § 18(a), 72 Stat. 1606, 1614.

76 *Id.*

77 *Id.*

78 *See* Treas. Reg. § 1.246-3(d)–(e) (1960).

79 TAX SECTION, N.Y. STATE BAR ASS'N, REPORT ON REGULATIONS TO BE ISSUED UNDER SECTION 246(C) RESTRICTING THE DIVIDENDS RECEIVED DEDUCTION (1993), Tax Analysts Doc. No. 93-2693; *see* Bradford L. Ferguson et al., *The Latest Stock Hedging Regulations*, 67 TAX NOTES 1795, 1796 (1995).

80 TAX SECTION, *supra* note 79; *see* Lee A. Sheppard, *Dividends Received Deduction Regulations: A Good Start*, 59 TAX NOTES 1447, 1448–50 (1993).

81 Deficit Reduction Act of 1984, Pub. L. No. 98-369, § 53(b)(1), 98 Stat. 494, 567.

82 S. REP. NO. 98-169, at 171–72 (1984); *see* H.R. REP. NO. 98-432, pt. 2, at 1186 (1984).

83 Deficit Reduction Act § 53(b)(3).

84 *Id.* § 53(b)(2).

85 S. REP. NO. 98-169, at 173–74.

86 H.R. REP. NO. 105-148, at 467 (1997).

87 I.R.C. § 246(c)(1)(A), (2).

88 *Id.* § 246(c)(4)(C); Treas. Reg. § 1.246-5(b) (1995); Reinstein & Goldberg, *supra* note 66, § VI(C)(5)(a)–(b).

89 I.R.C. § 246(c)(1)(B).

90 Prop. Treas. Reg. § 1.246-5, 58 Fed. Reg. 30,727 (May 27, 1993).

91 T.D. 8590, 1995-1 C.B. 15.

92 *See* Robert Willens, *Dividend-Stripping Proposed Regulations Broaden the Scope of Risk Diminution*, 79 J. TAX'N 138, 139–40 (1993) [hereinafter Willens, *Proposed Regulations*]; Robert Willens, *New Decision Expands Availability of Dividends*

Received Deduction, 74 J. TAX'N 276, 278–79 (1991) [hereinafter Willens, *New Decision*].

93 *E.g.*, I.R.S. Chief Couns. Adv. 2018-27-011 (Mar. 28, 2018); I.R.S. Nondocketed Serv. Adv. Review (Nov. 10, 2011).

94 Reinstein & Goldberg, *supra* note 66, § VI(C)(4) (emphasis added); *see* Willens, *Proposed Regulations*, *supra* note 92, at 142; Willens, *New Decision*, *supra* note 92, at 276.

95 Treas. Reg. § 1.246-5 (1995); Willens, *New Decision*, *supra* note 92, at 278.

96 Progressive Corp. v. United States, 970 F.2d 188, 189 (6th Cir. 1992).

97 *Id.*

98 *Id.* at 190.

99 Progressive Corp. v. United States, 91-1 U.S. Tax Cas. (CCH) ¶ 50,061, at 87,254 (N.D. Ohio 1990), *rev'd*, *Progressive Corp.*, 970 F.2d 188.

100 *Id.*

101 *Progressive Corp.*, 970 F.2d at 189–90.

102 *Id.* at 189.

103 Plaintiff's Trial Brief at 2, Duke Energy Corp. v. United States, 49 F. Supp. 2d 837 (W.D.N.C. 1999) (No. 3:97-cv-00040-GCM).

104 *Id.* at 2–4.

105 *Duke Energy*, 49 F. Supp. 2d at 837–38, 843.

106 *Id.* at 838–39.

107 David P. Hariton, *When and How Should the Economic Substance Doctrine Be Applied?*, 60 TAX L. REV. 29, 46 (2006); *see* Defendant's Trial Brief at 8–9, *Duke Energy*, 49 F. Supp. 2d 837 (No. 3:97-cv-00040-GCM).

108 *Duke Energy*, 49 F. Supp. 2d at 838.

109 Defendant's Trial Brief, *supra* note 107, at 2.

110 *Duke Energy*, 49 F. Supp. 2d at 839.

111 Plaintiff's Trial Brief, *supra* note 103, at 6.

112 *Id.*

113 *Duke Energy*, 49 F. Supp. 2d at 844.

114 Plaintiff's Trial Brief, *supra* note 103, at 25.

115 Hariton, *supra* note 107, at 46 n.73; *see* Treas. Reg. § 1.246-5(c)(1)(vi) (1995).

116 *Duke Energy*, 49 F. Supp. 2d at 838.

117 Minn. Tea Co. v. Helvering, 302 U.S. 609, 613 (1938).

118 *See* Jonathan D. Grossberg, *Attacking Tax Shelters: Galloping Toward a Better Step Transaction Doctrine*, 78 LA. L. REV. 369, 372–73 (2018); Yoram Keinan, *Rethinking the Role of the Judicial Step Transaction Principle and a Proposal for Codification*, 22 AKRON TAX J. 45, 45–46 (2007).

119 BORIS I. BITTKER & JAMES S. EUSTICE, FEDERAL INCOME TAXATION OF CORPORATIONS AND SHAREHOLDERS ¶ 12.02[5], Westlaw (database updated 2020); *see* Treas. Reg. § 1.368-1(a) (as amended in 2011).

120 I.R.C. § 1001(a), (c); *see* James C. Warner et al., *Corporate Overview*, 750-2nd TAX MGMT. PORTFOLIO (BNA) § VII(A) (2020).

121 Treas. Reg. § 1.1002-1(c) (1960).

122 *See* I.R.C. §§ 354, 356, 358, 361, 362(b).

123 BITTKER & LOKKEN, *supra* note 15, ¶ 94.1.1.

124 *Id.*

125 I.R.C. § 368(a)(1)(A); Treas. Reg. § 1.368-1(e)(2)(v), ex. 1 (as amended in 2011).

126 I.R.C. § 368(a)(1)(C), (2)(B).

127 BITTKER & EUSTICE, *supra* note 119, ¶ 12.02[1].

128 *Id.* ¶ 12.02.

129 Lawrence Zelenak, *The Story of* Seagram: *The Step Transaction Doctrine on the Rocks*, *in* BUSINESS TAX STORIES 261, 267 (Steven A. Bank & Kirk J. Stark eds., 2005).

130 *See* BITTKER & EUSTICE, *supra* note 119, ¶ 12.02[5].

131 Barnet Phillips IV, *Structuring Corporate Acquisitions—Tax Aspects*, 770-4th TAX MGMT. PORTFOLIO (BNA) § I(F) (2020) (footnotes omitted) (first quoting McDonald's Rests. of Ill. v. Comm'r, 688 F.2d 520, 524 (7th Cir. 1982), and then quoting King Enters., Inc. v. United States, 418 F.2d 511, 516 (Ct. Cl. 1969)).

132 Zelenak, *supra* note 129, at 269.

133 Keinan, *supra* note 118, at 74–77. For a European perspective, see Frederik Boulogne, *Tax, Time, and the Merger Directive*, *in* TIME AND TAX: ISSUES IN INTERNATIONAL, EU, AND CONSTITUTIONAL LAW 183 (Werner Haslehner et al. eds., 2019).

134 BITTKER & EUSTICE, *supra* note 119, ¶ 12.02[5].

135 *Id.*

136 *See, e.g.*, Treas. Reg. §§ 1.338(h)(10)-1(c)(2) (as amended in 2007), 1.368-2(k) (as amended in 2015); Rev. Rul. 2008-25, 2008-1 C.B. 986; Rev. Rul. 2001-46, 2001-2 C.B. 321; W. Eugene Seago & Edward J. Schnee, *Post-Reorganization Transactions and the Step Transaction Doctrine*, 128 J. TAX'N 6 (2018).

137 Grossberg, *supra* note 118, at 409; *see id.* at 433–36; Keinan, *supra* note 118, at 62–64.

138 BITTKER & EUSTICE, *supra* note 119, ¶ 12.02[5].

139 I.R.C. § 368(a)(1)(B).

140 Heverly v. Comm'r, 621 F.2d 1227 (3d Cir. 1980); Chapman v. Comm'r, 618 F.2d 856 (1st Cir. 1980); BITTKER & EUSTICE, *supra* note 119, ¶ 12.23[1].

141 *See* BITTKER & EUSTICE, *supra* note 119, ¶ 12.23[2]; H. Kirt Switzer & Gary B. Wilcox, *Corporate Acquisitions—(A), (B), and (C) Reorganizations*, 771-4th TAX MGMT. PORTFOLIO (BNA) § IV(A)(4)(a) (2020).

142 S. REP. NO. 83-1622, at 273 (1954); Treas. Reg. § 1.368-2(c) (as amended in 2015).

143 Treas. Reg. § 1.368-2(c).

144 *Id.*

145 Switzer & Wilcox, *supra* note 141.

146 Phillips, *supra* note 131.

147 399 F.2d 194, 200–01 (Ct. Cl. 1968).

148 Am. Potash & Chem. Corp. v. United States, 402 F.2d 1000 (Ct. Cl. 1968).

149 *See* Joshua D. Blank & Nancy Staudt, *Corporate Shams*, 87 N.Y.U. L. REV. 1641, 1662 (2012).

150 Grossberg, *supra* note 118, at 382.

151 TREASURY INSPECTOR GEN. FOR TAX ADMIN., REFERENCE NO. 2019-30-050, A STRATEGY IS NEEDED TO ASSESS THE COMPLIANCE OF COR-PORATE MERGERS AND ACQUISITIONS WITH FEDERAL TAX REQUIRE-MENTS app. 1, at 16 (2019).

152 *Id.* at 4.

153 *Id.* at 6; *see id.* at 7 fig.2.

154 104 T.C. 75 (1995).

155 Zelenak, *supra* note 129, at 263.

156 *Seagram*, 104 T.C. at 78.

157 *Id.* at 78–79.

158 *Id.* at 79; Zelenak, *supra* note 129, at 264.

159 *Seagram*, 104 T.C. at 79–80.

160 *Id.* at 82–83.

161 *Id.* at 81–86.

162 *Id.* at 87–88.

163 *Id.* at 88; Zelenak, *supra* note 129, at 266.

164 *Seagram*, 104 T.C. at 89.

165 *Id.* at 90.

166 *Id.* at 76, 91.

167 *Id.* at 93.

168 *Id.* at 99; Zelenak, *supra* note 129, at 271.

169 *Seagram*, 104 T.C. at 105.

170 Zelenak, *supra* note 129, at 271 n.43.

171 *Id.*

172 *Id.* at 276–77.

173 *Seagram*, 104 T.C. at 99.

174 Zelenak, *supra* note 129, at 281 & n.87; *see id.* at 271–73, 277–81; Brief of Petitioner-Appellant, J.E. Seagram Corp. v. Comm'r, No. 95-4109 (2d Cir. Aug. 25, 1995).

175 Zelenak, *supra* note 129, at 263.

176 *Id.* at 261.

5. FEARING THE POWER OF TAX TIME

1 *See* Matthew D. Shapiro & Joel Slemrod, *Consumer Response to the Timing of Income: Evidence from a Change in Tax Withholding*, 85 AM. ECON. REV. 274, 274 (1995).

2 LAWRENCE ZELENAK, FIGURING OUT THE TAX: CONGRESS, TREASURY, AND THE DESIGN OF THE EARLY MODERN INCOME TAX 29–63 (2018); Carolyn C. Jones, *Class Tax to Mass Tax: The Role of Propaganda in the Expansion of the Income Tax During World War II*, 37 BUFF. L. REV. 685, 685–86, 688–95, 699 (1988); Ajay K. Mehrotra, *"From Contested Concept to Cornerstone of Admin-*

istrative Practice": Social Learning and the Early History of U.S. Tax Withholding, 7 COLUM. J. TAX L. 144, 146–47 (2016).

3 ZELENAK, *supra* note 2, at 30–37; Mehrotra, *supra* note 2, at 151–62; *see* Ajay K. Mehrotra, *American Economic Development, Managerial Corporate Capitalism, and the Institutional Foundations of the Modern Income Tax*, 73 LAW & CON-TEMP. PROBS. 25, 54–55 (2010).

4 ZELENAK, *supra* note 2, at 46; *see id.* at 37–47; Mehrotra, *supra* note 3, at 55; Mehrotra, *supra* note 2, at 162–66.

5 ZELENAK, *supra* note 2, at 61; *see id.* at 52–63; Jones, *supra* note 2, at 695–97.

6 ZELENAK, *supra* note 2, at 49–52; Mehrotra, *supra* note 2, at 166–67.

7 Anuj C. Desai, *What a History of Tax Withholding Tells Us About the Relationship Between Statutes and Constitutional Law*, 108 NW. U. L. REV. 859, 903 (2014).

8 ZELENAK, *supra* note 2, at 62; Mehrotra, *supra* note 3, at 55–56; Mehrotra, *supra* note 2, at 149–50; *see, e.g.*, Leandra Lederman, *Statutory Speed Bumps: The Roles Third Parties Play in Tax Compliance*, 60 STAN. L. REV. 695, 697–700, 731–32 & n.205 (2007); Joel Slemrod, *Does It Matter Who Writes the Check to the Government? The Economics of Tax Remittance*, 61 NAT'L TAX J. 251, 260–61, 262–67, 272–73 (2008); Kathleen DeLaney Thomas, *The Modern Case for Withholding*, 53 U.C. DAVIS L. REV. 81, 84, 90–91, 93 (2019).

9 Thomas, *supra* note 8, at 128–43.

10 I.R.C. § 3402 (2017).

11 Tax Cuts and Jobs Act, Pub. L. No. 115-97, § 11041(c), 131 Stat. 2054, 2082 (2017).

12 *Id.* § 11041(c)(2)(B), (f)(2).

13 *The 2018 Tax Filing Season and Future IRS Challenges: Hearing Before the S. Comm. on Fin.*, 115th Cong. 12, 15 (2019) (statement of David J. Kautter, Acting Comm'r, Internal Revenue Serv.).

14 I.R.S. News Release IR-2018-05 (Jan. 11, 2018).

15 *Id.*

16 *See* Damon Jones, *Inertia and Overwithholding: Explaining the Prevalence of Income Tax Refunds*, 4 AM. ECON. J.: ECON. POL'Y, no. 1, 2012, at 158, 160, 182, 183; Shapiro & Slemrod, *supra* note 1, at 279; Thomas, *supra* note 8, at 115–24.

17 News Release, *supra* note 14.

18 Brian Faler, *The IRS' Election-Year Quandary: When to Boost Americans' Paychecks*, POLITICO (Jan. 10, 2018), www.politico.com; *see, e.g.*, Cristina Alesci, *Mnuchin Defends IRS Against Democrats' Attacks*, CNN (Jan. 11, 2018), www.cnn.com; William Hoffman, *IRS Issues 2018 Withholding Tables to GOP Praise, Dem Skepticism*, 158 TAX NOTES 295 (2018); Naomi Jagoda, *Treasury and IRS Release New Guidance on Tax Withholding*, HILL (Jan. 11, 2018), www.thehill.com; Richard Rubin, *Tax Overhaul's New Withholding Calculations for Paychecks Are Released*, WALL ST. J. (Jan. 11, 2018), www.wsj.com.

19 Letter from Ron Wyden, Ranking Member, U.S. Senate Comm. on Fin., & Richard E. Neal, Ranking Member, U.S. House Ways & Means Comm., to David Kautter, Acting Comm'r, Internal Revenue Serv. (Jan. 8, 2018).

20 Letter from Ron Wyden, Ranking Member, U.S. Senate Comm. on Fin., & Richard E. Neal, Ranking Member, U.S. House Ways & Means Comm., to Gene L. Dodaro, U.S. Comptroller Gen. (Jan. 8, 2018) (emphasis omitted).

21 I.R.S. News Release IR-2018-36 (Feb. 28, 2018).

22 *E.g.*, Ann Carrns, *With New Law, I.R.S. Urges Taxpayers to Review Withholdings*, N.Y. TIMES, Mar. 31, 2018, at B3; Laura Saunders, *Check Withholding or Risk a Painful Shock*, WALL ST. J., Mar. 3, 2018, at B4.

23 I.R.S. News Release IR-2018-73 (Mar. 26, 2018); *see* U.S. GOV'T ACCOUNT-ABILITY OFF., GAO-18-548, FEDERAL TAX WITHHOLDING: TREASURY AND IRS SHOULD DOCUMENT THE ROLES AND RESPONSIBILITIES FOR UPDATING ANNUAL WITHHOLDING TABLES 16–20 (2018).

24 Erica Werner, *Democrats' Attack Shifts as U.S. Paychecks Grow*, WASH. POST, Feb. 27, 2018, at A1; *see* Dave Min & Stephen B. Miller, *New Federal Tax Legislation Takes Effect*, 60 ORANGE CNTY. LAW. 42, 43 (2018).

25 William Hoffman, *Don't Rely Just on IRS Withholding Calculator, Preparers Say*, 159 TAX NOTES 1668 (2018).

26 *Id.* at 1669.

27 Laura Davison & Kaustuv Basu, *Trouble with Tax Withholding? Taxpayer Advocate Had Same Problem*, BLOOMBERG TAX (Mar. 7, 2019), https://news.bloomberg-tax.com.

28 Hoffman, *supra* note 25, at 1669.

29 U.S. GOV'T ACCOUNTABILITY OFF., *supra* note 23.

30 *Id.* at 13 tbl.1.

31 Marcy Gordon, *This Year's Big Paychecks Could Mean Next Year's Big Tax Bill*, CHI. TRIB., Aug. 2, 2018, § 2, at 1.

32 U.S. GOV'T ACCOUNTABILITY OFF., *supra* note 23, at 20; *see id.* at 19–20.

33 Press Release, U.S. Senate Fin. Comm. Ranking Member Ron Wyden, Wyden Statement on GAO Report, Estimate That 30 Million Taxpayers Will Be Underwithheld Next Year (July 31, 2018).

34 Marcy Gordon, *Auditors: 30M Taxpayers Will Owe More Due to Low Withholding*, ASSOCIATED PRESS, July 31, 2018, www.apnews.com; *see* Gordon, *supra* note 31; Marcy Gordon, *Auditors Say Many Will Owe More Taxes*, REC.-J. (Meriden, Conn.), Aug. 1, 2018, at A4; Marcy Gordon, *Report: 30 Millions Will Owe More Taxes Due to Changes*, TEL. HERALD (Dubuque, Iowa), Aug. 2, 2018, at A14.

35 INFO. REPORTING PROGRAM ADVISORY COMM., INTERNAL REVENUE SERV., 2018 GENERAL REPORT, at 25 (2018) [hereinafter IRPAC]; *see also* Darla Mercado, *Why These Taxpayers May Owe the IRS in 2019*, CNBC (Nov. 8, 2018), www.cnbc.com; Kathleen Pender, *Your 2018 Tax Cut Has Kicked In, but Pay Attention to Withholding*, S.F. CHRON., Nov. 15, 2018, at A1.

36 IRPAC, *supra* note 35, at 25; *see id.* at 9, 24–25.

37 Patricia Sabatini, *An Unkind Tax Surprise?*, PITT. POST-GAZETTE, Nov. 4, 2018, at F1.

38 Press Release, H&R Block, Only 46 Percent Feel Prepared to Update Their With-holding on Their Own (Dec. 20, 2018).

39 William Hoffman, *Millions at Risk for Underwithholding in 2018 Filing Season*, 161 TAX NOTES 1383, 1383 (2018).

40 *Children Could Determine Tax Bill*, L.A. TIMES, Mar. 11, 2018, at C2; Naomi Ja-goda, *One Year in, Trump's Tax Law Faces Test with Filing Season*, HILL (Dec. 22, 2018), www.thehill.com; Sabatini, *supra* note 37; Jim Spencer, *Accountants Warn Tax Reform Could Add Up to April Shock*, MINN. STAR TRIB. (Sept. 1, 2018), www.startribune.com; Jeff Stein, *IRS Online Calculator Can Check if Employer Do-ing Taxes Correctly*, CHI. TRIB., Mar. 4, 2018, § 2, at 4; *Taxpayers May Owe More Due to Low Withholding*, HERALD-DISPATCH (Huntington, W. Va.) (Aug. 1, 2018), www.herald-dispatch.com; Martha C. White, *Bills Too High, Paychecks Too Small*, MIAMI TIMES, Mar. 21, 2018, at 8B.

41 Editorial, *The Tax Cut That Wasn't: Why Americans May Owe the IRS*, BANGOR DAILY NEWS (Nov. 18, 2018), www.bangordailynews.com; Jerry Freda, Letter to the Editor, *Problem Lurking for Next Year in New Tax Law*, CHI. DAILY HER-ALD, Feb. 13, 2018, at 10; Mike Kistner, Letter to the Editor, *A Sugar High Comes with a Price*, WAYNE TODAY (Passaic, N.J.), Feb. 15, 2018, at A11; Alex Raskol-nikov, *The Tax Windfall That Wasn't*, N.Y. DAILY NEWS (Nov. 1, 2018), www.nydailynews.com.

42 I.R.S. Notice 2019-11, 2019-5 I.R.B. 430.

43 Laura Davison, *Senate Democrat Asks IRS to Waive Fines for Tax Filing Mishaps*, BLOOMBERG TAX (Jan. 3, 2019), https://news.bloombergtax.com; William Hoffman, *Underwithheld Taxpayers Get IRS Penalty Relief*, 162 TAX NOTES 328, 328–29 (2019); Allyson Versprille & Laura Davison, *IRS Won't Penalize Confused Taxpayers Following Changes to Code*, BLOOMBERG TAX (Jan. 16, 2019), https://news.bloombergtax.com.

44 Notice 2019-11, *supra* note 42; I.R.C. § 6654(e)(3)(A).

45 Notice 2019-11, *supra* note 42.

46 *Id.*

47 William Hoffman, *Don't Blame Smaller Refunds on Withholding Tables, Says Trea-sury*, 162 TAX NOTES 822, 822 (2019).

48 *Filing Season Statistics for Week Ending May 10, 2019*, INTERNAL REVENUE SERV., www.irs.gov (last updated Nov. 24, 2020).

49 Brett Ferguson, *2019 Filing Season Featured More Returns but Fewer Refunds*, 163 TAX NOTES 639 (2019); *see* Lynnley Browning, *Average Tax Refund Down 2% in Filings Under New U.S. Tax Law*, BLOOMBERG TAX (Apr. 24, 2019), https://news.bloombergtax.com.

50 *Compare Filing Season Statistics for Week Ending December 27, 2019*, INTERNAL REVENUE SERV., www.irs.gov (last updated Jan. 16, 2020), *with Filing Season Statistics*, INTERNAL REVENUE SERV., www.irs.gov (last updated Aug. 20, 2020) [hereinafter *FSS*] (2019 late-May filing season statistics by AGI).

51 *FSS, supra* note 50 (compared 2018 and 2019 late-May filing season statistics by AGI).

52 *Id.*

53 *Id.*

54 *Id.*

55 *Id.*

56 *Id.*

57 *Id.*

58 TREASURY INSPECTOR GEN. FOR TAX ADMIN., NO. 2020-44-007, RE-SULTS OF THE 2019 FILING SEASON, at 6–7 (2020).

59 *FSS, supra* note 50 (compared 2018 and 2019 late-May filing season statistics by AGI).

60 *Id.*

61 *See* Kay Bell, *Do You Want a Big Tax Refund or Bigger Paycheck?*, BANKRATE (Mar. 12, 2015), www.bankrate.com (Bankrate Money Pulse Poll).

62 Thomas, *supra* note 8, at 115–24; Michael Gelman et al., *Rational Illiquidity and Consumption: Theory and Evidence from Income Tax Withholding and Refunds* 3–4 (Nat'l Bureau of Econ. Rsch., Working Paper No. 25757, 2019).

63 John Tozzi, *Americans Are Delaying Health Care Until Tax Refunds Arrive*, BLOOMBERG TAX (Apr. 12, 2019); https://news.bloombergtax.com; *see infra* note 67 and accompanying text.

64 Brian Faler, *"Extraordinarily Angry and Very Upset Taxpayers": IRS Faces Chaotic Tax Season amid Shutdown*, POLITICO (Jan. 24, 2019), www.politico.com; Damian Paletta, *Trump Administration Opts for Speed over Accuracy in Implementing New Tax Law*, WASH. POST (Jan. 10, 2018), www.washingtonpost.com.

65 Eric Zorn, *Many Happy Returns: A Blue Wave Swamped Trump After All*, CHI. TRIB., Nov. 28, 2018, at 17; *see* Max Boot, *Now We Know the Full Magnitude of Trump's Defeat. Republicans Should Take Notice.*, WASH. POST: POST PARTI-SAN (Nov. 20, 2018), www.washingtonpost.com.

66 Jim Tankersley & Matt Phillips, *In Season of Upheaval, Tax Forecast Is Guesswork*, N.Y. TIMES, Jan. 28, 2019, at B1.

67 *See* DIANA FARRELL ET AL., JPMORGAN CHASE & CO. INST., FILING TAXES EARLY, GETTING HEALTHCARE LATE 4 (2018); DIANA FARRELL ET AL., JPMORGAN CHASE & CO. INST., TAX TIME: HOW FAMILIES MAN-AGE TAX REFUNDS AND PAYMENTS 2, 8, 11, 19–23 (2019).

68 *See* Howard Gleckman, *It's About Your Total Tax Liability, Not Your Refund*, TAX POL'Y CTR.: TAX VOX (Feb. 12, 2019), www.taxpolicycenter.org; Kathleen Del-aney Thomas, Opinion, *Misplaced Outrage over Tax Refunds Was Predictable and Preventable*, HILL (Mar. 5, 2019), www.thehill.com.

69 *Filing Season Statistics for Week Ending February 1, 2019*, INTERNAL REVENUE SERV., www.irs.gov (last updated Oct. 21, 2020).

70 *Filing Season Statistics for Week Ending February 8, 2019*, INTERNAL REVENUE SERV., www.irs.gov (last updated Nov. 24, 2020).

71 *See* Laura Davison, *Shrinking Tax Refunds Cast a Shadow on Trump's Signature Law*, BLOOMBERG TAX (Mar. 15, 2019), https://news.bloombergtax.com.

72 *Americans Shocked by Impact of New Tax Law: "My Jaw Hit the Floor,"* CBS NEWS (Feb. 19, 2019), www.cbsnews.com [hereinafter *Americans Shocked*]; Graham Brink, *The Many Tax Law Changes, Including to Withholding, Create Bottom-Line Surprises*, TAMPA BAY TIMES, Feb. 12, 2019, at A1; Daniella Cheslow, *Anger, Confusion over Dwindling Refunds. Is Trump's Tax Plan to Blame?*, NPR (Feb. 14, 2019), www.npr.org; Lee Davidson, *Tax Refunds Are Smaller for Utahns, Particularly for Large Families. One Accountant Says Half His Clients Have Been Disappointed.*, SALT LAKE TRIB. (Feb. 22, 2019), www.sltrib.com; Michael Finch II, *IRS Says Tax Filings, Refunds Down. Some Are Calling It a Scam*, SACRAMENTO BEE (Feb. 15, 2019), www.sacbee.com; Heather Long, *Millions of Americans Could Be Stunned as Their Tax Refunds Shrink*, WASH. POST (Feb. 10, 2019), www.washingtonpost.com; Darla Mercado, *If You Failed to Withhold Enough Tax in 2018, the IRS Has a Nasty Surprise for You*, CNBC (Feb. 7, 2019), www.cnbc.com; Alyssa Newcomb, *Under New Trump Tax Code, Average Refund Is 8.4 Percent Smaller*, NBC NEWS (Feb. 11, 2019), www.nbcnews.com; Donica Phifer, *MSNBC Panelist Says It's "Wonderful to Watch These Trump Voters Learn" as Some Americans Complain About Smaller Tax Refunds*, NEWSWEEK (Feb. 10, 2019), www.newsweek.com.

73 Tara Siegel Bernard, *Craving Relief, Early Tax Filers Are Frustrated*, N.Y. TIMES, Feb. 13, 2019, at A1.

74 Kristin Myers, *Trump's "Tax Scam": Some Taxpayers Get Unwelcome Surprise After Filing Returns*, YAHOO! FINANCE (Feb. 11, 2019), www.finance.yahoo.com; *see also* Bruce Leshan, *Tax Refunds Shrink, Twitter Explodes*, WUSA9 (Feb. 11, 2019), www.wusa9.com; Stephanie Sigafoos, *As Tax Refunds Shrink, #GOPTaxScam Blows Up Twitter*, MORNING CALL (Allentown, Pa.) (Feb. 11, 2019), www.mcall.com.

75 *Historical Twitter Trends (Beta)*, TRENDSMAP, www.trendsmap.com (last visited Mar. 10, 2020).

76 *#GOPTaxScam Promises vs. Reality: Tax Refund Edition*, NANCY PELOSI: SPEAKER OF THE HOUSE: BLOG (Feb. 11, 2019), www.speaker.gov.

77 Aaron Lorenzo, *As Tax Refunds Shrink, Republicans Scramble to Defend Trump Tax Cut*, POLITICO (Feb. 23, 2019), www.politico.com.

78 Letter from Annette Nellen, Chair, AICPA Tax Exec. Comm., to Steven T. Mnuchin, Sec'y, Dep't of Treasury, and Charles P. Rettig, Comm'r, Internal Revenue Serv. (Jan. 28, 2019).

79 Letter from Forty U.S. Sens. to Steven T. Mnuchin, Sec'y, Dep't of Treasury, and Charles P. Rettig, Comm'r, Internal Revenue Serv. (Feb. 15, 2019); *see* Jad Chamseddine, *Democrats Seek Penalty Relief for Underwithheld Taxpayers*, 162 TAX NOTES 942 (2019); Laura Davison & Kaustuv Basu, *Senate Democrats Ask IRS to Reduce Penalties for Confused Filers*, BLOOMBERG TAX (Feb. 15, 2019), https://news.bloombergtax.com.

80 I.R.S. Notice 2019-25, 2019-15 I.R.B. 942; Laura Davison, *Treasury Cuts Penalties for Taxpayers Confused About Withholding*, BLOOMBERG TAX (Mar. 22, 2019), https://news.bloombergtax.com; Asha Glover, *More Underwithheld Taxpayers to Get Penalty Relief*, 163 TAX NOTES 119 (2019).

81 Kelly Phillips Erb, *IRS Announces Automatic Penalty Waivers for 2018, Will Issue Refunds to Affected Taxpayers*, FORBES (Aug. 14, 2019), www.forbes.com; William Hoffman, *Penalty Waiver Highlights IRS Withholding Efforts*, 164 TAX NOTES FED. 1308 (2019).

82 I.R.S. News Release IR-2019-144 (Aug. 14, 2019).

83 *See supra* note 17 and accompanying text.

84 *See* Jad Chamseddine, *Treasury Rejects More Relief Because of TCJA Withholding Changes*, 162 TAX NOTES 1060 (2019); William Hoffman, *No Evidence That Withholding Tables Were "Goosed," Olson Says*, 162 TAX NOTES 1227 (2019).

85 *E.g., Americans Shocked, supra* note 72; Long, *supra* note 72.

86 *E.g.,* Long, *supra* note 72.

87 PROJET DE LOI DE FINANCES POUR 2017: PRÉLÈVEMENT À LA SOURCE DE L'IMPÔT SUR LE REVENU: ÉVALUATION PRÉALABLE DE L'ARTICLE 38, at 36 (2016) [hereinafter PROJET DE LOI]; 3 RAPPORT FAIT AU NOM DE LA COMMISSION DES FINANCES, DE L'ÉCONOMIE GÉNÉRALE ET DU CONTRÔLE BUDGÉTAIRE SUR LE PROJET DE LOI DE FINANCES POUR 2017, NO. 4125, Assemblée Nationale, 14ème Législature, at 21–22 (2016) [hereinafter RAPPORT 4125]; JEAN-LUC MONDON, LES MINI MÉMOS FOUCHER: LE PRÉLÈVEMENT À LA SOURCE § 1.1 (2019).

88 RAPPORT 4125, *supra* note 87, at 20.

89 Loi 90-1168 du 29 décembre 1990 de finances pour 1991 [Law 90-1168 of December 29, 1990 on the Budget for 1991], arts. 127–134, JOURNAL OFFICIEL DE LA RÉPUBLIQUE FRANÇAISE [J.O.] [OFFICIAL GAZETTE OF FRANCE], Dec. 30, 1990, pp. 16367, 16387–90; Ordonnance 96-50 du 24 janvier 1996 relative au remboursement de la dette sociale [Order 96-50 of January 24, 1996 regarding reimbursement of the social debt], J.O., Jan. 25, 1996, pp. 1226–29; *see* CODE GÉNÉRAL DES IMPÔTS [TAX CODE] arts. 1600-0G to -0J; CODE DE LA SÉCURITÉ SOCIALE [SOCIAL SECURITY CODE] arts. L136-1 to -8; MARTIN COLLET, DROIT FISCAL 283–85 (7th ed. 2019).

90 PROJET DE LOI, *supra* note 87, at 15–19, 41; RAPPORT 4125, *supra* note 87, at 19; *see infra* note 107 and accompanying text.

91 PROJET DE LOI, *supra* note 87, at 19–24.

92 *Id.* at 336–37.

93 *Id.* at 24; Loi 2016-1917 du 29 décembre 2016 de finances pour 2017 [Law 2016-1917 of December 29, 2016 on the Budget for 2017], art. 60, J.O., Dec. 30, 2016.

94 Ordonnance 2017-1390 du 22 septembre 2017 relative au décalage d'un an de l'entrée en vigueur du prélèvement à la source de l'impôt sur le revenu [Order 2017-1390 of September 22, 2017 on the One-Year Delay in the Entry into Force

of Withholding at Source of the Income Tax], art. 1(1°), J.O., Sept. 23, 2017; Ingrid Feuerstein, *Une ordonnance sur le prélèvement à la source*, LES ÉCHOS, June 22, 2017, at 5.

95 RAPPORT FAIT AU NOM DE LA COMMISSION DES AFFAIRES SOCIALES SUR LE PROJET DE LOI D'HABILITATION À PRENDRE PAR ORDONNANCES LES MESURES POUR LE RENFORCEMENT DU DIALOGUE SOCIAL, NO. 19, Assemblée Nationale, 15ème Législature, at 291 (2017).

96 DIRECTION GÉNÉRALE DES FINANCES PUBLIQUES, DOSSIER DE PRESSE: PRÉLÈVEMENT À LA SOURCE: FICHES PRATIQUES POUR 2019, at 1–2 (2019); Aurélie Lebelle & Matthieu Pelloli, *Prélèvement à la source: La note qui affole le gouvernement*, LE PARISIEN (Sept. 2, 2018), www.leparisien.fr.

97 Ingrid Feuerstein, *Prélèvement à la source: Récit d'une première année sans heurts*, LES ÉCHOS, Dec. 30, 2019, at 2; Guillaume Guichard, *L'histoire d'une réforme mouvementée . . . qui finit bien*, LE FIGARO, Jan. 4, 2020, at 16.

98 *E.g.*, Pauline Chateau, *Prélèvement de l'impôt à la source: "Nous sommes bien loin de la simplicité avancée,"* L'EXPRESS (June 18, 2015), https://lexpansion.lexpress. fr; *Le gouvernement lance la réforme du prélèvement à la source de l'impôt sur le revenu, mais de très nombreuses questions restent à trancher*, BULLETIN QUOTI- DIEN, June 18, 2015, at 8; Cyrille Pluyette, *Le principal syndicat des impôts fustige le prélèvement à la source*, LE FIGARO (June 2, 2015), www.lefigaro.fr; Marianne Rey, *Pourquoi le prélèvement à la source risque de complexifier encore la paie*, L'EXPRESS (June 18, 2015), https://lentreprise.lexpress.fr; Patrick Roger, *Le casse-tête du prélèvement à la source*, LE MONDE, June 17, 2015, at 10; Frédéric Schaef-fer, *Impôts: Les questions que pose le prélèvement à la source*, LES ÉCHOS (June 17, 2015), www.lesechos.fr.

99 *E.g.*, Laurence Allard, *Prélèvement à la source: L'État gagnant mais le citoyen per-dant*, LE POINT (June 18, 2015), www.lepoint.fr; Serge Berini, Letter to the Editor, L'EST RÉPUBLICAIN, Jan. 12, 2015, at 34; Frédéric Douet, Opinion, *Impôt sur le revenu: "Le serpent de mer du prélèvement à la source refait surface,"* LE MONDE (May 22, 2015), www.lemonde.fr; *Impôt sur le revenu. Vers un prélèvement à la source?*, LE TÉLÉGRAMME (May 21, 2015), www.letelegramme.fr; Sophie de Menthon, *François Hollande et les impôts: Une grande histoire d'amour*, ÉCONO-MIE MATIN (Jan. 12, 2015), www.economiematin.fr; Caroline Monnot & Thomas Wieder, *Prélèvement à la source: Terra Nova décrète l'urgence*, LE MONDE, May 23, 2015, at 9; Cyrille Pluyette, *Un projet toujours repoussé*, LE FIGARO, May 26, 2015, at 4; Marc Vignaud, *Impôt: Le prélèvement à la source, une vraie fausse propo-sition*, LE POINT (May 21, 2015), www.lepoint.fr.

100 *E.g.*, PROJET DE LOI, *supra* note 87, at 288; Francis Brochet, *Impôt: Prélevé à la source?*, L'EST RÉPUBLICAIN, May 21, 2015, at 36; Ingrid Feuerstein, *Le chantier du prélèvement à la source entre dans une phase cruciale*, LES ÉCHOS, Dec. 30, 2015, at 5; Elsa Grenouillet, *Impôt sur le revenu: Ce que change le prélèvement à la source*, LA VOIX DU NORD, May 29, 2015, at 38.

101 Marc Le Fur, *Retenue à la source: Une révolution funeste*, VALEURS ACTUELLES, June 18, 2015, at 88; Cyrille Pluyette, *Le secret des données, problème numéro 1*, LE FIGARO, June 12, 2015, at 18.

102 *E.g.*, Pluyette, *supra* note 101; *Prélèvement à la source: Le pour et le contre*, AGENCE FRANCE PRESSE, June 8, 2015, Nexis Uni.

103 Claire Bauchart, *Prélèvement à la source: Plus de la moitié des patrons de PME inquiets*, LES ÉCHOS, May 4, 2016, at 5; *Jugé "complexe" et "contraignant," le prélèvement à la source inquiète les patrons*, AGENCE FRANCE PRESSE, May 3, 2016, Nexis Uni; Fabien Piliu, *Le prélèvement à la source, un casse-tête pour les entreprises?*, LA TRIBUNE, July 28, 2016, at 27; Catherine Quignon, *Le prélèvement à la source inquiète les DRH*, LE MONDE (Dec. 5, 2016), www.lemonde.fr.

104 CODE GÉNÉRAL DES IMPÔTS [CGI] [TAX CODE] arts. 204A–B, 1671(1); Direction générale des finances publiques, Bulletin officiel des finances publiques-impôts [BOFiP-Impôts], BOI-IR-PAS-10-10-10, Revenus soumis à la retenue à la source (2018); BOFiP-Impôts, BOI-IR-PAS-30-10-10, Personne tenue d'effectuer la retenue à la source ou "collecteur" § 20 (2018); LE PRÉLÈVEMENT À LA SOURCE 11–13, 89–91 (Béatrice Hingand ed., 2018) [hereinafter LEFEBVRE].

105 CGI arts. 204C, 1663C; BOFiP-Impôts, BOI-IR-PAS-10-10-20, Revenus soumis à l'acompte (2018); BOFiP-Impôts, BOI-IR-PAS-30-20-10, Modalités de versement et de paiement de l'acompte (2019); LEFEBVRE, *supra* note 104, at 14–16, 107–12.

106 *See* LEFEBVRE, *supra* note 104, at 22.

107 PROJET DE LOI, *supra* note 87, at 73–80; *see* Nathalie Cheysson-Kaplan, *Prélèvement à la source: Ce qu'il faut savoir en 7 questions*, LES ÉCHOS (May 18, 2018), www.lesechos.fr.

108 LEFEBVRE, *supra* note 104, at 35–39, 89–90, 95–97.

109 CGI art. 204H(I); BOFiP-Impôts, BOI-IR-PAS-20-20-10, Taux déterminé pour le foyer fiscal ("taux de droit commun") § 80 (2021); LEFEBVRE, *supra* note 104, at 39.

110 *See supra* note 109.

111 CGI art. 204H(III); BOFiP-Impôts, BOI-IR-PAS-20-20-30-10, Taux par défaut— Situations et modalités d'application (2020); LEFEBVRE, *supra* note 104, at 46–58.

112 CGI arts. 204F–G; BOFiP-Impôts, BOI-IR-PAS-20-10-10, Assiette de la retenue à la source (2020); BOFiP-Impôts, BOI-IR-PAS-20-10-20-10, Assiette de l'acompte—Dispositions communes (2018).

113 CGI art. 204I; BOFiP-Impôts, BOI-IR-PAS-20-30-10, Actualisation du prélèvement—Changements de situation (2020); LEFEBVRE, *supra* note 104, at 63–72; Thierry Lamulle, *Prélèvement à la source et modification de la situation familiale*, AJ FAMILLE, Apr. 2019, at 187.

114 CGI art. 204J.

115 *Id.* art. 1729G(2)–(3); LEFEBVRE, *supra* note 104, at 81–82.

116 *See* Mathieu Castagnet, *Le prélèvement à la source bute sur la confidentialité*, LA CROIX (July 26, 2016), www.la-croix.com; Pauline Chateau, *Protection de données: Bercy ajuste le prélèvement à la source*, LE FIGARO (July 25, 2016), www.lefigaro.fr.

117 CGI art. 204H(IV)(1); BOFiP-Impôts, BOI-IR-PAS-20-20-30-20, Option pour le taux par défaut §§ 10–70 (2020); LEFEBVRE, *supra* note 104, at 59–60, 97.

118 CGI art. 204H(IV)(2); BOI-IR-PAS-20-20-30-20, *supra* note 117, §§ 80–210; LEFEBVRE, *supra* note 104, at 60–62.

119 CGI art. 6(1), (4), (5).

120 *Id.* arts. 204E, 204M; BOFiP-Impôts, BOI-IR-PAS-20-20-20, Taux individualisé (2020); LEFEBVRE, *supra* note 104, at 41–46.

121 Menthon, *supra* note 99; *"Prélèvement à la source: Ce que les socialistes ne disent pas,"* LA DÉPÊCHE DU MIDI, June 23, 2015, at 29 [hereinafter *PAS*].

122 *See* Chloé Bossard, *Pas si simple à mettre en place,* LA NOUVELLE RÉPUBLIQUE DU CENTRE OUEST, May 25, 2015, at IG-19; Philippe Crevel, *Prélèvement de l'impôt à la source: Le miroir aux alouettes,* FIGAROVOX: VOX ÉCONOMIE (June 17, 2015), www.lefigaro.fr; Grenouillet, *supra* note 100.

123 *E.g.,* Justine Simon Degouey, *"Payer deux années d'impôts pendant la transition vers le prélèvement à la source? Non merci!,"* FIGAROVOX: VOX ÉCONOMIE (May 26, 2015), www.lefigaro.fr; Benoît Georges, Opinion, *Prélèvement à la source: une fausse bonne idée,* LES ÉCHOS, Aug. 20, 2015, at 6; Menthon, *supra* note 99; Jean-Pierre Thelliez, Letter to the Editor, L'EST RÉPUBLICAIN, Jan. 12, 2015, at 34.

124 Frédéric Douet, Opinion, *Faire du prélèvement à la source un outil de relance,* LES ÉCHOS, Aug. 13, 2015, at 6.

125 Jérôme Barré, *Impôt à la source: Une mesure compliquée à instaurer,* ÉCONOMIE MATIN (June 9, 2015), www.economiematin.fr; *Le casse-tête de l'année de transition,* SUD OUEST, June 11, 2015, at 3 [hereinafter *Casse-tête*]; Clotilde Mathieu, *Les dessous du prélèvement à la source de l'impôt sur le revenu,* L'HUMANITÉ (June 16, 2015), www.humanite.fr; Monnot & Wieder, *supra* note 99.

126 *Casse-tête, supra* note 125.

127 Marc de Boni, *Prélèvement à la source et "année blanche": L'opposition dénonce "une combine,"* LE FIGARO (June 17, 2015), www.lefigaro.fr; *see* Allard, *supra* note 99; Mathieu Castagnet, *Impôt, le prélèvement à la source sera mis en œuvre en 2018,* LA CROIX (June 18, 2015), www.la-croix.com; Jean-Francis Pecresse, Editorial, *Une source d'inquiétude,* LES ÉCHOS, June 18, 2015, at 11; *Prélèvement à la source des impôts: Le gouvernement met en place des garde-fous pour éviter une année blanche fiscale,* PARIS-NORMANDIE, Aug. 20, 2016, at 25; Frédéric Schaeffer, *Prélèvement à la source de l'impôt: Le casse-tête de "l'année blanche,"* LES ÉCHOS (June 17, 2015), www.lesechos.fr; Marc Vignaud, *Huit questions sur le prélèvement à la source,* LE POINT (June 18, 2015), www.lepoint.fr.

128 Cyrille Pluyette, *Impôts à la source: Un gros cadeau pour les riches héritiers,* LE FIGARO (June 19, 2015), www.lefigaro.fr; *see* Mathilde Damgé et al., *Prélèvement à la source: "L'année blanche" ne signifie pas qu'on ne paiera pas d'impôt,* LE MONDE (Aug. 31, 2018), www.lemonde.fr.

129 Ingrid Feuerstein, *La droite contre le prélèvement à la source en 2018,* LES ÉCHOS, Apr. 13, 2016, at 4 (quoting Hervé Mariton, LR-Drôme).

130 Loi 2016-1917 du 29 décembre 2016 de finances pour 2017 [Law 2016-1917 of December 29, 2016 on the Budget for 2017], art. 60(II)(A), J.O., Dec. 30, 2016 (consolidated text); BOFiP-Impôts, BOI-IR-PAS-50-10-10, Crédit d'impôt pour la modernisation du recouvrement—Calcul et imputation (2018); LEFEBVRE, *supra* note 104, at 117.

131 *See supra* note 130.

132 Loi 2016-1917, art. 60(II)(C)–(F); BOFiP-Impôts, BOI-IR-PAS-50-10-20, Revenus non exceptionnels ouvrant droit au bénéfice du CIMR (2018); LEFEBVRE, *supra* note 104, at 121–61.

133 MONDON, *supra* note 87, § 3.1; Anne-Aël Durand, *Année blanche, vie privée, taux appliqué: Le vrai et le faux sur le prélèvement à la source*, LE MONDE (Jan. 4, 2019), www.lemonde.fr.

134 DIRECTION GÉNÉRALE DES FINANCES PUBLIQUES, RAPPORT D'ACTIVITÉ: CAHIERS STATISTIQUES 2018, at 53 (2019) [hereinafter RAPPORT D'ACTIVITÉ]; Ingrid Feuerstein, *Impôt sur le revenu: Les 2% de foyers les plus aisés concentrent 40% des recettes*, LES ÉCHOS (Aug. 2, 2017), www.lesechos. fr.

135 *See* Vincent Touzé, Opinion, *Prélever à la source l'impôt sur le revenu: Une réforme compliquée et coûteuse*, LA TRIBUNE (Sept. 16, 2015), www.latribune.fr.

136 *See* Nathalie Cheysson-Kaplan, *Prélèvement à la source: Les dispositifs anti-abus*, LES ÉCHOS (May 17, 2018), www.lesechos.fr; Ingrid Feuerstein, *Impôts sur le revenu: Ce qui change dès 2018 avec le prélèvement à la source*, LES ÉCHOS, Jan. 8, 2018, at 4.

137 Pierre Chaillan, *Faut-il mettre en place un prélèvement de l'impôt à la source?*, L'HUMANITÉ (June 12, 2015), www.humanite.fr; Romain David & Solenn de Royer, *Au PS, l'impôt à la source relance le débat sur la fiscalité*, LE FIGARO, May 26, 2015, at 4.

138 Le Fur, *supra* note 101.

139 Berini, *supra* note 99; Albert Bonnefant, Letter to the Editor, *La supercherie de l'impôt à la source*, VALEURS ACTUELLES, June 25, 2015, at 92; Sébastien Crépel, *Le retour du bouclier fiscal des très riches*, L'HUMANITÉ (Aug. 11, 2015), www.humanite.fr; Paul-Henri du Limbert, Editorial, *À la source du mal*, LE FIGARO (June 11, 2015), www.lefigaro.fr; Yves de Kerdrel, Opinion, *Contre le prélèvement à la source*, LE FIGARO, Sept. 14, 2016, at 17; *PAS*, *supra* note 121; Pluyette, *supra* note 99; Frédéric Schaeffer, *Nathalie Kosciusko-Morizet: "Il faudra baisser les impôts de 100 milliards d'euros dès 2017,"* LES ÉCHOS (May 26, 2015), www.lesechos.fr.

140 Le Fur, *supra* note 101; Charles Sannat, *SCANDALE, le prélèvement à la source? Déstructurer la famille et augmenter les impôts!*, ÉCONOMIE MATIN (Oct. 22, 2015), www.economiematin.fr; *PAS*, *supra* note 121; *cf.* Lise Chatain, *Le PAS: Une affaire de famille*, AJ FAMILLE, Nov. 2018, at 598; Christiane Marty & Olga Trostiansky, Opinion, *Prélèvement à la source: Une réforme contre les femmes?*, LA TRIBUNE, Oct. 17, 2015, at 98.

141 *E.g.*, Crevel, *supra* note 122; Roland Hureaux, *Impôt: La folie du prélèvement à la source*, LE FIGARO, Sept. 2, 2016, at 16; Roger, *supra* note 98; Pascal Salin, Opinion, *Le prélèvement à la source, une réforme dangereuse*, FIGAROVOX: VOX ÉCONOMIE (Apr. 5, 2016), www.lefigaro.fr.

142 *Impôts sur le revenu: Plus de 60% des Français favorables au prélèvement à la source*, LA TRIBUNE (May 21, 2015), www.latribune.fr; Ingrid Feuerstein, *Impôts: Deux tiers des Français sont favorables au prélèvement à la source*, LES ÉCHOS, June 16, 2016, at 5; Ingrid Feuerstein, *Impôts: La crise des "gilets jaunes" n'a pas entamé le soutien des Français au prélèvement à la source*, LES ÉCHOS (Dec. 20, 2018), www.lesechos.fr.

143 Marie Bellan, *Prélèvement à la source de l'impôt: La majorité veut accélérer*, LES ÉCHOS, May 26, 2015, at 3; Ingrid Feuerstein, *Prélèvement à la source: La grande peur du bug de l'an 2019*, LES ÉCHOS, Sept. 17, 2018, at 9; Aurélie Lebelle & Matthieu Pelloli, *Prélèvement à la source: Les trois raisons qui font douter Macron*, LE PARISIEN (Sept. 1, 2018), www.leparisien.fr; *Une semaine de cacophonie gouvernementale autour du prélèvement à la source*, LE MONDE (Sept. 2, 2018), www.lemonde.fr.

144 *E.g.*, Allard, *supra* note 99; Benoît Floc'h, *Les doutes du gouvernement sur le prélèvement à la source*, LE MONDE (Aug. 29, 2018), www.lemonde.fr; Benoît Floc'h & Virginie Malingre, *Le prélèvement à la source, une mise en œuvre redoutée*, LE MONDE (Jan. 1, 2019), www.lemonde.fr; André Gauron, Opinion, *Le prélèvement à la source, une redoutable erreur*, LES ÉCHOS, June 18, 2018, at 10; Cyrille Pluyette, *Le prélèvement à la source va-t-il simplifier la vie des Français?*, LE FIGARO, Apr. 19, 2016, at 13; Adrien Sénécat, *Prélèvement à la source: Les quatre risques qui font hésiter l'exécutif*, LE MONDE (Aug. 31, 2018), www.lemonde.fr; Marie-Christine Sonkin, *Les effets pervers du prélèvement à la source*, LES ÉCHOS, July 2, 2018, at 19; Vignaud, *supra* note 127.

145 *See* Douet, *supra* note 124; Le Fur, *supra* note 101; Schaeffer, *supra* note 98.

146 CODE GÉNÉRAL DES IMPÔTS [CGI] [TAX CODE] art. 1664(1) (before abrogation by Loi 2016-1917 du 29 décembre 2016 de finances pour 2017 [Law 2016-1917 of December 29, 2016 on the Budget for 2017], art. 60(I)(B)(15°), J.O., Dec. 30, 2016); *see* PROJET DE LOI, *supra* note 87, at 373–76.

147 CGI arts. 175, 1664(3) (before abrogation by Loi 2016-1917, art. 60(I)(B)(15°)); BOFiP-Impôts, BOI-IR-DECLA-20-10-10, Personnes tenues de souscrire une déclaration §§ 340–350 (2016); *e.g.*, DIRECTION GÉNÉRALE DES FINANCES PUBLIQUES, PRÉCIS DE FISCALITÉ 2018, at avant-propos, § 316 (2017).

148 RAPPORT D'ACTIVITÉ, *supra* note 134, at 47; *see Impôt sur le revenu: Seuls 58% des ménages ont choisi la mensualisation, contre 70% il y a cinq ans*, LE MONDE: LES DÉCODEURS (Aug. 31, 2018), www.lemonde.fr.

149 CGI arts. 1681A, 1681B (both before abrogation by Loi 2016-1917, art. 60(I)(B)(22°)); *see* PROJET DE LOI, *supra* note 87, at 377–78.

150 CGI art. 1681C (before abrogation by Loi 2016-1917, art. 60(I)(B)(22°)); *see* PROJET DE LOI, *supra* note 87, at 378.

151 *See supra* notes 108–10, 146, 149, and accompanying text.

152 *Prélèvement à la source, promesses et inquiétudes*, MIDI LIBRE, June 18, 2015, Nexis Uni; Touzé, *supra* note 135; *see* Damgé et al., *supra* note 128.

153 Christian Guichard, *Calcul du taux du prélèvement à la source*, AJ FAMILLE, Apr. 2019, at 182.

154 *See supra* note 112 and accompanying text.

155 Cheysson-Kaplan, *supra* note 107.

156 *See supra* notes 114–15 and accompanying text; *see also* Marie-Christine Sonkin, *Les pièges du prélèvement à la source*, LES ÉCHOS, Dec. 14, 2018, at 33.

157 PROJET DE LOI, *supra* note 87, at 16–18; *see* Charly Tournayre, *Le traitement des avantages fiscaux à l'heure du prélèvement à la source*, AJ FAMILLE, Apr. 2019, at 195; Bruno Parent, *Dix idées fausses sur le prélèvement à la source*, LES ÉCHOS, Oct. 12, 2016, at 11.

158 Ingrid Feuerstein, *Prélèvement à la source: Les doutes montent sur le calendrier de la réforme*, LES ÉCHOS, Mar. 30, 2017, at 4; Renaud Honoré, *Prélèvement à la source de l'impôt: La droite sénatoriale propose une solution alternative*, LES ÉCHOS, Nov. 4, 2016, at 5; Juliette Mickiewicz, *Prélèvement à la source: La droite fait échouer l'adoption de la mesure à l'Assemblée*, LE FIGARO (Nov. 17, 2016), www.lefigaro.fr; Patrick Roger, *Contretemps pour le prélèvement à la source*, LE MONDE (Nov. 18, 2016), www.lemonde.fr.

159 CODE DU TRAVAIL [LABOR CODE] arts. L3242-1 to -4; Floc'h & Malingre, *supra* note 144.

160 *See* Renaud Honoré, *Les doutes gagnent l'Élysée sur le prélèvement à la source*, LES ÉCHOS, Aug. 30, 2018, at 3.

161 *See* David Gamage & Darien Shanske, *Three Essays on Tax Salience: Market Salience and Political Salience*, 65 TAX L. REV. 19, 41–43 (2011). *But cf.* Gregory Klass & Kathryn Zeiler, *Against Endowment Theory: Experimental Economics and Legal Scholarship*, 61 UCLA L. REV. 2 (2013).

162 *See, e.g.*, Albert B. Crenshaw, *Paychecks Experience Some Withholding Pains*, WASH. POST, Mar. 22, 1992, at H3; Karen Hosler, *Taxpayer Refrain to Bush: "No New Withholding!,"* BALT. SUN (Mar. 17, 1992), www.baltimoresun.com.

CONCLUSION

1 Michael A. Livingston, *Women, Poverty, and the Tax Code: A Tale of Theory and Practice*, 5 J. GENDER RACE & JUST. 327, 327 (2002).

2 That certainly seems to be the *New York Times*'s go-to adjective for describing all things tax-related. In fact, a June 9, 2020, Nexis Uni search in the *New York Times* database for articles with the word "arcane" within eight words of some variant of the word "tax" produced more than 150 hits between 1980 and 2020.

3 BARTOSZ BROŻEK, THE LEGAL MIND: A NEW INTRODUCTION TO LEGAL EPISTEMOLOGY 5, 39–67 (2020).

4 Obergefell v. Hodges, 576 U.S. 644 (2015); United States v. Windsor, 570 U.S. 744 (2013).

5 *See generally* ANTHONY C. INFANTI, OUR SELFISH TAX LAWS: TOWARD TAX REFORM THAT MIRRORS OUR BETTER SELVES (2018).

6 Est. of H.H. Weinert v. Comm'r, 294 F.2d 750, 755 (5th Cir. 1961).

7 For yet further detail, see INFANTI, *supra* note 5, at 109–33.

8 Anthony C. Infanti, *Tax Reform Discourse*, 32 VA. TAX REV. 205, 218 (2012); *see* INFANTI, *supra* note 5, at 141–43.

9 EMMANUEL SAEZ & GABRIEL ZUCMAN, THE TRIUMPH OF INJUSTICE: HOW THE RICH DODGE TAXES AND HOW TO MAKE THEM PAY, at ix-x, 45–87 (2019).

10 *See* INFANTI, *supra* note 5, at 4–6.

11 *Cf.* 114 CONG. REC. 9395, 9397 (1968) (reprinting Martin Luther King Jr.'s sermon "Remaining Awake Through a Great Revolution," in which Dr. King famously states: "We shall overcome because the arc of a moral universe is long, but it bends toward justice.").

12 *E.g.*, Caroline Lucas, Opinion, *Here's How We Can Help the Covid-19 Recovery, Tackle the Climate Crisis and Fight Disillusionment with Our Democracy*, INDEP. (June 27, 2020), www.independent.co.uk; *"Non à un retour à la normale": De Robert De Niro à Juliette Binoche, l'appel de 200 artistes et scientifiques*, LE MONDE (May 6, 2020), www.lemonde.fr; Lee Stevens, Opinion, *How COVID Has Challenged Our Theories About Poverty*, CALGARY HERALD (June 25, 2020), https://calgaryherald.com; Ekemini Uwan, *There's No Going Back to "Normal,"* ATL. (June 13, 2020), www.theatlantic.com; Muhammad Yunus, *"La crise du coronavirus nous ouvre des horizons illimités pour tout reprendre à zéro,"* LE MONDE (May 5, 2020), www.lemonde.fr.

13 Eric Garcetti, L.A. Mayor, 2020 State of the City Address, at 7 (Apr. 19, 2020), www.lamayor.org.

14 *Id.*; *see* Tim Arango & Thomas Fuller, *Why Liberal Californians Don't Want to Go Back to Normal*, N.Y. TIMES (May 5, 2020), www.nytimes.com; *see also* Jamelle Bouie, Opinion, *Another Way the 2020s Might Be Like the 1930s*, N.Y. TIMES (Apr. 28, 2020), www.nytimes.com.

15 *See, e.g.*, Noah S. Diffenbaugh & Marshall Burke, *Global Warming Has Increased Global Economic Inequality*, 116 PROC. NAT'L ACAD. SCI. 9808 (2019); Stephane Hallegatte & Julie Rozenberg, *Climate Change Through a Poverty Lens*, 7 NATURE CLIMATE CHANGE 250 (2017); S. Nazrul Islam & John Winkel, *Climate Change and Social Inequality* (U.N. Dep't of Econ. & Soc. Affs., Working Paper No. 152, 2017).

16 *See, e.g.*, INFANTI, *supra* note 5; *Green Tax Solutions Symposium*, 17 PITT. TAX REV. 1 (2019).

17 *See* CRITICAL TAX THEORY: AN INTRODUCTION (Anthony C. Infanti & Bridget J. Crawford eds., 2009); FEMINIST JUDGMENTS: REWRITTEN TAX OPINIONS (Bridget J. Crawford & Anthony C. Infanti eds., 2017); Tracey M. Roberts, *Picking Winners and Losers: A Structural Examination of Tax Subsidies to the Energy Industry*, 41 COLUM. J. ENV'T L. 63, 75–93 (2016).

INDEX

Page numbers in *italics* indicate Figures.

ABA. *See* American Bar Association

abnormal act of management (*acte anormal de gestion*), 35, 36

abus de droit fiscal (abuse of tax law), 35, 201n35

abuse: antiabuse, 29, 35–36, 54, 154–55; curtailing, 127–28, 133–34, 147–49

abuse of tax law (*abus de droit fiscal*), 35, 201n35

accelerated cost recovery system (ACRS), 102–5, 110

accelerated depreciation, 101, 102, 212n28

accountability, 93, 94, 188

accounting methods, 11, 115–16; accrual, 9–10; cash, 9, 10

accrual method, 9–10

acquisitions: corporate, 146, 150–54; foreign, 118, 119, 121–22, 123; multistep (creeping) stock, 148–49, 151–52

ACRS. *See* accelerated cost recovery system

acte anormal de gestion (abnormal act of management), 35, 36

actor, 60, 61–62, 156, 181, 189

adjusted gross income (AGI), 162–63

administrability, equity and, 30

advantage, tax, 43, 66, 74, 139, 182

advisers, tax, 12, 28, 54, 60, 133, 135, 181

aggressiveness, 153

AGI. *See* adjusted gross income

aid: federal, 83–84, 89, 209n108; state, 82–83, 117, 118, 122, 123

alchemy, 109

allowances: immediate expensing, 106–7, 108; withholding, 158, 162

all-times, law as, 16, 91, 193n11

ambiguity, 141–42

amended returns, 13–14

American Bar Association (ABA), 67, 68–70

American Indians, Time, and the Law (Wilkinson), 22–23

American Institute of Certified Public Accountants, 165

American Potash & Chemical Corp. v. United States, 149–50

amortization: of financial goodwill, 26, 96, 115–17, 118, 120–22; in US, 115

analysis: constitutional, 90–92; statutory, 92–94; tax-expenditure, 84, 87

année blanche (blank/lost year), 171–72, 173

annual reporting period, 8

anthropology, 17

antiabuse, 29, 35–36, 54, 154–55

Arrowsmith doctrine, 8–9

assets, income-producing, 97–98

Associated Press, 161

Asymmetries in Time (Horwich), 1

auctions, 119

audits, 150

Auerbach, Alan, 105–6

authors, 61–62

autobiography, 17, 18–19

Averill Corporation, 38, 39, 41

avoidance, tax, 37, 105, 135–36

backlash, 156, 176–77, 178
basis, 58; recovery of, 52, 53, 59; stepped-up, 126–27, 128, 129–30, 137, 184–85
becoming, 17
benefits, tax, 154; disparate distribution of, 112–14; rule, 9; for schools, 84, 85; unwarranted/unintended, 12
Biden, Joseph, 108
Birnbaum, Jeffrey, 103–4
blank/lost year (*année blanche*), 171–72, 173
Board of Tax Appeals, US, 37, 39, 42
Bob Jones University v. United States, 87, 88, 89, 91–92, 93
bonus depreciation, 105–7, 108, 112
Bork, Robert, 17–19
borrowed time, 130, 132, 136, 137, 155
bright-line rules, 128–29, 141
brother-sister corporations, 47, 53
Brown, E. Cary, 98
Brown v. Board of Education, 63, 78, 81, 111
Bush, George W., 106

calculator, withholding, 159, 160–61
Canada, 33, 34, 36, 102
capital cost recovery, 26, 96, 154
capital gains, 46–47
capitalization, 97–102; defining, 97; depreciation following, 99, 100, 109
cash, as property, 54
cash method, 9, 10
Cauble, Emily, 131
change: climate, 191; social, 20; in wage, 176, 178, 187
charitable contributions, 78, 83, 85; classification of, 87; defining, 79–81, 86
Charney, Gil, 160
le cheval de Troie (Trojan horse), 172–73
Chief Counsel's Office, IRS, 66, 67, 80–85
Child Tax Credit, 158
choices, 25, 62, 63, 156, 185–86
civil law, 34
civil rights, 84

civil unions, 63, 65–66, 67, 71, 74
class, socioeconomic, 4, 25, 28, 130–31
classifications, 30–31, 87
climate change, 191
Clinton, Bill, 15–16
clubs, social, 87, 209n122
Code § 179, 105, 106–7, 108, 110, 113–14
Code § 246(c), 139–40, 141, 145
Code § 304, 29, 45–59, 182; example of, 52–53; fictions of, 57–59; the past and, 57–59, 61; prerequisites, 53–54; on sales as redemptions, 55–57; text excerpt of, 49–51
Code § 368, 146
Code § 501(c)(3), 78, 79–80, 87
Code § 1014(e), 128–30, 131, 137
Code § 1031, 132, 135, 136–37, 221n37; example use of, 133; US Congress on, 133–34
Commissioner, IRS, 32–33, 158, 159, 160
commodity: labor as, 25, 96; time as, 25, 26, 95, 124, 126, 155, 182, 184
common law, 19, 20, 34
common market, 123
companies: foreign, 116; Fortune 500, 112–13. *See also* corporations
comparative tax law, 6
competition, 117, 119
compression, of time, 109–12, 120, 124, 189
confirmation hearings, 17–19
Congress, US, 29, 31, 56, 59, 61; ACRS and, 103, 105; on bonus depreciation, 106–7; on Code § 1031, 133–34; on depreciation, 100–101; on dividends-received deduction, 139–42; on immediate expensing, 109; inaction of, 70, 73; on inherited property, 126–27; time compression of, 109–12; on withholding, 158–59
Congressional Research Service, 113
Conoco, Inc., 150–52
Conseil d'État, 35, 36
consequences, tax, 30–31

Constitution, US, 15–16
constitutional analysis, 90–92
constructive ownership, *50*, *51*, 53, 54, 57
contexts, for substance-over-form principles, 33–36
contribution pour remboursement de la dette sociale, 168
contribution sociale généralisée (CSG), 168, 174
control, 48, 53, 54, 55
Cooper v. Aaron, 82
corporate acquisitions, 146, 150–54
corporate distributions, 47
corporate privileges, 145, 153–54
corporate reorganization, 41, 44, 145, 146–49, 151
corporations, 46; brother-sister, 47, 53; Conoco, Inc., 150–52; Duke Energy Corp., 143–44; E. I. DuPont de Nemours & Co., 151–54; J. E. Seagram Corp., 150–54; parent-subsidiary, 47, 48–49, 125; Progressive Corp., 143; 21st Securities Corp., 143–44
court cases: *American Potash & Chemical Corp. v. United States*, 149–50; *Bob Jones University v. United States*, 87, 88, 89, 91–92, 93; *Brown v. Board of Education*, 63, 78, 81, 111; *Cooper v. Aaron*, 82; *Green v. Kennedy*, 85, 87, 88, 89; *Griffin v. State Board of Education*, 82; *J. E. Seagram Corp. v. Commissioner*, 150; *Obergefell v. Hodges*, 66–67, 68, 72, 77; *United States v. Windsor*, 66, 68, 69, 70, 71, 73, 77. See also *Gregory v. Helvering*
Court of Appeals for the Second Circuit, US, 31, 40–42, 100
Court of Justice of the European Union, 120
courts, 85–88, 147; Board of Tax Appeals, US, 37, 39, 42; Conseil d'État, 35, 36; Court of Appeals for the Second Circuit, US, 31, 40–42, 100; Court of Justice of the European Union, 120;

General Court of the European Union, 119–20; Supreme Court, Canada, 34; Tax Court, US, 29, 32, 100. *See also* Supreme Court, US
COVID-19 pandemic, 2, 27–28, 187, 190, 191
creativity, 14, 94, 122; of tax imagination, 123–24, 129–30; of tax lawyers, 181–82
credits, tax, 103, 104, 110, 158, 172
criminal punishment, 21
CSG. See *contribution sociale généralisée*
currency, time as, 6, 95, 111

data, 168–69, 176
death, 127, 132
debate, 90–91, 125
deductions, tax, 8–9, 96, 97; dividends-received, 138–45, 153, 185; unlimited marital, 127–28
Defense of Marriage Act (DOMA), 65, 66, 68, 70
delayed-payment regime, in France, 157, 168, 175, 176, 177
Democrats, 159, 160–61, 165, 166, 167
demographics, 114
depreciation, 184; academic justification for, 97–99; accelerated, 101, 102, 212n28; bonus, 105–7, 108, 112; capitalization followed by, 99, 100, 109; economic, 98–99, 102; in economic expansion, 107–8; nonacademic justification for, 99–100; purpose of, 97; recessions and, 106–7; straight-line, 99; US Congress on, 100–101, 106–7
disability, 25, 131, 186
disadvantaged groups, 25, 62, 114
discrimination, 73, 186, 190, 191; governmental, 88, 89, 91, 93; sexual orientation based, 72, 75, 77, 89–90. *See also* racial discrimination
disguised interest, 11, 12
distribution: corporate, 47; dividend, 45–49, 58–59; of tax benefits, 112–14

distributive injustice, 130–32, 136–38, 142–45, 150–54
dividend-capture strategies, 142–44
dividend distribution, 45–49, 58–59
dividends-received deduction, 138, 143, 153, 185; regulations for, 140–42, 144, 145; US Congress on, 139–42
doctrines, 24, 25; *Arrowsmith*, 8–9; judicial, 29, 30–45, 60; step-transaction, 145–54. *See also* substance-over-form principles
DOMA. *See* Defense of Marriage Act
domestic partnerships, 63, 65, 67, 71, 74
Duke Energy Corp., 143–44

economic depreciation, 98–99, 102
economic expansion, 107–8
E. I. DuPont de Nemours & Co., 151–54
Einstein, Albert, 1, 2
empathy, 164
employers, 168–69
Engel, David, 20–21
Enright, Máiréad, 75
equity: administrability and, 30; health, 131–32; tax, 25
errands, 4
estimated tax payments, 169, 170, 175, 176, 177–78
ethnicity, 25, 131, 132, 186
European Commission, 117, 121, 122; aftermath, 119–20; decisions, 118–19
exceptional income, 172
exceptions, to rules, 181
exchanges, 32. *See also* like-kind exchanges
exemptions, 125, 158
expansion, economic, 107–8
expectations, frustrated, 69–70
expensing, full, 98. *See also* immediate expensing

faces, of substance-over-form principles, 186

facts, of *Gregory v. Helvering*, 37–39
Fair Labor Standards Act, 22
farmland, 32
fear, 156, 157, 172–74, 177, 178
federal aid, 83–84, 89, 209n108
Fellows, Mary Louise, 12
fictions, 5, 57–59
financial goodwill (*fondo de comercio financiero*), 26, 96, 115–17, 118, 120–22
firms, women-owned, 113–14
Fogg, T. Keith, 160
force, 110
foreign acquisitions, 118, 119, 121–22, 123
foreign companies, 116
Form 1040, 13
Form 1040-X, 13
Form 2210, 163
Fortune 500 companies, 112–13
foyer fiscal (tax household), 169
frame, spatiotemporal, 90, 91, 92, 93, 183
France, 27, 35–36, 125; delayed-payment regime of, 157, 168, 175, 176, 177; social security taxes in, 168. *See also* withholding, in France
Franklin, Benjamin, 95
full expensing, 98
fundamental public policy, 88, 91, 92, 93
the future, 19–20, 44

GAAR. *See* general antiavoidance rule
gains: capital, 46–47; recognition of, 132–33
Garcetti, Eric, 190–91
Geier, Deborah, 97–98
gender, 25, 76–77, 96, 114, 131
gender identity, 25, 186
general antiavoidance rule (GAAR), 34
General Court of the European Union, 119–20
gifts, 127–29
GOA. *See* Government Accountability Office, US
goals, 28

Goldberg-Hiller, Jonathan, 21
goods, public, 4
goodwill, 184; defining, 115; financial
 goodwill, 26, 96, 115–17, 118, 120–22; tax
 treatment of, 115–17
#GOPTaxScam, 164–65
Government Accountability Office, US
 (GOA), 102, 159, 160–61
governmental discrimination, 88, 89, 91,
 93
Great Recession, 106, 107, 110
Greenhouse, Carol, 2–3, 16–19, 27, 91,
 193n11
Green v. Kennedy, 85, 87, 88, 89
Gregory, Evelyn, 37–38, 39, 40, 41, 42,
 44–45, 55–56
Gregory v. Helvering, 29–30, 36, 55–56, 60,
 134; facts of, 37–39; IRS time rewriting in, 39–40; substance-over-form
 principles and, 37–45, 61, 182; time
 suspension in, 43–45; time travel and,
 42–43
Griffin v. State Board of Education, 82
groups, 20–21; disadvantaged, 25, 62, 114;
 income, 162–64; minority, 64; privileged, 150

harvesting, loss, 11
hashtags: #GOPTaxScam, 164–65; #Pay-
 checkCheckup, 160; #TrumpTaxScam,
 164–65
health care, 131–32, 164
hearings, confirmation, 17–19
hedging, 140, 142, 143
heterosexual privilege, 74, 75, 88, 183
hierarchies, 39
history: of French tax withholding, 167–
 68; of US tax withholding, 157–58
holding periods: minimum, 126, 130, 140,
 141, 145; two-year, 134, 135
homogeneity, of time, 75
Horwich, Paul, 1
H&R Block, 65

Human Rights Campaign, 67–68
husband, 76, 77
hybrids, rule/standard, 125, 126, 135, 141–
 42

identity, gender, 25, 186
Illinois, 65, 66
Illinois Department of Revenue, 66
imagination, legal, 6, 13, 40, 85, 155, 156,
 192
imagination, tax, 5, 6–7, 14, 23–24; breadth
 of, 155; creativity of, 123–24, 129–30;
 engaging, 94; messages from, 185–88;
 positive use of, 188–92; power of, 95,
 157, 179, 182, 192; unleashed, 60–62
immediate expensing, 102–5, 110–11, 113,
 184; allowances, 106–7, 108; US Congress on, 109
immigration, 25, 186
inaction, of US Congress, 70, 73
incarceration, 21
incentives, tax, 106, 113, 118, 123
income, 10, 25; AGI, 162–63; assets
 producing, 97–98; exceptional, 172;
 groups, 162–64; nonexceptional, 173
income tax, 5; inherited property and,
 126–27, 128; integrity of, 100–102; reporting periods for, 7–8; in Spain, 116
Indian law, 22–23
industrial plant, 20–21
inequality, 96, 130–31, 190, 191
inflation, wartime, 157
Information Reporting Program Advisory
 Committee (IRPAC), 161
inheritance, of property, 126–29, 132, 191
injustices, 71, 77, 93; correcting, 189;
 distributive, 130–32, 136–38, 142–45,
 150–54; past, 183
Institute on Taxation and Economic
 Policy, 112–13
instrumental time, 20–21
insulation, against time, 22–23
integrity, of income tax, 100–102

intent, 54
interest, 11–12, 13
Internal Revenue Code, 13, 26; Code §
    179, 105, 106–7, 108, 110, 113–14; Code §
    246(c), 139–40, 141, 145; Code § 302, 47,
    57, 58; Code § 368, 146; Code § 501(c)
    (3), 78, 79–80, 87; Code § 1014(e), 128–
    29. See also Code § 304; Code § 1031
Internal Revenue Service (IRS), 10, 31;
    Chief Counsel's Office, 66, 67, 80–85;
    Commissioner, 32–33, 158, 159, 160;
    Form 1040, 13; Form 1040-X, 13; Form
    2210, 163; on Gregory v. Helvering, 39–
    40; IRPAC, 161; 1967 legal memoran-
    dum, 80–81; policy shifts, 79
International Fiscal Association, 36
inventories, 11
IRPAC. See Information Reporting Pro-
    gram Advisory Committee
IRS. See Internal Revenue Service
Isenbergh, Joseph, 33
items, special, 10–11

J. E. Seagram Corp. v. Commissioner, 150
Johnson, David, 21
Johnson, Olatunde, 78
Joint Committee on Taxation, 101–2, 112
judging, 20
judicial doctrines, 29, 30–45, 60
justice, 28, 111–12, 188, 239n11. See also
    injustices
justices, US Supreme Court, 16–19
justifications, for depreciation, 97–100

Kahn, Douglas, 99
King, Martin Luther, Jr., 239n11
knowledge, 188

labels, 68, 69, 71, 73
labor, 25, 96
language, 24, 74
largesse, 111, 113, 122, 123, 154
Latour, Bruno, 74–75

law: all-times notion of, 16, 91, 193n11;
    civil, 34; common, 19, 20, 34; cultural
    force of, 19; Indian, 22–23; state, 68–69;
    time and, 14–23, 28; time constructed
    by, 21–23. See also tax law
lawmaking, time and, 15–20
lawyers, 23–24, 181–82
layers, of privilege, 187
leasing, safe-harbor arrangements for,
    103–4, 105, 111
legal imagination, 6, 13, 40, 85, 155, 156,
    192
legal propositions, 81
LGBTQ+ community, 42, 67, 71, 75, 77, 183
like-kind exchanges, 132–38, 155, 184–85;
    defining, 132; example of, 133; nonrec-
    ognition treatment for, 134, 136–37
like-kind properties, 32
Likhovski, Assaf, 38
linear time, 2–3, 8, 12–13, 90, 95, 183
liquidation, 38
Livingston, Michael, 181
living will, 129–30
LLM. See Master of Laws
loans, 163
Lokken, Lawrence, 11
long positions, 139
losses: harvesting, 11; net operating, 8,
    194n31; revenue, 101–2, 105, 108, 112;
    sustained, 98

manipulation, 140; abusive, 173, 179;
    political, 159, 166, 174; rule, 128–30,
    135–36; standards, 149–50
market, common, 123
marriage: alternatives, 67–68, 69, 70, 71–
    74; defining, 64–66, 77
marriage equality, 25, 42, 63, 183; deci-
    sions, 66–67, 89; regulations, 67, 71–73,
    76
Massachusetts, 65
Master of Laws (LLM), 7
McCaffery, Edward, 127

McCumber, John, 1–2
mechanics, of French tax withholding, 168–70
Mellon, Andrew, 37
memorandum, IRS, 80–81
mergers, 31, 116, 119, 146, 151–53
messages, from tax imagination, 185–88
methods, accounting, 11, 115–16; accrual, 9–10; cash, 9, 10
minimization, tax, 38
minimum holding periods, 126, 130, 140, 141, 145
minimum wage, 190
minority groups, 64
mirror, 185
Mississippi, 85
moderns, 74–75
A Moment's Notice (Greenhouse), 17, 19
money: time as, 25, 26, 95; time value of, 11–13
Monitor Securities Corporation, 37–38, 39, 44
motives, 129
Murray, Alan, 103–4
myths, 28, 131

National Taxpayer Advocate, 160
net operating losses, 8, 194n31
new property, 11, 101, 105, 146
New York Times, 79, 164, 238n2
nonexceptional income, 173
nonrecognition treatment: corporate re-organizations, 146; like-kind exchange, 132–34, 136–37, 221n37
normality, 190, 191

Obergefell v. Hodges, 66–67, 68, 72, 77
obligations, 140
offers, tender, 150–51, 152, 153
openness, 155
opportunity, 191
opprobrium, 112
optimism, 192

Organisation for Economic Co-operation and Development, 167
organized time, 22
original returns, 13, 14
others, 123, 188
ownership: constructive, *50, 51,* 53, 54, 57; of property, 96, 130

pace, of modern life, 19
pandemic, 2, 27–28, 187, 190, 191
parent-subsidiary corporations, 47, 48–49, 125
participation exemptions, 125
partnerships, domestic, 63, 65, 67, 71, 74
the past, 14, 29; Code § 304 and, 57–59, 61; fragment of, 75; meaning of, 40–42; preprogrammed changes to, 56
paths, 44, 54, 60–61
patience, 135–36, 137
pay, take-home, 159, 165, 171, 174, 178
#PaycheckCheckup, 160
payments, estimated tax, 169, 170, 175, 176, 177–78
Peabody, Bruce, 15–16
Pelosi, Nancy, 165
penalties, 161, 162, 163, 165, 167, 170
performativity, 41, 42, 43
period, reporting, 7–9. *See also* holding periods
philosophy, 1–2
Pittsburgh Post-Gazette, 161
planning, tax, 43
plant, industrial, 20–21
pleats, 110
policies, IRS shifting, 79. *See also* public policy
political manipulation, 159, 166, 174
positions, long and short, 139
post related party sale, *48*
power, 27, 28, 188; purchasing, 171, 174; of tax imagination, 95, 157, 179, 182, 192
practical mergers, 146
prerequisites, Code § 304, 53–54

presidency, vice, 15–16

privacy, 168–69, 170, 176

private face, of substance-over-form principles, 186

private schools, segregated, 64, 78, 79, 81, 83–86

privileges, 26, 64; corporate, 145, 153–54; groups with, 150; heterosexual, 74, 75, 88, 183; layers of, 187

Progressive Corp., 143

property, 106, 133–35, 154; cash as, 54; inheriting, 126–29, 132, 191; like-kind, 32; new, 11, 101, 105, 146; ownership of, 96, 130; qualified, 107–8; real, 137, 221n37; requirements for, 55, 56; similar, 140, 141, 144; taxes, 4; transactions, 11; transfer of, 32, 135; used, 101, 103, 105, 111

propositions, legal, 81

provisions, tolling, 139, 141, 142, 143

proxy, time as, 125, 129

public face, of substance-over-form principles, 186

public goods, 4

public opprobrium, 112

public policy: fundamental, 88, 91, 92, 93; restrictions, 89; violating, 82, 83, 87–88; well-settled, 81

punishment, criminal, 21

purchasing power, 171, 174

race, 25, 64, 81, 87, 130–31, 186

racial discrimination: IRS Chief Counsel's Office on, 81–82, 86; by tax-exempt entities, 78–81, 209n122

Rakoff, Todd, 21–22, 198n116

rates: French tax withholding, 169–70, 176; wage, 113

Read, Donald, 67, 68, 69, 70

realization event, 11

real property, 137, 221n37

recessions: depreciation and, 106–7; Great Recession, 106, 107, 110

recognition, of gains, 132–33

recovery: ACRS, 102–5, 110; of basis, 52, 53, 59; capital cost, 26, 96, 154

redemptions, 45–49, 52, 57–59; Code § 304 on, 49–51; sales as, 55–57; of stock, 46

refunds, tax, 27, 156, 162–64, 166–67, 178

regulations, 148, 205n19; dividends-received deduction, 140–42, 144, 145; marriage-equality, 67, 71–73, 76

related party sale, 48

relationships: civil unions, 63, 65–66, 67, 71, 74; domestic partnerships, 63, 65, 67, 71, 74; same-sex, 64–65, 66, 183. See also marriage

relativity, 1

Relativity (Einstein), 1

reorganization, 43; defining, 146; tax-free corporate, 41, 44, 145, 146–49, 151

reporting periods, tax, 7–9

reports, country, 36

Republicans, 159, 164, 166, 167, 185

requirements, for property, 55, 56

research, 14–15, 189

resources, 192

returns, amending, 13–14

revenue: losses, 101–2, 105, 108, 112; tax, 5, 112, 113, 173

Revenue Act of 1913, 157

rights: civil, 84; Human Rights Campaign, 67–68

rolls, 144

rules: bright-line, 128–29, 141; Cauble on, 131; exceptions to, 181; GAAR, 34; interest, 11–12; manipulating, 128–30, 135–36; standards versus, 125; tax benefit, 9

rule/standard hybrids, 125, 126, 135, 141–42

Saez, Emmanuel, 131–32

safe-harbor-leasing arrangements, 103–4, 105, 111

sales, 32, 45–49, 52; as redemptions, 55–57; related party and post related party, 48; of tax breaks, 104 same-sex relationships, 64–65, 66, 183

scams, tax, 164–65

scholar, 6

schools: segregated private, 64, 78, 79, 81, 83–86; tax benefits for, 84, 85

Seagram, 150–54

segregation, 64, 78, 79, 81, 83–86

semitransparent stock, 120–22

sexual orientation, 25, 63, 64, 72, 75, 77, 89–90

shell game, temporal, 165–67

shelters, tax, 12, 31, 139

short positions, 139

Showdown at Gucci Gulch (Birnbaum and Murray), 103–4

Simons, Henry, 12

skepticism, 33

sleight of hand, 91

social change, 20

social clubs, 87, 209n122

social justice, 3, 6, 92, 189

Social Security, 67, 69, 70, 158

social security taxes, in France, 168

social time, 22

society, 3, 4, 7, 27, 28, 186–87, 190

socioeconomic class, 4, 25, 28, 130–31

solutions, 191

Spain, 184; amortization of financial goodwill in, 26, 96, 115–17, 118, 120–22; corporate income tax in, 116

spatiotemporal frame, 90, 91, 92, 93, 183

special items, 10–11

speed, of time, 2

spin-off, 38, 39, 40

spouse, 76, 77

standards: hybrid of rules and, 125, 126, 135, 141–42; manipulating, 149–50; rules *versus*, 125

state aid, 82–83, 117, 118, 122, 123

state law, 68–69

status quo, 175–76

statutory analysis, 92–94

stepped-up basis, 126–27, 128, 129–30, 137, 184–85

step-transactions, 145–54, 185; nebulousness of, 150; Seagram, 151–54; standards manipulation of, 149–50; tests for, 147–48

stimulus, 101, 103, 111

stock, 45–49; long and short positions in, 139; multistep (creeping) acquisitions of, 148–49, 151–52; redemptions of, 46; semitransparent, 120–22

straight-line depreciation, 99

strategies, dividend-capture, 142–44

substance-over-form principles, 24, 25, 29, 63, 70, 74; comparative contexts of, 33–36; faces of, 186; *Gregory v. Helvering* and, 37–45, 61, 182; importance of, 94; judicial doctrines of, 30–45, 60; public and private faces of, 186

Supreme Court, Canada, 34

Supreme Court, US, 8, 9, 13, 14, 145, 193n12; on depreciation, 99–100; on *Gregory v. Helvering*, 43–44; justices, 16–19

Surrey, Stanley, 83–84

suspense, time in, 43–45

sustained loss, 98

tables, for US tax withholding, 159–61, 165–66

take-home pay, 159, 165, 171, 174, 178

tax, 3; actor/author, 60, 61–62; advisers, 12, 28, 54, 60, 133, 135, 181; avoidance, 37, 105, 135–36; consequences, 30–31; credits, 103, 104, 110, 158, 172; equity, 25; estimated payments for, 169, 170, 175, 176, 177–78; incentives, 106, 113, 118, 123; lawyers, 181–82; minimization, 38; planning, 43; property, 4; refunds, 27, 156, 162–64, 166–67, 178; revenue, 5, 112, 113, 173; scams, 164–65; scholar, 6. *See also specific topics*

tax breaks, sale of, 104

Tax Court, US, 29, 32, 100

Tax Cuts and Jobs Act (TCJA), 27, 107–8, 112–13, 156, 158–59, 187

tax-exempt entities: defining, 83, 85, 86; racial discrimination by, 78–81, 209n122

tax-exempt status, 78–80, 82–88, 183, 209n122; debate over, 90–91; revoking, 92, 93

tax-expenditure analysis, 84, 87

tax-free reorganization, 41, 44, 145, 146–49, 151

tax household (*foyer fiscal*), 169

tax imagination. *See* imagination, tax

tax law, 3; as arcane, 28, 155, 181, 187–88, 238n2; Canadian, 34; comparative, 6; examining, 4–7; French, 35–36; as mirror, 185; time and, 23–28; timing issues in, 7–14. *See also specific topics*

TCJA. *See* Tax Cuts and Jobs Act

tender offers, 150–51, 152, 153

terms, gender-based, 76–77

tests, for step-transactions, 147–48

Thomas, Clarence, 17, 18–19

time, 1, 6; borrowed, 130, 132, 136, 137, 155; as commodity, 25, 26, 95, 124, 126, 155, 182, 184; compression, 109–12, 120, 124, 189; elasticity of, 153, 154–55; forms of, 17; frozen, 109; Greenhouse on, 2–3; instrumental, 20–21; insulation against, 22–23; law and, 14–23, 28; law constructing, 21–23; lawmaking and, 15–20; linear, 2–3, 8, 12–13, 90, 95, 183; as money, 25, 26, 95; prolonging, 126; as proxy, 125, 129; reifying, 95, 122–23, 184; rigidly pliable, 73–77; suspension of, 43–45; tax law and, 23–28; US tax withholding and, 165–67; value of money, 11–13. *See also specific topics*

Time and Philosophy (McCumber), 1–2

A Time for Every Purpose (Rakoff), 21–22

timelessness, 91

time travel, 24, 29, 74; Code § 304 and, 52–53; refusal of, 42–43, 63

tolling provisions, 139, 141, 142, 143

transactions, 31, 32; abusive, 35, 201n35; property, 11; two-step, 151. *See also* step-transactions

transfer, of property, 32, 135

transition, to withholding in France, 171–73

travel, time. *See* time travel

Treasury Department, US, 205n19; on accelerated depreciation, 101, 102, 212n28; pressure on, 159; on tolling provisions, 139; on withholding allowances, 158; withholding tables updated by, 165–67

treatise, 133, 142, 147, 148, 149, 152

Treaty Establishing the European Community, 117

Trojan horse (*le cheval de Troie*), 172–73

Trump, Donald, 42, 108, 158, 164, 186

#TrumpTaxScam, 164–65

21st Securities Corp., 143–44

2019 US tax filing season, 162–64

Twitter, 164–65

two-step transaction, 151

unions, civil, 63, 65–66, 67, 71, 74

United Mortgage Corporation, 37–38, 39–40

United States (US), 4, 5, 14–15; amortization in, 115; Board of Tax Appeals, 37, 39, 42; Constitution, 15–16; Court of Appeals for the Second Circuit, 31, 40–42, 100; DOMA, 65, 66, 68, 70; Fair Labor Standards Act, 22; GOA, 102, 159, 160–61; immediate expensing in, 102–6; Revenue Act of 1913, 157; Tax Court, 29, 32, 100; TCJA, 27, 107–8, 112–13, 156, 158–59, 187; 2019 tax filing season, 162–64. *See also* Congress; Treasury Department; withholding, in US

United States v. Windsor, 66, 68, 69, 70, 71, 73, 77
unlimited marital deduction, 127–28
US. *See* United States
used property, 101, 103, 105, 111

values, of society, 3, 7, 27
vice presidency, 15–16
violence, 190

wage, 30; changes in, 176, 178, 187; minimum, 190; rates, 113; withholding on, 4, 156, 157, 168, 169, 170
wartime inflation, 157
Washington Times, 95
wealth, 98, 130–31
White, James Boyd, 23–24
wife, 76, 77
Wilkinson, Charles, 22–23
will, living, 129–30
windfall, 166, 172–73
Wistrich, Andrew, 19–20
withholding, 26–27, 125, 179, 189; allowances, 158, 162; calculator, 159, 160–61;

as timing mechanism, 156; on wages, 4, 156, 157, 168, 169, 170
withholding, in France, 167–79, 185; fears around, 172–74; history of, 167–68; mechanics of, 168–70; rates for, 169–70, 176; timing concerns for, 171; transition to, 171–73; as Trojan horse, 173–74; workers perspectives on, 175–79
withholding, in US, 157–67, 179, 185; history of, 157–58; new tables for, 159–61, 165–66; tax scams with, 164–65; TCJA and, 158–59; time and, 165–67; 2019 tax filing and, 162–64
Wojcik, Mark, 76
women-owned firms, 113–14
workarounds, to Code § 1014(e), 129–30
workers, on tax withholding in France, 175–79
World War II, 157, 168

x-ray specs, 120

Zelenak, Lawrence, 147
Zucman, Gabriel, 131–32

ABOUT THE AUTHOR

ANTHONY C. INFANTI is the Christopher C. Walthour, Sr. Professor of Law at the University of Pittsburgh School of Law. He teaches and writes in the area of tax law, with a focus on comparative tax law and critical tax theory.